The Employee Revolution
Corporate Internal Marketing

The Employee Revolution

CORPORATE INTERNAL MARKETING

Kevin M. Thomson, M.C.I.M.

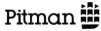

Pitman Publishing
128 Long Acre, London WC2E 9AN

A Division of Longman Group UK Limited

First published in 1990

© Kevin M. Thomson 1990

British Library Cataloguing in Publication Data

Cataloguing in publication data for this book is available from the British Library.

ISBN 0-273 03295 X

Typeset, printed and bound in Great Britain

This book is dedicated to my wife Lesley Ann without whom I would not have met the deadlines; and who spent many hours reading the script contributing her ideas as a management consultant in human resources.

It is also dedicated to my son Marc who will hopefully be the ultimate winner, when he grows up to join organisations dedicated to practising what will one day be commonplace – Corporate Internal Marketing.

Contents

Foreword

This book is aimed at key decision makers and influencers in the fields of both human resources and marketing. The nature of the title and subject matter will also be of interest to managing directors, who are now beginning to recognise that it is not enough to leave the subject of communication solely to personnel specialists, many of whom have had difficulty in adapting to the dynamic changes affecting organisations.

In the wake of Tom Peters with *Excellence,* and Philip Crosby, Juran, Demming *et al.* with *Quality* there is also the recognition that it is not enough to *want* cultural change to occur: the only way to make things happen in the internal environment is to win the hearts and minds of every single employee. In simple terms 'Excellence' and 'Quality' are both products and they need to be marketed in a way that the internal customer wants to buy into them.

This book will address what Peters and Crosby have only been able to uncover as tactical examples of good communications. The work done by the author and his team within major organisations and also in small companies is based on the fundamental practices of marketing. This expertise is brought together with years of experience in human resource development using the methods of communicating through training, developing, briefing, presenting, and so on. In short, if organisations are to take their people with them into the next century then the only way they can do this in today's extremely marketing conscious and sophisticated environment is by practising internally the emerging business disciplines of Corporate Internal Marketing.

The definition

Corporate Internal Marketing takes a holistic view of an organisation. It creates an inspiring climate in which, by developing a framework of targeted communication aimed at everyone in the organisation, motivation and morale thrive. Corporate Internal Marketing ensures that both the internal people relationships and the business's resources are working in harmony to achieve the organisation's strategic and tactical goals.

Preface

The holistic approach

The term 'holistic' tends to suggest that 'if you don't do the whole (istic!) lot at once then you are sunk'. Fortunately, this is not the case. The Corporate Internal Marketing model, which will be built up progressively throughout the book, does not offer a closed loop where you cannot break in if you don't do it all. Entry points are to be found everywhere.

It will be surprising if, with much of what is described in this book, you won't be nodding, and saying to yourself, 'Yes, we do that'. It might be trite but still a truism to say, 'You didn't get where you are today without doing something right'.

What is advocated strongly is that those things that you *are* doing right can be done that much better, once viewed through the eyes of Corporate Internal Marketing. This happy state, however, does require one thing which can variously be described as 'The big picture', 'The overview', 'The strategic plan', or – the latest buzz-word – 'The holistic view'. Unfortunately, the problem with a holistic view is that unless you can see the whole, then the parts may in themselves not appear as clear as you might like them to be.

This book can therefore best be described as a jigsaw. You can start anywhere. You can pick it up and go back to it at any time. You will start to see smaller pictures emerging as you build up each section of the jigsaw that you are looking at.

To continue with the analogy, the problem that you may have, depending on your background, is how much of the picture on the box lid you can see already, and how much you are simply enjoying putting the pieces together as opposed to discovering the picture as you go along. Until the late 1980s the same jigsaw analogy applied to myself and the team and the organisations we worked with; except that we had no picture – and often no pieces.

I have been involved in this tremendously exciting area for ten years now and much of the Corporate Internal Marketing work until a few years ago was of a tactical nature. During the 1980s, for example, the biggest area of concern for many organisations was in the field of customer service, so this was where the big internal marketing budgets were spent.

The pattern of a *total approach* has only recently emerged. This has evolved with the increasingly complex needs of the internal customer becoming increasingly more like demands! This book explores the background, processes and methodologies that can be used to tackle these needs, while not taking a 'rose tinted view' of the internal customer. Unlike the external customer, the internal customer does not have a choice when it comes to some of the very tough demands the organisation increasingly places on them.

Throughout the book each piece of the jigsaw is built up to give as much of a mini-picture as possible and, by incorporating a few graphics into the text and creating obvious points of reference, some of the chapters will be provided with a 'jigsaw piece' summary.

And now for some targeting!

THE 'STRATEGIC' THINKER

If you need to 'see' the big picture first and then fill in the details, please go straight to Chapter 5 – The model.

THE 'TACTICAL' THINKER

If you prefer first to build up the details about the subject you are interested in, then head for Chapter 9– The internal marketing mix.

THE 'ACADEMIC'

I am delighted to say that I have been assisted in this work by David Maitland, who is in the process of doing his MBA on the subject of Corporate Internal Marketing. His academic background and penchant for the subject have enabled him to categorise and augment my personal views, which have been built on practical experience backed up by avid reading, rather than academic research. David has therefore been able to validate them by providing references and suggested reading. He has produced what I have called 'The back of the book – for the academically inclined'. (See Appendix II)

THE 'IMPLEMENTERS' AND 'INFLUENCERS'

For those looking to introduce change through a focus on the internal customer and believe that Corporate Internal Marketing might assist in this process, I have spent a long time on the build-up to the arguments needed. I am constantly in front of decision makers who need the reassurance that what they can see immediately as the big picture is backed up by people who know what they are talking about. The first third of the book is devoted to the 'features', to the organisation and its people. It does not attempt to provide answers – only background. These features and, later, the benefits are purely tools to be used by the people who intend to market or sell the concepts and ideas to others in the organisation.

THE DECISION MAKER

Decision makers usually like to know two things: what something will do for their career, and by implication what it will do to improve the organisation. 'The Benefits' is the key section that pulls together all the features and turns them into what can best be described as 'the nice thing for your organisation is . . .

The reader will be pleased to note that just like external marketing, the nice thing about Corporate Internal Marketing is that there are lots of nice things about it!

THE MARKETEER

As with the word 'bucaneer' I prefer this way of spelling 'marketeer', rather than 'marketer', which conveys none of the spirit employed by the pirates of old! As someone who will be up and running with much of the marketing jargon in this book I would point you towards Chapter 8 – the SWOT analysis. Under Weaknesses (see page 227) you will find the one thing which I soon discovered will hopefully prevent you from doing what I heard one large advertising agency had done, that is 'introduced a Corporate Internal Marketing campaign and deliberately did not involve the human resources department'. If only it were as easy as appealing to external customers. *They* don't spend half their life actually living and breathing in the environment which makes the products and services you have to market.

THE TRAINING/PERSONNEL/HRD PEOPLE

For those of you who are on the look-out to photocopy ideas for your next course you may be disappointed. This book is not a 'handbook'. It has been written as a strategic approach to the internal issues facing organisations in the 1990s and beyond into the next century.

Having said that, I have set out to demonstrate that under the total banner of human resource development, personnel and training is being increasingly perceived as part of a total pro-active solution to organisational development – *and this means that a customer focus must permeate everything, both internal customers and external customers.* This also means it is no longer the backwater department reacting to specific, and often operational problems.

The reader is well advised to read the book from cover to cover! If you are not *au fait* with everything that is involved in Corporate Internal Marketing, then my vision of the future tells me that you will soon be left behind.

Acknowledgements

To all the people in my career who have supported my creative and innovative nature and allowed me to be amongst the first to break new ground.

To the Internal Marketing team and all at HRD who helped me develop the concepts included in the book, and then put them into practice, especially Mike Moon, Kathy Whitwell, Andrew Flint, Julia Christian, Cathy Sweetman, Candy James, Lesley Ann Thomson and Alison Snelling.

To the people and organisations with whom I have been involved, and who have sometimes taken the risks needed to break new ground, especially Frank Whittaker – now at Sutcliffe Catering (P&O); Alan Reed and Peter Hazzard – Gardner Merchant (THF); Steve Tucker and David Howell – Butlins Holiday Worlds (The Rank Organisation); Trevor Baker – Esso; Alistair Hall and Mark Lucas – Lloyds Bank; Melanie Harvey – The Burton Group; Diane Smith and Ross MacLennan – Royal Mail; David Young and Graham Couldwell – Midland Bank, Dieter Merz, Renault Trucks and Ian Brooks and Carl Christon of Unsworth Sugden Advertising.

To all those contributing their time and experiences to allow the many examples to be quoted throughout the book.

To David Maitland for Appendix II.

To Chris Downs who inspired me through his unswerving belief: 'You can if you think you can!'

To you, my target audience. If this inspires you to introduce new thinking that benefits yourself and the people in your organisation then I have achieved my Mission. You will also be amongst the first to start to fulfil my Vision. Please let me know how you get on, your experiences will help the next book, which is more on the tactics, take shape.

Kevin M. Thomson MCIM

1 | *The mission and the vision*

A two-minute summary

It is necessary to establish at the outset that the fundamental starting point of Corporate Internal Marketing uses the wealth of knowledge and experience of two key disciplines that have affected the dynamic changes in business today. These are marketing and human resource development.

The language and concepts of marketing together with human resource development (HRD), provide an amazingly powerful tool to tackle the strategic and tactical ramifications that 'change' has on all organisations.

One of the first concepts to explore in this new language is one which is starting to reach the very heart and soul of organisations – the mission. Starting at the 'top', this is being discussed in boardrooms throughout the world, and from there generally – and often not successfully – cascades (i.e. falls in a downward direction) towards the 'employee'. However, we have now hit the first snag: these are the same employees who for years have been left very much to the vagaries of their immediate boss. They are now expected to partake in a new direction for the company which has taken the 'bosses' often days of painstaking debate. Even worse, the new direction is thus communicated under the mystifying title of 'The mission statement'. This in turn is either given to the employee verbally by managers who themselves wonder what it really means, or it goes up on the wall as a paragraph on a piece of paper. Some of the employees may actually read it.

The mission of Corporate Internal Marketing aims to put a stop to this type of internal advertising, PR and promotional activity that would put most organisations out of business if practised externally.

Does this sound a harsh judgement on the way the internal customer is treated? Turn then to the external customer and the vast amounts of time and money that are being put into 'customer care'. Even after all the spending, there is still a huge gulf between what the external customer should expect in terms of the way he is treated and what actually happens. A fair assumption can therefore be made that this is because all too often internal people may not be treated as well as the external customer. Indeed, the internal customer is usually perceived as someone who is *paid* to take on anything that is given to them (or thrown at them), and not seen as someone who should be 'sold' to, or even marketed to professionally.

The 'mission' statement referred to is therefore only to provide an overview of the function of Corporate Internal Marketing. It will also raise an awareness that concepts like this don't stand on their own; they need to be put into context. This will be done in the Corporate Internal Marketing mix. It is also only a 'statement' because you, the target reader, cannot be expected to buy into a set of words on a piece of paper. It matters not a jot that these words have been lovingly produced. Nor that they should mean anything, or even that they should be assumed to increase your propensity to want to act on them. A lot more needs to happen.

Corporate Internal Marketing is all about getting into the psyche of the target buyer and creating someone who is 'ready, willing and able' to change his attitudes, understanding, and behaviour towards the new and the different.

The vision

The 'vision' is something usually held by the leaders of an organisation – a picture in their minds of the future. My vision of Corporate Internal Marketing is that within the next decade the Employee Revolution will have created an environment where the strategies and tactics advocated by internal marketing will be the norm in all 'Excellent' organisations.

The first part of the jigsaw

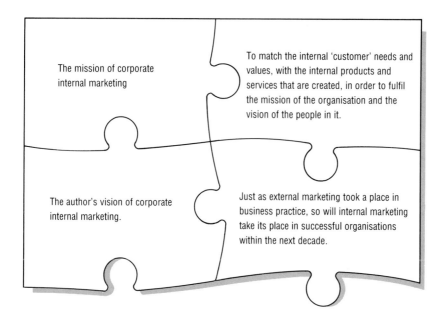

The mission of corporate internal marketing

To match the internal 'customer' needs and values, with the internal products and services that are created, in order to fulfil the mission of the organisation and the vision of the people in it.

The author's vision of corporate internal marketing.

Just as external marketing took a place in business practice, so will internal marketing take its place in successful organisations within the next decade.

2 | *Fear and other human reactions to 'change'*

As will be seen, there are four *major* strategic changes that are the result of Corporate Internal Marketing e.g. total customer focus. They can also be predetermined as being the areas that need to be tackled when looking to introduce 'changes'. Either way, they are fundamental to the process of achieving the 'mission' of those organisations which want to rely on their people to help them achieve their goals in a positive and motivated way.

In those organisations that have recognised that 'change' needs to take place, some or all of the four strategic changes may be seen as important by the leaders of the organisation. In practice, they may be seen in numerous other ways as well, usually negatively, especially by the people who are likely to be affected by them most, often the people at the 'sharp end'!

Therefore it is worth exploring the human reactions that the introduction of any 'change' will produce before examining the results. These reactions will, in turn, need to be taken into account when considering the internal marketing strategy for a future shift of attitude, of practice, or culture.

Fear of 'change' itself

Does fear sound too strong a word? I don't believe it is. And not just one aspect of fear arises out of 'change'; there are, unfortunately, a number.

One of the greatest challenges in any programme of 'change' is to tackle the inherent fear that people feel when looking to a *different* future. It may be that the future is better, but if there is the slightest chance of any uncertainty about it, it can safely be assumed that the internal marketeer is going to face barriers. These barriers are actually intended to destroy – or at least hinder – the new order of things being introduced.

The future may or may not concern people; it is the fact that their view of it is unclear that causes the problem. So, fear and the resulting barriers produce one of the greatest challenges to any introduction of change. My grandfather used to say, 'You can't change a man against his will!' The corollary of which is that you can't communicate to people who don't want to listen!

It is usually fear which produces a 'knee jerk' response in the individuals in organisations. This is not unrecognised of course; but all too often there is an attempt to calm the fears of individuals, which then goes too far the other way to appease, and results in totally negative reactions. This occurs when individuals feel they are in a strong position because people are going out of their way to placate them. They know that what is being introduced is fundamentally right, although they may not be happy about it personally. It is at this very early stage in the process of 'change' that key individuals can be detected who are likely to become major sources of discontent and disruption. This is simply 'hitting out' as a means of protection. They are afraid of 'change'.

I am often asked by human resource professionals (especially when introducing an attitudinal campaign, such as happy people serving our customers) what to do about the desperately negative people who are already undermining or will quite likely undermine the major investment. Surprisingly, experience suggests that these people are a primary target market! They need to recognise the hooks, and be given the opportunity to see that their world is not going to be turned upside down. They are, indeed, likely to end up as greater 'champions' of the new ideas than those who already appear to be practising many of them.

Why is this? The reason is simple. When people are coming from a low attitudinal base, the removal of the fear barrier allows them to make enormous changes. In short, the simplest analogy is well documented for those looking for something to substantiate personal observation. Consider the hundreds of thousands of people who have been 'converted', in religious terms, to any of the causes that one could care to mention.

Personal experience of many a training course shows that the last thing that should be done with 'Fred in the corner', who is causing havoc with his negative vibes, his caustic comments, and pointed remarks, is to kick him out. In most cases the 'Freds' of this world are afraid of the changes that are apparently being forced on them. However, once they 'see the light' then woe betide anyone who tries to criticise the trainer or the programme! In essence, they are now in a new comfort zone. This will produce a level of acceptance of anything new that will be absorbed into their *modus operandi*. Interestingly enough they will probably then accept almost anything that the instigator of the change wants to throw at them. The fear will be removed through a belief in the person who can 'see' into the future and will make sure that Fred is OK.

Very often, surprisingly, it is the person who seems to be the paragon of virtue who is the one to watch out for. Why should this be? Perhaps they fear that they will lose the status they had prior to any change. Not only is everyone else taking on board the new ideas that often only they thought they were practising, but also they are no longer the focus of attention. This results in a loss of standing or visibility, and hence may even affect their chances of promotion. They feel that the attention is not on them but on a new leader who is driving forward new ideas and concepts.

The net result for targeting internal marketing or sales messages is that these people can become the most difficult to reach. They don't want to listen. As far as they are concerned, they are already doing what is being asked of them. They seem to feel (judging by the blank looks and sometimes supercilious attitude of people on many a training course or workshop) 'I don't have to bother with this.' In reality, it is another type of fear, the kind that is well known to the people we all aspire to emulate – the Japanese.

Fear of loss of face

This kind of fear is not an Oriental phenomenon, it affects every organisation. It is this fear which creates entrenched positions and negative attitudes in people. Examples of how the internal marketeer can overcome this serve to illustrate the severity of the problem, as in the following copy:

> **This customer service programme will help you build on your strengths**

Translated into what it really means – but you dare not say it:

> **We have had a number of complaints from our customers about the appalling attitudes and practices of our staff and we are taking immediate steps to change the way you do things!**

or:

> **You are invited to attend a 5-day management development workshop in leadership skills**

Translated, this means:

> **The people reporting to you are having big problems with the way you are treating them.**

Is this overstating the case? Is there more than a grain of truth behind these statements? The real problem is that if anyone says that they have a *better* way of doing things – as opposed to saying, for example, 'here is a *different* way of doing things that you *might* like to consider', people get defensive. This automatically assumes that the way they were doing it before was, at best *worse* than what is being suggested now, or at worst totally the *wrong* way of going about it! This of course, to people who don't like criticism, means a loss of face.

Hence, the introduction of 'change', which almost implies things being 'better', also implies that what went before was 'worse'. For those people who are not prepared to admit infallibility, or for those who believe that what they are doing is right, it comes as a shock to be told that this is not the case. The 'soft sell' is inevitably necessary.

Yet, compare this to external marketing; when anyone launches a 'new' and 'improved' product it is usually eagerly awaited! The manufacturer is not criticised for making it better. Why? Because the consumer is not personally involved. With no personal involvement in producing the product, it is unlikely that they will say, 'I'm not going to buy this because you didn't do it better before'. They are more likely to praise you for improving and developing it.

The fear of 'loss of face', is just one of the many reasons why Corporate Internal Marketing will always be more difficult than external marketing. Internally, in most organisations, there will be an aversion to anything new. In contrast, in the external market place people are always demanding almost everything to be new!

Fear of losing job

Is fear of losing one's job a major consideration when thinking of 'change', or is this another example of possibly overstating the case? First-hand experience of a number of projects shows that it is one of the biggest concerns of many employees, of both large and small organisations. Think of the introduction of information technology (IT, i.e. computers!). People's past experience would suggest that this 'service' provided for the internal market, while ostensibly being done to improve the efficiency of the organisation and to enable it to meet the needs of the customer, is introduced to reduce costs. Therefore IT is perceived to save money, and so it 'must cut jobs'.

This is a fairly gross example of a method of changing an organisation for the better, which can be perceived to have a *major negative impact on the individual*.

If you think about it, almost any change in an organisation could do the same. For example, better management development programmes produce the need for fewer managers. This is generally accepted as a part of the current methodology for bringing about 'flatter structures'. Many managers are running scared about flat structures, and the effect not only on their future prospects but on the job they are doing now.

Unfortunately, the same can be said about improvements of almost any kind. If the individual perceives them to be a threat to their position or their future, then they will resist them. This makes the role of Corporate Internal Marketing a lot more difficult than external marketing.

Fear of failure

Taking on anything new as a task or hobby at home allows for a period of private experiment 'where no one can see'. It might take hours to put the flat-pack kitchen cupboard up, but it's done in the privacy of your own home. The same is not true at work. Under the full glare of colleagues and bosses, the pressures to adapt and adopt to new practices and principles are increasing daily.

These are real pressures to those who feel they cannot cope. The individuals who refuse to accept that they are unable to change will once again self-justify their incapability as being someone else's fault, e.g. 'they are throwing too much at us again'. However, it may be that they feel that the end result will be that the organisation will sooner or later not require their services. In the meantime any failure, whether it is accepted by others as part of the learning curve or not, will often be perceived by the individual as something personally unacceptable.

Matters are made worse by the prevalent culture in most organisations that failure is unacceptable. The QED to this is that creativity and innovation are stifled.

If people don't attempt anything new, then they can't be seen to be failing. Resisting change protects people from the glare of failure

In one organisation, this fear had created a culture which spawned long memos blaming everyone else for failure, or even potential failure. These memos were universally recognised by the mnemonic

'TCIC'—thank Christ I'm covered!

This may be amusing, but recent analyses of how managers spend their time would suggest some frightening statistics. In one management survey the figures looked like this:

TIME SPENT JUSTIFYING YOUR EXISTENCE: one-third

TIME SPENT COVERING YOUR BACK (TCIC):   one-third

TIME SPENT ACTUALLY BEING PRODUCTIVE: one-third

If you think of the amount of time spent writing and reading unnecessary memos, and the wasted time spent in meetings because of the fear of exposure and failure, the figures become more familiar.

What has this got to do with Corporate Internal Marketing? It is against this attitudinal background that the new messages need to penetrate. To give a concrete example, which will be covered in greater depth later, in one of the UK's largest clearing banks I encountered an unspoken cultural axiom which virtually all the managers seem to adhere to. Summed up it can be expressed in a way akin to a government warning about smoking:

'SPEAKING UP CAN DAMAGE YOUR FUTURE WEALTH'

If it is accepted that communication is a two-way process, this kind of barrier does create a major problem for the internal marketeer!

Other attitudinal barriers to introducing 'change'

Pride

This is often referred to as 'NIH' – Not Invented Here. Once again this arises through an unwillingness of people to admit that they couldn't or didn't think of something. Alternatively, even to think that they can agree that someone else has improved on what they have done is tantamount to failure.

If every new product in the external marketplace was rejected

because the potential customer hadn't thought of the idea, there would be very few products on the shelves.

What this means in the internal market place is that the key word being bandied about when it comes to gaining acceptance in organisations, is 'ownership'. This is all well and good, but when taken too far is akin to another word used when dealing with people's attitudes, which is 'pussyfooting'.

In one organisation, I came across a very competent administration manager who expressed astonishment that a quality circle had spent eight man-days designing a form for a new system that he had produced in eight minutes. His view that it was his job was correct. Indeed the practice of consulting others to provide 'ownership' is so widespread that the costs must be horrendous. Is it necessary? The answer is that in a thriving organisation it is probably only necessary on critical issues. Individuals who do not feel that they are not communicated with, and who do not perceive themselves to be under threat, and even more, who are very busy, will, I believe, willingly accept someone else's ideas.

It may be worth stating that while these negative attitudes may need to be altered, they also have to be accepted. Until the day arrives when the individual feels safe, secure, motivated, rewarded, etc. in the job that they are doing, then the barriers are put up simply as a survival mechanism. If everyone in the organisation is doing the same, then you have a cultural problem. It is up to the internal marketeer to tackle the attitudinal barriers as well as finding ways of working around them.

Complacency

There is a lot that can be placed under this heading, including such attitudinal barriers as lack of commitment, lack of enthusiasm, etc. These are perhaps a greater threat to organisations than the stronger emotions already covered, and typified by one office in a Welsh Regional Health Authority that I visited. The only colourful thing about the office, its people, and its atmosphere was a host of postcards on the notice board, all of which were of the same fundamentally sad nature:

YOU DON'T HAVE TO BE MAD TO WORK HERE
– BUT IT HELPS!

The same can be said of the mnemonic about Fridays, i.e. POETS day.

P*** OFF EARLY TOMORROW'S SATURDAY

It shows a basic flaw in how work is perceived – as a bore! Yet these individuals are the same target markets who will enthusiastically fly half way round the world to do the same thing day after day, getting sunburnt on a beach. It is not the monotony of jobs which causes the attitudes to be negative, it is how people react to the monotony. These negative attitudes form the fundamental stumbling blocks to any Corporate Internal Marketing campaign.

This book is not intended to compete against the myriad of self-improvement books now appearing in station and airport bookshops throughout the world. There is a general recognition by human resource specialists that attitudes are a major cause for concern, and need tackling. This concern, however, is often seen as only impacting on training, on getting on with the job, and perhaps in a more nebulous way on the 'culture'. To the internal marketeer it is absolutely vital to know all of the barriers to communication, if any *successful* activity is to take place. These problems must therefore be researched and analysed, as part of what will later be discussed in the Corporate Internal Marketing mix.

The picture unfolds . . .

Fear of change itself is one of the fundamental problems to be faced by the internal marketeer.

People feel they are admitting they have done something wrong by accepting a 'new' way of doing things. This creates a fear through loss of face. It creates a resistance to new methods and practices.

The role of corporate internal marketing is made much more difficult through the well-founded fear of job loss from flatter structures and new technologies.

Any new introduction will be resisted if it is felt it will adversely affect people. Internal marketing is basically concerned with new introductions!

With no personal interest by the consumer in the introduction of new ideas, external marketing is not faced with one of the big internal problems – NIH – not invented here.

3 | *The features*

Corporate Internal Marketing, like its sister discipline of external marketing, centres around one key aim.

In order to entice people to do anything that needs some form of persuasion, it is necessary to find what creates or reinforces the 'need' for them to *want* to act in a positive and motivated way.

This 'need' itself is a concept that people must be able to accept and buy into. To help this happen, the organisations I have worked with found that it is more emotive, and therefore more powerful, to call these enticements the 'hooks'. This chapter is concerned with finding the hooks for you.

The hooks are quite likely to be the involvement in the strategic changes that will affect your organisation. In Corporate Internal Marketing terms, however, your hooks will not be the same for all individuals or for the organisation itself. Therefore to continue to use the terminology and concepts of the marketing world, of which selling is a part, the hooks to both the organisation and the individuals have been entitled the 'benefits', and the strategic changes that are necessary to produce the hooks are the 'features'.

Constant customer focus through the language of marketing

It is not enough just to keep repeating how important the customer is; there must be a strategic methodology for ensuring that *every* decision has the customer as its focus.

And now for the good news. There is no need to go out and reinvent the wheel to make sure this happens. There are thousands of man-years of experience behind the practices and disciplines of external marketing. With the careful addition of the practices and disciplines of human resource development (i.e. what used to be called Personnel and Training), the methods of achieving a constant customer focus are waiting to be applied.

By putting external marketing and human resource development skills together and adding the vital techniques needed to merge the two business disciplines, only then can Corporate Internal Marketing take place.

From this strategic base, a constant customer focus requires an often enormous attitudinal shift as well as an organisational shift. These shifts *must* be away from the classic heavy industrial stance of asset facing. Certainly they *must* be away from the classic employee stance of inward facing. They *must* also be away from the supplier stance of stock facing. Finally, the shift *must* be away from the all-too-often-seen stance of a simple revenue focus – dare I say – a 'screw the customer' philosophy. The supposed stalwarts of customer focus, the salesforce, often have to adopt this stance (be it retail, finance, or any salesforce) when the pressure is on to generate the revenue.

The reason why the focus within organisations is on things other than customers is a simple one – it is because of the *measures* that are put on people. These measurements *must* now force them to see customers as their key criteria. In many organisations the moves to start any constant customer focus are in fact totally thwarted by the often useless traditional management measures used to drive the business. But more of this later.

Suffice it to say that all too often these measures are cost or simply revenue driven, when the need is for market and customer driven requirements. In order to create the two changes that are necessary for a constant customer focus – on people and on the organisation, there needs to be a shift from existing practice. Corporate Internal Marketing provides the climate to achieve this.

The attitudinal shift to a total customer focus

The basis of attitudes is in repeated behaviour. If this repeated behaviour is given a new input that forces it to adopt new concepts through a constant use of a new 'language', the shift can start to occur. (See Figure 3.1.)

Existing word(s)	Existing focus	New word	New focus
Communication	Verbal/written	Corporate internal marketing	Targeted/multi methods of reaching people
Employee	Inward/with a 'downward' looking type of disrespect	Internal target market	Internal customers/ with a marketeer's respect for their nature and variety
Attitude survey	Inward/problems	Internal market research	Internal customers/ opportunity
Manuals/memos	Downward/ instructions	Internal support material	Targeted/ internal customers
Conference	'Tell'	Internal launch event	'Sell'
Training	'Tell'	Workshop	'Sell'
Inform	'Tell'	'Sell the idea'	'Sell'
Briefing	'Tell'	Issues	Consult

Figure 3.1   Beginners' guide to CIM language

And so the list goes on, allowing organisations to pick up the language of their marketing departments, of which sales should be a part.

The organisational shift to a total customer focus

Having established the power that marketing and its language has on the attitudinal aspects of the people, the same holds true for the organisational side. Before looking at this, however, it is necessary to establish the one common link between the two. That link is very simply created by perceiving everyone in the organisation as an *internal customer*.

The time has now come for what Tom Peters calls 'A blinding flash of the bloody obvious'. If it is accepted that all employees *are* internal customers (and this concept is crucial to all quality programmes along the Crosby style) then two key concepts must follow:

1 The internal customer must need an internal salesperson

This means that people are able to say: 'If I am your internal customer then all internal verbal transactions to do with the business involve you "selling" to me'.

2 The internal customer buys products and services from the organisation

'If I am an internal customer then anything that the organisation wants me to "buy into" must be a product or service that it is provided to assist me to meet our goals.'

Thus the concept of the internal customer is fundamental to adopting and adapting the concepts of external marketing to any organisation. In simple terms, internal people are the customers for the products and services of the organisation.

The nice thing is that it is so easy to grasp that everyone in the organisation can start to perceive the need for a fundamentally new approach. As an added bonus, for those organisations that have bought into the quality programmes, which use the concept of the customer/supplier chain, the methodology of matching the needs of the internal customers through Corporate Internal Marketing *must* be the next logical step to take. It cannot be enough to accept that internal customers exist, without giving the people the sales skills, or the organisation the internal marketing techniques, to be able to deal with these new found customers.

If the organisation is now viewed as a supplier of the internal goods and services, then the people who are responsible for these goods and services also need to have the skills necessary to be able to get these to the internal market place. This may range from producing a memo to a dissemination of the five-year plan.

The organisational shift to a total customer focus must then start to take place, once the pragmatic skills and techniques of marketing are being used to define, design and refine those internal products and services. From there the move for the people in the organisation to one that is focused on the external customer is but a step away.

If a manager knows that in order to get something accepted internally he or she has to go through a *process*, and that the process will create a greater chance of success, then they will buy into it. If, in addition to providing a process, the chances of success are considerably enhanced, then the system will be more widely used. Furthermore, if the system actually allows the user to be more creative, more efficient, more effective and – most of all – more successful, then they are even more likely to want to adopt it to meet their needs.

There are numerous other features to entice managers to adopt Corporate Internal Marketing. However, it is only when sufficient numbers develop a total customer focus that the organisation will begin to shift. This will be covered in greater detail later. In the meantime, here are one or two other features that will encourage the process.

DO YOU THINK I'M SEXY?

The first feature is that in most organisations marketing is perceived to be 'sexy'. The same is also true of Corporate Internal Marketing. It is an exciting area to be involved in, often with large budgets! It is always easier to shift attitudes if managers who are implementing plans know that they have the financial, as well as the emotional backing. The investment in people through Corporate Internal Marketing should be at the very least greater than the investment in traditional internal communication. Bigger budgets mean more to play with!

DO YOU THINK IT'S WORTH IT?

The other features to be mentioned at this stage are those that many organisations greatly desire. These include lower staff turnover, more involvement in improving quality, more and better suggestions, more innovation, etc.

The payoffs must of course also outweigh the investment. To prove this, the one thing that then becomes vital is the quality of the measures and the levels of success. Marketing techniques can be used to provide these measures.

So, the concept of shifting the organisation to a total customer focus through Corporate Internal Marketing looks like a good idea. The question is, how to go about it? Fortunately, the same language of marketing that is used to create the 'attitudinal' shift is also used in the methodologies and practices that are required for an 'organisational' shift. Figure 3.2 shows some examples.

A word about marketing jargon

Having now stated that the 'language of marketing' is a fundamental part of the process of moving attitudes and organisations towards the total customer focus, it is worth backing this up. It could be said that Figures 3.1 and 3.2 merely show the same meanings put into marketing jargon.

Existing word(s)	Existing focus	New word(s)	New focus
Standards	Production/'must do's'	Internal products or 'Best Practice'	Internal customers/ targeted messages
Plans	Top down/'must do's'	Internal services	Targeted to meet internal customer needs
Purchasing	Cost/price	External customer supplier chain	Competitiveness/ long-term relationships/ responsiveness

Figure 3.2 The organisational shift

In all organisations the language used is not a trivial part of the culture that builds up. For example, the word 'punter' is often used in those organisations which have a basic contempt for their customers – no matter how much it is protested that it is an 'affectionate term'. The level of swearing is also indicative of a culture that breeds bravado and often fear. The use of terms like 'screw the business' (or the customers) are also part of the language of an organisation which is likely to have future problems.

By the same token there are many organisations which have not established any common language that its people can understand when it comes to information about its practices or successes. If no one talks about revenue, profit, strategies, tactics, mission, vision, values, etc. then the people are hardly likely to be able to get involved in the discussions.

A corporate language is the bedrock of a corporate culture

It must be said that it is only 'jargon' if a select few are privy to its meaning and its daily usage. Jargon is therefore taboo! The constant use of the language of marketing is vital. It provides a 'focus on the customer' that is so strong, it is almost impossible not to get hooked into it.

Imagine, then, the leaders, managers and staff in an organisation using these words and concepts to describe their interactions and relationships. This language of marketing produces a commonality between individuals that either creates cultures or starts the shift towards customer focused ones.

We now look at this language of marketing together with the language of human resource development, with a view to merging the two.

External marketing terms

Target market The term 'target' is a graphic one, describing exactly what the marketeer would like to do with the main message to be portrayed, i.e. strike right into the heart of the person at the centre of his aim. The term is never far from the lips of the marketing person and provides a constant and continual reminder of the *raison d'être* for almost everything that is being done.

It may seem obvious but the marketeer never attempts just to 'tell' people about the products and services that are being marketed: that would soon create a major problem in the number of sales! The 'targeting of messages' ensures that a number of things happen:

1 *The right message is produced.* This may range from creating awareness, through to encouraging extra purchase via a promotional campaign.

2 *The right medium is used.* This may mean any form of the printed page through to audio and visual, including TV and radio.

3 *The right people are targeted.* This is probably the most important of all and may mean a specific segment of a market, or the whole of that market. It is worth saying that today, there are very few marketing people who would suggest that whole markets, or mass markets exist. That is because the level of sophistication of the customer has created a whole series of niche markets.

Niche markets   It was Tom Peters who said, 'There are only niche markets'. What he meant was that all marketing is about reaching smaller groups of people with far more tightly aimed messages about more highly specific products and services. The same is true internally.

TIME FOR A QUICK PAUSE

Should there be any marketing orientated people reading this they may be getting impatient. 'Who is he to be teaching me to suck eggs?' they may be saying.

The whole point of this exercise is to place these external marketing terms in the context of the internal market. For example, at present, internal people are called '**employees**'; what would happen if they are perceived as '**target markets**'? The internal person not used to the marketing terminology or techniques needs to understand how they are used and can then be applied. For the marketing person, getting back to basics may serve to reflect on the last time they saw internal people as target markets.

This is the greatest challenge to marketing people in the world today. The world's largest untapped target market – the 'em-

ployee'. The single biggest opportunity to reach people with new products and services, all of which need totally new methods of design and distribution that 'ordinary above and below the line' methods cannot reach.

Two things emerge from this. Firstly, to the external marketeer, it is worth questioning the insular stance that might have been taken in the past. They usually acted as though the changes that they tried to bring about with new products and services needed only to be communicated to the external market. Secondly, to the person responsible for HRD – watch out. It won't take long for marketing people to take up the challenge of seeing internal people as their next target market. Indeed, at a conference held in 1989 on internal marketing – the first of its kind in the UK – one marketing director talked of his 'ex-personnel director', i.e. the function of internal communication and all other people aspects, was now driven by his marketing department!

The basic personnel type issues can be transferred to where they belong, to the managers who should have ownership of dealing with all aspects of the people for whom they are responsible.

Yet another personnel director of an international chain of outlets each with up to 200 people is looking to be rid of all personnel departments in these outlets. This places the onus on the managers to be totally responsible for people they bring into the organisation. It also then ensures that the ongoing responsibility of communicating issues like induction, career paths, company policy, etc. are placed on the manager. As will be seen, these are the very issues which become the products and services that need to be conveyed by Corporate Internal Marketing. So there are implications to both human resource development people, and to marketing people in this whole area.

It is therefore worthwhile examining the fundamentals of both disciplines in order to see how they can be applied and how they will impact on each other. For example, if employees are now target markets, how do you go about defining them? Is it by traditional marketing techniques as outlined on the following pages?

ABC analysis This is a somewhat outdated but simple way of classifying people in the UK. It sprang out of a realisation that it was too simplistic to call people 'upper, 'middle', and 'lower' class. Generally, however, it stuck to these same very broad definitions. However, money became just as important as status – a real revolution at the time; and it was only in the 1960s that it really took hold as a common marketing tool. This method is less used now, but its sentiments serve to illustrate how easy it would be to start off internal marketing with this type of classification before moving on to more sophisticated models.

It may be worth pointing out at this stage that the imposition of corporate culture and other factors within the workplace do not allow the external marketing classification techniques to apply.

Socio-economic group 1 – the 'A's Before starting with what the 'A' stands for it is probably best to define 'socio-economic'. This really is jargon, simply for 'class' and 'money', thus socio-economic! The 'A's are those with both! You could therefore be an 'A' if you were a Lord with no money, or a barrow boy with lots of it. In the liberal 1960s it was perceived that by combining 'socio' and 'economic', this would lead to common needs as target markets. So a Rolls-Royce was targeted at the 'A's. Among this group would probably be the 'leaders' of companies, such as the chairman, the managing director and members of the board.

Socio-economic group 2 – the 'B's These are the upper income bracket managerial types and the next best thing to the 'A's. They are recognised today as being among the people with the least disposable income, that is the ones with very little to spend, having used it all up at the end of the month on very large mortgages. Among this group would probably be the senior managers, such as the divisional heads, and those with the title Director.

Socio-economic group 3 – the 'C1's and 'C2's This is where things get really interesting, because the two groups are classified under the same general heading of 'C', it being safe to assume that they roughly have the same amount of disposable income once they have paid all the basics. The sub-classification then splits out roughly into C1 as 'white collar' and C2 as 'blue collar'. In today's internal market terms this would probably be converted to 'administrative staff' and 'the workers'. This distinction of course is tremendously blurred because today's technology allows 'workers' to work by pressing the same sort of keyboard buttons that the typist does.

Socio-economic group 4 – the 'D's and 'E's The 'D's are those in society who have little money, for example pensioners. The 'E's are those with no money, i.e. the homeless. Both of these terms are shorthand ways of classifying people for whom the marketeer rarely has products and services that they can afford. And even if they could, they are not in a big enough group to target. In Corporate Internal Marketing terms these people exist outside the workplace anyway so they would not be seen as relevant.

The point of introducing these concepts in external terms is that at least they provide a simple classification for many marketing people to hang their hats on, and from which more sophisticated techniques can be developed. This is not to suggest that the ABC definition should be used, but in broad terms the classifications do correspond to the perceptions of levels of individual employees, be they worker or administrative as in the 'C1' and 'C2's, the manager in 'B', and the ultimate bosses, the 'A's.

With a little tweaking, this base classification could provide Corporate Internal Marketing with just as good a start as external marketing. It is only from a common base such as individual, manager and leader, that greater degrees of sophistication can be added. Other techniques described below are also in common use in external marketing.

ACORN analysis This is an acronym for 'A Classification Of Residential Neighbourhoods'. This technique is often used in direct mail to target people to buy products and services through those delightful letters saying, 'Dear Mr Thomson, We are delighted to tell you Mr Thomson, that you Mr Thomson, have won the opportunity to enter a competition that could bring you Mr Thomson, the amazing sum of £1,000,000.'

The way that this targeting is done, that is hitting only certain market segments in certain geographical areas, is through a system which has used the base data of the UK 1981 census. The targeting is based on research that showed there were almost identical buying patterns by people who live in similar household types, for example farmhouses in the country. Could this be applied to Corporate Internal Marketing?

It may be that in the future people looking for jobs could be targeted in this way, or that they could be screened by their address when they apply. It could also be that an ACORN analysis on an organisation produces a marked propensity to certain ACORN types. This information could be used as the basis for an internal marketing campaign. As part of the battery of tests now becoming available this could prove to be extremely valuable. Once employed, the targeting of messages to the various ACORN types could become progressively easier. It could also be used to highlight different ACORN types in different geographic sectors of the business, for example, the South East/London and the North West could well attract different people to a particular industry.

Just as the external marketing person would build different messages and graphics for a piece of communication material to, say, an 18-year-old from an urban council estate, or to a 50-year-old from a rural village, so the same should happen in Corporate Internal Marketing.

'Lifestyle' classifications There are a number of organisations, including research companies and advertising agencies, who have produced new models based around the way a person lives, rather than their income, social background or their abode. The most famous of the terms (although not necessarily an accepted target group, but it serves to give an understanding of the meaning of 'lifestyle') is another acronym – the 'YUPPIE' – for the Young

Upwardly Mobile Income Earner. Other terms have crept into this lifestyle folklore, such as 'DINKIE' – Dual Income No Kids.

The essential point about lifestyle classifications is that they pinpoint certain key attitudes in individuals' perceptions of the world and how they fit into it. Current work in research seems to be reinventing the wheel of Maslow, and giving it 'sexy' new marketing titles such as 'lifestyle'.

In essence, Maslow developed a theory of the 'Hierarchy of needs' which forms the basis of what drives individuals. For now it suffices to suggest that the more sophisticated forms of targeting like lifestyles will be just as valid in the internal market as in the external market.

OTS This is yet another piece of jargon created to pinpoint one of the measures of success of an advertising campaign, usually run on television. As such it provides a pointer to what may well become one of the measures for the Corporate Internal Marketeer. The term simply means 'opportunities to see', yet behind it lies a tremendous debate about the validity of the measure. Just like a memo which may have been circulated to, say, 20 people, a TV advertising campaign may also be transmitted with a view to reaching its target audience. But how many people does it need to reach and how often do they need to see it to make the type of impact that is deemed necessary? These are the two key measures. Things start to get complicated at this stage because, just like the unread memo, so the TV commercial may not be seen. How does the advertising agency know that someone has seen it? They don't. The only measure that is currently available is taken from a sample panel of people who have their TV sets monitored as to when they are on, and which TV station is on at the time. *Whether anyone is watching the set when an advert is on is not measured.*

Hence, like the memo which goes out, targeted at 20 people, how do you know that all 20 people actually see it? Of course, you know even less about what impact it has and changes in behaviour it causes unless you further research the sales, or the behaviour and attitude of the target audience.

This highly unsophisticated tool, still used today, caused one advertising agency to be dropped by its client, a TV station, when it publicly declared their concern at its validity.

What chance then has the internal person, sending out a piece of communication, of trying to assess its impact? Sending out 20 memos or 4000 Corporate Newsheets may well produce a warm glow of satisfaction as the 'opportunities to see' can be clearly defined. However, these are not like newspapers which people buy to read; they are more like the TV adverts which are transmitted without their consent. The 'opportunity' may be there, but that doesn't mean they will take it up.

How does this relate to Corporate Internal Marketing? Let us take a real example which is typical of today's corporate life – that of the document going out to announce a new policy or practice. I came across a manager who had received one such document sent to him to describe the massive changes that were about to hit him and his staff regarding the large-scale installation of IT equipment. The manager was one of 12 being researched about the implications of this upheaval and fundamental change in method and focus of working practice. He said of the document, which he had received some two months previously, 'I hope you aren't going to ask me too many questions about this, I only read the document last night, knowing that I was coming here today.' He was, in fact, the only one to have read it at all!

In summary, the OTS of a memo, document, etc. is very similar to that of a TV ad: it can be measured by its circulation, just like counting the number of times an advert is being shown in people's homes. Whether or not it is seen is difficult to measure, and a crude tool – the OTS – becomes the one that has to be used. The message is clear – even though you may be fired for saying it – the 'opportunity' to do something is not the same thing as actually doing it.

This leads on to two other external marketing definitions that focus on the gathering of information needed to justify the activity and to prepare for the future – qualitative and quantitative research.

Qualitative research This is the gathering of information which provides an in-depth or 'quality' piece of data. It is acquired through discussion in small groups, rather than through a questionnaire to large numbers. This type of research is ideal for certain needs. Usually an in-depth analysis of the issues is necessary to get 'under the skin' of the problem or opportunity. Qualitative research is therefore ideal when testing out new products and services. The group will interact to debate their perceptions of what is under discussion.

This type of research is also ideal when the marketeer knows that something is not right about the existing products and services out in the market place. It can also be used where a steer is needed on which way the quantitative data should be positioned, and which questions are pertinent to ask.

What is fascinating about the process of qualitative research is that it has an inherent characteristic of involving people in the change process. This is of little use to the external marketeer but can be of tremendous use to the whole process of Corporate Internal Marketing. The process uses two key techniques, that of open questioning, and of facilitation of the discussion to encourage the in-depth analysis necessary to get to the real issues. When this is used in the external marketing situation the customer leaves the research group and that is the end of their involvement. In the Corporate Internal Marketing process however, a fundamental change will often have taken place. Through the professional questioning and facilitation, group members will have had the opportunity to debate and consider the issues. This will often lead to them reappraising the issues. In short, they may change their minds about something which they may not have considered before. This becomes a powerful tool in the hands of the person who knows how to use it.

Quantitative research This type of research provides a 'quantity' of information, usually enough – a representative sample – to ensure that it is a valid basis on which to work. It is interesting that the word most typically used to describe research in HRD terms is 'survey'. This implies something that provides interesting information on events that have occurred, or are likely to occur, for example a survey on voting. It does not imply a pro-active measurement process used to provide data on which to make decisions.

External marketing uses the much more specific terminology of qualitative and quantitative research. This indicates that it is one part of a total external marketing methodology. This should be used in Corporate Internal Marketing if it is to be viewed by the decision makers in the same light. The decision makers are in fact those most likely to want this type of information about the Corporate Internal Marketing process. They will use quantitative data to examine the effectiveness of the investment made in HRD, and qualitative research to back up their own value judgements about past issues and future events.

Until quite recently qualitative and quantitative research has been a neglected area for human resource development. Now is the time to change.

The same view about the investment made in HRD was made famous about advertising in the quote that goes something like: 'I know that half of the money spent on advertising is wasted – I just don't know which half!'

The only way to persuade decision makers of the long-term validity of any investment decision is to keep providing the data which shows that it is working. Marketeers have learned this lesson very well and will go into board meetings with some very impressive figures that somehow always seem to back up their case – even if the figures are questionable, such as OTS!

It is up to those who are going to drive forward the concepts of human resource development and Corporate Internal Marketing to make sure the figures are there for all to see. Otherwise, the training and internal marketing budgets – as is classically the case for training and external marketing – will be the first to be cut.

There is no arguing with the type of statement made by Bass, one of the UK's major brewers, that 'The figures in the test sites for the northern division, as researched by Sheffield Business School, following a customer service campaign, showed an 81% increase in beer volume against a declining market.'

It is clear that top line and bottom line information like that, together with the 'softer' data on attitudes and 'harder' data on staff turnover, recruitment costs, etc. will go a lot further than the all-too-often heard comment about internal campaigns, 'it was extremely well received'.

Some definitions of key issues of human resource development affecting Corporate Internal Marketing

The main purpose of raising some of the definitions in both human resource development and Corporate Internal Marketing has been to set the scene for future terminology and to begin to allow a merging of the two disciplines of external marketing and HRD as practised to date by personnel and training specialists. This whole process of merging will in itself produce the key strategy of 'total customer focus', the starting point for this section. So, having reminded you why we are going down this route, it is worth persevering with the human resource development issues that will crop up when practising this new discipline.

Training The Oxford English Dictionary defines training as: 'Train: Bring (person, child, animal) to desired state or standard of efficiency etc. by instruction and practice.' What I find interesting about this definition is that it makes no mention of whether or not the person (child, animal) actually wants to be trained. It then goes on to say that the methodology is by instruction and practice. This would infer a situation where people are told what to do, and then they must go about doing it once they have had the chance to try it out through practice.

It reflects the still prevalent view of many unenlightened trainers (the type of people who wouldn't read this book so they won't be upset by my calling them that) who have what I first discovered in the catering industry – 'must do' mentality. This happens because trainers, managers and supervisors feel that they have the power of the organisation behind them to instruct employees to act in such a way as to achieve set standards. Today, the final desired outcome may be exactly the same, but the methods of achieving it via an autocractic 'tell' mode will be less successful.

Training has come a long way and, as a subject, is well covered by others. Almost by default, training people are beginning to adopt many internal marketing techniques.

Coaching, Counselling, Appraisal, Influencing: In human resource development terms these are called inter-personal skills. What have they to do with Corporate Internal Marketing? The answer is that they could be dramatically enhanced if, in the appropriate circumstances, people were viewed as customers who need to be sold to. Then it is necessary to use the much more powerful and sophisticated techniques of selling. There is a huge need in the area of training, and in all internal contact, to accept that the concept of the internal customer means that internal sales skills are needed. I would call this Corporate Internal Selling. This concept will be explored in outline later.

At this point, to prevent people switching off if they view selling as something a little bit sordid, it is worth telling the story of one executive who had similar views. He came to a course he had been asked to attend on corporate internal selling, entitled 'Selling Yourself'. His boss telephoned me some two months afterwards to say how during his salary review the executive had used all the principles he had been taught. The boss had given him more than double he had intended.

If this is not enough to convince you, and there is no reason why it should be, then simply reflect that the internal manager has only the same basic tools as the salesperson on the road. To get the most out of the people they deal with, salespeople have only their brains and their mouths. They are perceived to need training to deal with external customers. Their level of revenue is dependent on the skills they bring to bear when influencing the potential buyer. Is it not true then that within organisations massive amounts of revenue are lost through an inability to communicate and persuade people? If the internal customer needs to buy into the products and services then the internal salesperson has to sell.

Workshop This is the term often used to describe a training session. Workshops are more popular and therefore more fully subscribed than they are when promoted as training sessions. Assuming that people need to be 'sold' via an interactive process that creates debate and persuasion, the term 'workshop' should mean just what it implies. It should be an opportunity to work through ideas and concepts which need time to be bought into. The fact that they are, or should be, interesting and fun, is not an added bonus; it is part of the process necessary to create the maximum absorption.

It is sad and indicative, however, that some senior people only feel comfortable attending 'workshops', or the even more euphemistically named short training course, an 'appreciation'. But they do expect employees to go on training courses, assuming that there is a budget for such unproductive activity!

Conferences Having chaired a conference on Corporate Internal Marketing, I can give you the type of feedback from many of the 100 delegates that I am increasingly hearing. It is totally indicative of the way things are moving in the way that people want to learn. People feel that the conference process inhibits learning. It is a one-way flow of information which does little to create that key stimulus to learning – interaction.

This is not to say that conferences do not have a place in the field of human resource development, because they very much do. The huge, and perhaps main, benefit to holding them is that they can create a great deal of *impact*. This may be vital when the perceived need of the people is to see commitment to the subject in question being demonstrated. If, however, they themselves are already committed, and feel that the organisation is committed, then a conference may be one of the most expensive ways of getting the fewest number of messages through. This, of course, excludes the memo!

Another benefit of the conference, if it is held in an exciting place, is for pure reward, for example sales conferences. Again this may be very valid, and once started is difficult to stop; but the mechanism, as a vehicle for increasing understanding, is very limited.

In one organisation in which I worked the annual conference for approximately 300 people cost £250,000 – and that was in the early 1980s! It was held abroad. The total time away was two days, but the total conference time was just two hours!

If impact or reward are the only objectives then the conference may well be the answer. Some serious questions must be asked if the main requirement is absorption, especially given the propensity of people to 'have a good time'. In addition to this, it becomes a problem because of the very nature of such exciting and prestigious events; to know how to make them even more exciting and prestigious year after year. This leads to an escalation of cost, an escalation of expectation, and a diminution of the main aim of the conference, *impact*, as delegates watch 'yet another hyped up event'.

In short, in terms of Corporate Internal Marketing, events and conferences alike are very limited vehicles. They may be extremely valid in external marketing when impact is necessary to launch that new car or plane in a blaze of publicity, but to the internal customer they can have negative impact.

There is one such case extremely well known in the brewing industry. The marketing people decided that the best way of advising over 1000 pub managers of the 'way forward', was to fill the Albert Hall and inform them that they were not just part of one concept, i.e. pubs, but of 16 newly created brands. This gathering coincided with a dramatic reduction in the number of pubs due to increased competition and falling volumes. So, all this money was being spent on the event and people were being made redundant! To add insult, the managers were being 'told' that the product they knew and loved would be shoved into a concept that they could not relate to. The resulting effect on the business can be imagined.

So marketeers beware! The same thing happens internally as happens externally if people are upset – they can be put off the products and services for ever. According to the well told tale, the ex-MD of this brewery company will testify to that!

This leads us on to the next type of event which is gaining more and more critics.

The one-day road show   As with a conference, the aim is to create *impact*, on a large, but more limited number of people, e.g. between 30–100. But only skilled presenters working from pre-arranged scripts can control these sorts of numbers. Again, the level of impact may be high, but the absorption level is likely to be correspondingly low. These events can have their place in a well-orchestrated campaign, but by themselves they are of limited value.

IV   Training jargon for 'interactive video'. Through the use of laser video discs the trainee can be led down a maze of learning suited to his speed and ability. It is the visual version of the old language lab without the linear methodology of learning. It is excellent for skills based training and for creating awareness of what needs to be done. Because it is used by the individual sitting in front of a screen, the attitudinal aspects of learning may not be as powerful as those created through group or personal discussion with peers or managers.

Role play is of course not possible, and physical skills are also difficult to impart and practise. However, IV training is becoming extremely sophisticated and cost effective, although the capital expenditure is initially high. Also called Computer Based Training (CBT), and latterly called Technology Based Training (TBT), it is a powerful way of ensuring that messages get through to the internal market place.

The scene is set

Whether you are a marketeer or human resource development professional you may have cause for concern at this point. Well, that's great! The whole point of every form of Corporate Internal Marketing is to create debate and challenge existing thinking. It sounds extremely American, which is no bad thing (especially if you are American), but the best word to describe this process, is 'internalise'. In external marketing the level of internalising of the messages about a new packet of soap powder, for instance, may be very limited. In Corporate Internal Marketing, many of the issues faced by the target markets will require a great deal of internalising. Issues such as culture, vision of the leaders, information technology, selling skills, etc. are all extremely complex, especially when viewed holistically. To make things worse, because the speed of change is so rapid, by the time something has been internalised it is likely to have changed! An example of this would be 'Knowledge Workers'. These are people who are extremely well paid, who do very specialised jobs, which may suddenly become defunct through something like a change in technology. The absorption levels required to become a knowledge worker, are considerable. The same is true when someone is required to change jobs. This puts a great deal of onus not only on the individual, but on the quality of the Corporate Internal Marketing to create the right environment in which new learning is maximised.

This somewhat sideways look at just a few of the definitions of both external marketing and human resource development is part of the build-up of the language that becomes the bedrock of the corporate culture. It is this language that creates the first major strategic change, that of **constant customer focus.**

Using terms like 'target', questioning the impact and quality of the messages from conferences, and introducing measures into the organisation which are driven by internal research, will all result in a new focus.

It is no longer sufficient to call people 'employees'; to just train them and to assume that by sending out information, it will be read. It is also naive to assume that just because people are paid they will do what is demanded of them.

The external focus begins

Focusing on *internal* customers' needs will ensure that the focus on *external* customers' needs is at least understood. Then the process of everyone understanding external marketing can really begin.

The mechanisms for succeeding with externally focused campaigns like customer services, will be more readily accepted once the internal market perceives that it can benefit from them. The philosophy of embracing the external customers' needs will also be accepted if the individual can see that the organisation embraces his/her needs. Tools such as marketing and selling, which are used to reach the external customer, will be valued if the individual perceives a benefit to himself by developing these skills. In short, if the move to customer facing is to happen externally, it must happen internally.

A good example of this is to look at the early attempts at customer service campaigns. They all had one very simple thread: 'Be nice to the customer'. It did not take very long for the resounding answer to come back: 'Why should I be nice to the customer when my manager is not very nice to me!' Today's organisations are faced not only with their competitors attempting to differentiate themselves by giving 'excellent service', but also with the need to bring in sales.

One of the big four banks, Barclays, has recognised the need to introduce selling skills into all levels of the bank. They have introduced trained sales staff who sit at desks in the banking hall and respond to customer needs by using their sales skills. The managers have also been trained to apply and manage the process.

Imagine however, organisations only training front line staff in professional skills. There are some very sophisticated techniques used to enable them to 'open the sale', to get to the root of the customer's needs through 'open questions', and to 'close the sale' by gaining commitment with little 'yes' questions. It would not take the staff very long to realise that these same techniques were not being applied to them internally. They would soon react by saying: 'Why should I bother?'

In addition to this, if all other internal customers are not practising the same techniques, the lack of reinforcement will soon result in the investment in the training and development being totally wasted. In other words, it is not just the way that they are expected to behave that is important. They also need to see champions of the behaviour whom they can emulate, and constant reinforcement from colleagues.

Once the benefits are realised, this becomes an iterative process, that will make people buy into it.

The beauty of Corporate Internal Marketing is that it forces people down the route of looking for the benefits because they are a fundamental part of its methodology. Once people realise that it is OK to say, 'What is in it for me?', they will soon be coming out with it 'in the open', rather than, at present, muttering it under their breath. The external customer has no problem *demanding* to know 'What's in it for me?' If organisations don't respond to the needs of the internal customer then they will soon end up having difficulty attracting and keeping them. It is also a fact of life that if your competitor is in the process of becoming more responsive to his internal customers, you are going to have to respond also!

The examples of organisations in the UK going down the Corporate Internal Marketing route will soon be legion. Midland Bank now have (at the time of writing) the UK's very first internal marketing manager, David Young, and Trusthouse Forte have the UK's very first internal brand manager, Robin Turner. The many programmes being introduced now, often by newly appointed communications managers, are all examples of Corporate Internal Marketing, such as those run by British Airways for the last 10 years on customer service.

The concept of the internal customer and the strategy of good internal customer relations is at the heart of these programmes. For example, programmes such as the one being run by Butlin's Holiday Worlds, part of The Rank Organisation, entitled 'The People Development Programme'. It's aim is to meet the needs of every individual coming into the company, thousands of whom will only work for a very short period, often a matter of weeks. Yet the recognition is that if they do not meet the needs of the internal customer then the internal customer will look elsewhere. The net result will be that the external customer focus will not succeed.

All of these, and the many other examples, have at their base the principles and practices of Corporate Internal Marketing. The people putting into practice these exciting changes in culture and working practice may not recognise that they have been doing this under the holistic model developed in this book, but they will certainly recognise the elements in their programmes that make them succeed – and sometimes fail.

The strength of Corporate Internal Marketing is that at least there is a plan, and a methodology against which the results can be measured. The first of these is **constant customer focus**.

A word about external and internal customers

It has already been said that marketing as a language includes targeted products and services. It also encompasses the practices required for selling and distribution. The whole emphasis is therefore on the customer. What this has meant in the past, however, is that the focus for the marketing departments has been almost totally external, unless of course one or other of the internal departments was seen to be preventing the marketing plan from being realised. This then creates the basis for a mutually enjoyable meeting of minds, often asking 'who is to blame this time?' Once this conflict is resolved, the marketing people climb back into their respective shells muttering strange noises like 'OTS', 'Saatchi and Saatchi', and other equally bizarre sayings, and continue on with their weird and wonderful ways. At least that is the view of some internal people. Today's external marketing will only succeed if internal marketing is also focused on the final customer.

This focus is also of a very special nature because the customer needs to become the single driving force of the marketing-based organisation. Rightly so. It gives the external marketeer a very simple aim, that of meeting the customer's needs. These words 'meeting the needs' are important because they show that the customer has a choice. Indeed they can very easily change allegiance to products and services, often on the most irrational basis. They are in a buyer's market and are under no obligation to do anything they do not want to do. They have an amazing amount of choice, not only of all products in direct competition, but also of other products in indirect competition. It is therefore up to marketing and advertising departments to do everything in their power to build the allegiance of the customer. Unless the customer's loyalty is strong enough they will 'vote with their feet'.

This is seen as the biggest challenge to the marketing orientated company. It is a challenge that is made doubly difficult by the onslaught of the competition. A phrase that springs to mind which drives the marketeer (but unfortunately does nothing for many shop-floor assistants who do not perceive customers as a challenge, but a pain) is 'the customer is king'.

Now imagine the statement 'the employee is king'! It suddenly smacks of unions, worker power, loss of control of the organisation by its management and its leaders, etc. Why is this? Because in the past, employees have not had the power to do all the things that they can do when they are outside the workplace, i.e. be as demanding and as fickle as they like. There is no retribution on them if they suddenly opt out of buying into products or services that they may have been buying for any length of time before.

But we come back to it again: 'Times they are a changin'. The fickleness of people is a part of the 'me' culture. Today, if people don't like doing something then they simply won't do it. They will sometimes accept unemployment rather than a job they don't like. Is this any different to the external customer stopping buying products and services?

We are beginning to move towards the employee being king, and there is very little that can be done about it. Recent reports suggest that the labour shortage in the United States in the catering industry is such that wage demands are rising way beyond what the consumer is prepared to pay for the end product, such as a hamburger. The only thing that can be done is to either create a very high level of efficiency that masks the high labour costs, or provide a very low level quality product and environment. Hence, with the former, the McDonalds type operation will survive the demands that employees are making on it, and with the latter so will the Momma and Poppa operation. The organisation in the middle will get squeezed out. And it is not just wages which are creating the increased costs associated with a fickle internal customer. Recruitment and retention costs are also much higher.

Are things really so bad that organisations have to give up their sovereign right to be able to pursue their interests in making a profit? Must they lie on their backs and roll over to this new breed of internal customer? The answer is No! Even if times get really tough, the organisation must have its own needs. Sometimes these organisational needs will not meet the needs of the individual, or indeed may be in conflict with them.

This is one of the most fundamental differences between Corporate Internal Marketing and external marketing. The difference actually lies in the simplest of words, which impacts on the way the internal person is marketed to. The word replaces the term 'meeting' as in 'meeting the needs of customers' in the short definition of external marketing. It is the word 'matching', and is used in the context of 'matching the needs' of the internal customer. I'm not playing with semantics. It is a way of demonstrating that the internal customer is as much a 'king', as the organisation itself. The organisation cannot become subservient to the needs and wants of the individuals. Therefore both needs must be 'matched' wherever possible and this is where external and internal marketing really differ.

The external marketeer must react totally to the customer's needs. Gone are the days when products could be made in isolation of customer's needs. If a product does sell without going through the formal marketing mix then it is either good intuitive marketing thinking, or just good luck. Either way, the producer is at the mercy of the consumer, or at the mercy of the ability of the advertising, promotion and PR professions to affect their thinking.

The internal customer, on the other hand, cannot dictate his terms to the supplier of goods and services if the organisation is to remain profitable. He cannot simply opt out when he chooses if the organisation needs his position filled. The internal customer has no choice in complying with certain requirements; therefore the organisation does not exist solely to 'meet' their needs.

However, in these days of fickle people, some internal customers may believe, rightly or wrongly, that they do not have to 'meet the needs' of the organisation.

And so to the crunch. Do they have to live as two opposing factions? No, it is simply a question of attempting to **'Match the needs of the individuals to those of the organisation'**. The word 'match' is hereafter used to demonstrate that both have a right to have wants and needs but they must be compatible.

In the world of external marketing, the producer has no such consumer-given right, so the marketing function does not have the dual role of marketing the product, and ensuring any compliance of the purchaser to reciprocate in a certain way – apart from parting with their cash!

Strategy from below

'Do as I say, not as I do' was once the war cry of 'The Boss'. It represented his (and I use the pronoun advisedly!) ability to be able to do a number of things:

1 Tell people what to do.
2 Not allow them to answer back (unless of course it was with the backing of the unions).
3 Not bother with what they think.
4 Not be concerned about being a role model for the behaviour that was being demanded.
5 Not be concerned about them as individuals.

It also made the inherent assumption that 'The Boss' knew it all, and could literally command 'his' people in a way that was akin to military rule. In accountancy, it is recognised that people are not an asset as they cannot be 'owned' by the organisation. However, this does not translate into reality, judging by the behaviour of some managers.

All too often they will perceive that the people working 'for them' are 'their people', that they work 'under them', and are their 'subordinates'. This type of thinking labels people as lesser beings in comparison to the person they work for:

- less important;
- less capable;
- less valued;

- less intelligent;
- less experienced;
- less likely to be able to contribute;
- less motivated;
- less enthusiastic.

It also makes an assumption that they are 'more' likely to be a number of undesirable things:

- more in need of being closely watched;
- more likely to 'cock it up';
- more in need of castigating when they get it wrong;
- more trouble than they are sometimes worth.

The net result of the traditional employee/boss relationship is a lack of respect. This respect is what the external customer is beginning to command. Without it, it is not felt necessary to *listen* to them. The same respect must be given internally.

There is no way of uncovering internal customer needs if the organisation does not listen. If it doesn't, those needs definitely cannot be met. The often staggering number of quality ideas and feedback on ways to improve will not be heard if the organisation does not listen.

It is through the teaching, and indeed preaching, of Corporate Internal Marketing that the needs, wants, desires and *ideas* of the individuals in the organisation will be respected. Too much is happening now for the average manager to 'do it themselves'. They haven't got the time: so the people 'get on with it'. But this can only happen if the people are given more information. This is the crux of the second strategic change.

It all points to a very simple rule: information is power

This rule has been instinctively recognised for generations by people who have worked their way up the organisation. They ensure that they are 'indispensable' by simply keeping things to themselves. Everyone knows the people in their organisation who withhold things from their 'subordinates', who tell the boss only the 'good news', who block information that would harm their position, who filter information that enhances their cause, who feed information into the grapevine that damages other people. This type of information control leads to massive time wasting, upset and damage to the organisation.

How can Corporate Internal Marketing prevent information control? It is all about information gathering and dissemination in all directions.

To cite just one example. In days gone by the manager who had unhappy staff could keep that information from those who mattered. It may not have even been considered important that staff turnover was high. Morale was probably not a major issue, motivation would probably be considered to be immeasurable, and there may have been organisational 'Brownie Points' for being seen as a 'bastard'. This state of affairs was prevalent in a number of organisations. The hire and fire manager was feared in case they made it to the top and did unto others what he wouldn't want done to him!

Suddenly however, the transfer of power has resulted in the employees being important. It became fashionable in the 1980s to hold attitude surveys. They often produced damning statistics, and managers who had unhappy staff were being examined under the microscope. In short, the surveys were pieces of information gathered by research and disseminated by internal marketing. The information, once held by the individual, became the weapon to be used to make demands that were listened to.

Look at the concern an employee might feel about the quality of 'communication' they receive. This in itself is a classic sign of the level of dissatisfaction with an organisation. There are a number of other issues e.g. management attitude. This will affect the morale, motivation and ultimately the effectiveness of that employee. The organisation will then be affected. If the numbers in the research are 'statistically significant', then positive action should be taken.

There is only one conclusion – the gathering of all data from individuals, *en masse*, will create a picture which will provide the data for future strategy, both internally and externally. The people in the organisation who are most able to do this are those who are closest to the external customer, and can provide the fastest response times in information feedback. These are the people 'at the bottom'. They are the ones who can spot the needs, spot the trends, spot the gaps. They may not be able to verbalise them as well as marketing specialists, but they are exposed to what is happening.

And so to MBWA

There are two main reasons for Chief Executive Officers (CEOs) wearing out their shoe leather when practising the Tom Peters' observed technique of MBWA. It is my belief that one is 'top down'. It is a selling function. It is all about the leader having one-to-one discussions which allows the people to buy into the enthusiasm, vision and mission of that leader – whoever they be in the organisation. The other function of MBWA is 'bottom up' and is a pure research one. Collecting both qualitative research data and enough quantitative research data on the internal and external issues affecting the organisation can provide the future strategy. This information can come from anyone in the organisation but it comes primarily from the people who have the closest contact with the customer.

There is a slight niggle with the title MBWA (Management By Wandering About). While stirring the might of corporate management, it vastly undervalues the vital importance of the results it produces, by focusing on and almost trivialising the process, i.e. wandering.

> **No one entitles research 'Information by wandering about'. No one entitles professional selling 'Securing orders by wandering about'.**

Yet now we have a generation of managers who have been led to believe that the way to the hearts and minds of the people is through wandering about. Of course if you are a successful CEO you are likely to have acquired the skills of selling, and the skills of getting people to respond to you. You will be sufficiently aware of what marketing is, to recognise the strategic importance of what you are hearing. You will be able to add up all the anecdotal evidence that is beginning to accumulate, and make some assumptions about what you should be doing. The successful organisations that Tom Peters identified had CEOs who were doing all of this instinctively.

> **He has extolled the virtues of MBWA, yet fundamentally the success has nothing at all to do with wandering – indeed if you are lousy at selling, researching, and making decisions on that research, then the safest place for you is in the office.**

He is really extolling the virtues of Corporate Internal Marketing. He is advocating that time must be spent carrying out the fundamental front-end research, for the products and services you need to have. Time must also be spent on the selling of your own organisation and its future, to the people who need to be sold to, i.e. the internal customer. If this is not done, the organisation will stagnate and die.

To give a concrete example, the Chief Executive of Eagle Star shows his commitment to the people in the organisation, firstly in a published internal article in a highly targeted *Quarterly News Bulletin*, and by actually practising what he preaches. It is worth quoting extensively from the article as this gives the flavour and shows the methodology of getting across the deep-seated belief in the value of listening and talking – or in marketing terms *researching and selling*.

Taken from 'LIFELINK' Summer 1989 – Eagle Star, Life Division: 'The Steve Melcher Interview'

Q   How do you plan to get to know people in the Life Division?

(Note the use of interview style rather than an article)

A   Well if you looked at my diary, you'll see that I am spending more than half of my time on the road talking to people and meeting them, so that's a big commitment in time.

(A commitment to research)

Q   Will this travelling around include Cheltenham?

(Targeted research)

A   Yes, of course. I am concentrating on the branches, and the plan is to get to each branch by the end of October. That should help me to get a good feel for the distribution of the business, which is the critical area at this time.

(Strategy from below)

Q   Coming on to the challenges facing the Life Division, do you think we have the products to cope?

(Providing marketing data to the people in the organisation)

A   Yes, we certainly have the products to cope, but our success does not depend upon our products as much as on our ability to sell them, i.e. their distribution. In fact we probably have too many products. What we have to do is cut back on the number of products, concentrate on the ones we are good at and on those which are profitable, and then build a market share in those products.

(Not holding back on the 'bad news' validates the sincerity of the sales message)

Q   We all face a great deal of change in the months ahead. What are your comments on change?

(And now for some classic sales techniques, which are embodied in all 'excellent' leaders. Note the 'hooks', note the use of analogies, people see things much better in pictures, and note the assumptive close by saying the word 'we', and note the actual close which leaves no room for doubt that everyone is contributing to the strengths, and helping provide strategy from below)

A   Change is difficult and it's all relative to what people are used to. I believe that in order even to keep up with what's going on in the market place, we must not only change but we must also be constantly changing: we must all get used to change as a 'status quo'. We must take on the attitude that there is always a better way to build a mouse trap and once we have built it, we have to rebuild it, keep rebuilding it, and through the rebuilding process, we end up doing things better.

Change need not be threatening, but can actually be a motivating force, getting people to want to perform better. We have a lot to do and we are not going to do it all in one month, or even in one year. I advocate change not for change's sake, but to enable our Division to be more responsive to the changing environment in which we compete. To bring about and lead this change is like rolling a large object. Once you get it rolling, you have got to keep pushing or you will lose the momentum. I plan to have the corporate reorganisation really on the road by year end. But changing people's minds, habits and attitudes acquired over many years is not going to happen overnight.

We must be careful not to change the wrong aspects of our Division, like the loyalty and dedication to hard work of our staff. I am very optimistic about the future of Eagle Star Life. We have great strengths, a clear idea of the way forward and a workforce which is eager to participate in the process.

So, the 'information' from the Chief Executive is clear, and provides the targeted reader with the power to act on it. It states that there is a 'top down' demand for change, but also a 'bottom up' demand to participate in the change. Additionally, it shows both the individual and the manager that the time to listen and talk, that is, research and sell, is vital. It therefore encourages the people to provide 'strategy from below'. Terrific stuff! The people are given the information on which they can act. Information is power, and the nice thing is that this works to everyone's benefit.

How much can Corporate Internal Marketing bring about 'Strategy from below'?

The answer to this will only become clear once organisations start to practise Corporate Internal Marketing. For the moment, one piece of research exists which shows the extent of the overall 'communication' and attitude problems that are impeding this two-way process. It would be unfair to name the organisation. The temptation of the reader might well be to say, 'Well of course we could not be like that'. My experience of this organisation is that it is extremely well regarded by the staff and also extremely well regarded by the customers – it is among the UK's largest companies. To add credibility to the research I can say that it was commissioned by the organisation in order to publish the data internally, and to give it credence the research company chosen was MORI. The findings are, I believe, not too dissimilar from what might be discovered in many organisations today.

The message that the following statistics contain is that things can really only get better by improving 'communication'; this can only get infinitely better if it is done professionally by Corporate Internal Marketing techniques such as research.

1 Communication

A massive 68% of people feel there is not enough opportunity to tell the organisation about the things that affect their work.

2 Freedom to speak

A frightening 59% of people feel that speaking up can damage their career prospects.

3 Appreciation

Over half, 56%, feel the organisation is below average in showing appreciation for the things they do.

4 Training

58% feel that training is ineffective on new services.

5 Communication via the grapevine

Almost 50% feel that communication is via the grapevine; 95% of people do not want to receive information this way.

6 Communication from meetings

Only 30% of information is felt to come from communication meetings. Over 50% would prefer meetings as a part of the communication process.

This is not an untypical set of results from organisations, many of whom are trying extremely hard to 'communicate', but are finding it difficult. The message that the data is giving is that people not only want to be informed, but they also want to inform. Unless this two-way process does start then, according to the Henley Centre research produced for Luncheon Vouchers, they will end up citing poor 'communications' as one of the main reasons for leaving.

So, it is for the good of the organisation, in terms of the wealth of information, that makes it worth gathering 'strategy from below'. It is also vital to the individuals. The individual members of the organisation must increase their involvement and thereby reduce their propensity to leave.

This feature of Corporate Internal Marketing is achieved by targeting messages and information to everyone in the organisation. However, the way this is done now, through news sheets, circulars, videos, training, conferences, etc. is often deliberately targeted directly at the individual. It skirts around the manager. Why? Because there is a recognition that the manager often 'filters' information to suit his needs.

This leads on to the next feature of Corporate Internal Marketing. It is one that obviates the problem of filtering as far as is possible.

There does come a time when the 'soft' approach is not working with certain individuals, and they need to go. It is a managerial decision as to how much they are positively contributing to the organisation, its strategies, its goals and its team-work. Most people have had experiences where for no fault of their own they have not 'fitted'. People who may not work well in one environment may thrive in another. However, if the problem of management filtering information is a generic one, then the issue must be addressed as an organisational matter.

The words being increasingly used today when referring to improving the effectiveness of managers, in their dealings with others is Added Value.

Added Value

To look at a specific example of the power of Added Value, the experience of Esso is one that many organisations might like to emulate. The sting in the tail is that they would have to release total control of the ability to manage their managers, making them answerable only to themselves. How many organisations would be prepared to do that? Then again, with the massive demographic changes and much looser organisational ties, the days are not far off when this example may be more the norm.

Esso Retail UK supply approximately 2500 sites up and down the highways and by-ways. These range from the large urban, extremely busy forecourts to much smaller rural sites. These sites, even those owned by Esso, are run and managed by independent retailers who are not employed by Esso. The relationship therefore is totally different from an ordinary one. Like the future patterns, there are no 'direct reporting' lines of authority.

As a result, the owner/manager of a site is his own boss. Yet, because there are so many of them, it is possible to approach them as a large enough target market to provide credible and meaningful data. These managers are constantly being researched, as would be expected of an organisation that needs to market its products and services to individuals who can make their own decisions about buying into them or not. One extremely interesting fact came out of one of the qualitative pieces of research that was carried out on the subject of 'Staff Development'. The research by MORI showed that the individual staff member felt very strongly about the 'level of involvement and interest' in their jobs. *This was three times higher than the average, MORI found.*

The reasons for this, I can only speculate on, but would suggest the following:

1 *Flat structures – i.e. the Boss and the Staff!*   A simple two-tier structure. The net result would be excellent communication and little feeling of lack of communication on bigger issues (even though in many organisations these would have no relevance to the average person).

2 *Devolved responsibility.*   The nature of a service station means jobs involve a great deal of responsibility in a number of seriously important areas (health and safety, theft, cash control, etc.). Often these jobs are delegated to the one person left on the site to run it. The manager cannot be there on every shift.

3 *Fast feedback.*   As a result of 1 and 2, the feedback would be much quicker than in an organisation where the decision makers are remote.

The net result is that when looked at in terms of the amount of input that an employee gives because they feel 'interested and involved' it provides the Added Value that organisations are now desperately seeking – and not just at employee level. It is also at the manager level. Their job is to run the site. If they can do it putting much less time and effort into the day-to-day managing, and devote more time to, for example, planning, training, building the business, researching customer needs, etc. then this is the 'added value' that is generated.

Do structured organisations create Added Value?

There are in essence three human requirements that can be projected to provide a model for the targeting of messages and information. They are fundamental to the understanding of the people when it comes to the output that is expected of them. They form the basis for all Corporate Internal Marketing.

Once again, I believe that it is important that the language used to describe these is kept simple, memorable, and above all usable in every instance where Corporate Internal Marketing is necessary. I call these requirements or needs 'The Three A's'.

1 **Attitude**   How do people feel about what they are doing?
2 **Awareness**   Why are they doing what they are supposed to be doing?
3 **Ability**   What way are they supposed to do it?

The order of tackling these is vital. It depends on the situation (for those who are interested, see Blanchard's *Theory of Situational Leadership*) but in most cases where Corporate Internal Marketing is required rather than one-to-one managing of an individual, the order is as above.

Attitude, Awareness, Ability

To put this into everyday terms:

1 *Attitude*
   People need to feel 'good' about what they are doing if they are to put in the enthusiasm and effort.
2 *Awareness*
   People need to know 'Why the hell am I doing this?' or even 'Why the hell are we all doing this?'
3 *Ability*
   Once they feel good and know why they are there, they can be shown what to get on with.

All too often *Ability* is all that is tackled, as it is felt that it is all that 'employees' need. In other words, 'I'll show you what to do then you can damn well get on and do it!'

The time has arrived where it no longer matters if individual managers do not believe that they need to cater for the attitudes and awareness of the employee. The individual will, and is, demanding to enjoy what they do, understand why they are doing it and then, not just be capable enough to do it, but be left alone while they are doing it. These needs must therefore be met if the organisation is to ensure that it is reaching the people.

These 'three As' are worth exploring further. I first came across the concept that 'Attitude training precedes knowledge and skills' when working for Trusthouse Forte. The theory was put to us by Chris Downs, the founder of Customer Service Training (since acquired by the Handley Walker Group). The basis behind this concept was first developed by an American called Maxwell Maltz. Simply put, it runs along similar lines to the teachings of the Dale Carnegies *et al.*, and states, 'You are what you think you are', and 'you can if you think you can.'

In the many years that I have known Chris Downs, he has been one of the UK's leading exponents of the now universally accepted notion that excellent customer service leads to excellent reputations, sales, and repeat business. Having joined the organisation, I have had first-hand experience of seeing the massive power of generating in people a belief in themselves. The list of organisations that have successfully run customer service training programmes reads like a Who's Who of Britain's top companies.

All of these organisations have doubly benefited from this approach because the Added Value is gained not only at staff level. Unlike many other directly targeted 'one-day events', the Attitude training is generally given first and foremost to the manager, who then personally targets and delivers the messages to the staff.

The internal marketing of attitudes doesn't just happen in training. It applies to everything.

Awareness

Philosophers are ultimately concerned with the simplest of questions, 'Why?'. The same is true of almost every individual you care to meet. The question 'Why?', however, was often left unanswered in the workplace, and for many years everyone was expected to 'get on with it'.

The question is now a major preoccupation with Chief Executives, boards, and senior management of organisations throughout the world. This has become the search for the corporate holy grail. It is this search for the direction and meaning of life of the organisation, that has prompted the days and weekends away, to come up with 'The Mission Statement'!

Once a mission statement is produced, the Added Value that comes from the senior people can almost be felt palpitating through the corridors. There is the renewed zest for all things corporate. Enthusiasm and team spirit are rekindled in often previously warring factions. The desire to rush out and publish the words of wisdom grips the creators of this new born babe with fervour. Why? Because they have found out 'WHY?'. They have come to a personal and common consensus about their raison d'être. Life is no longer just about shuffling paper or juggling budgets, it has meaning and purpose.

It is the same need that everyone has at every level in the organisation. Yet, just like the 'Mission Statement', it has taken years to recognise the necessity for viewing 'Awareness' as a prime area of communication. Organisations have been too preoccupied at all levels with the skills of individuals, i.e. their Ability. This must be changed.

As discussed earlier, the methodology for *creating* Awareness is not achieved by simply running promotional or advertising campaigns. Just as it takes time for the senior people to think things through and absorb the implications, time will also be required by everyone else.

Once the internal marketeer has established the best ways of individuals absorbing the required awareness, then Added Value will also be forthcoming.

The need to create awareness may be very different in the target people in the organisation. The youth of the past few decades have been brought up in a different educational system than post- and pre-war. They have been taught to question. They are expected to think things through. They discuss politics, economics and philosophy and are able to rationalise, as well as produce the creative thinking that leads to cognitive leaps. The UK's exams that pupils sit at 15 and 16 years of age have been described as much tougher than degrees of only a few decades before.

Television, computers, social changes and parental attitudes to the rights of children ensure that they will not sit meekly by and say nothing to the 'boss'. Yet, compare this to the generations before. Their sense of loyalty means an acceptance of an authority which is no longer valid in the context of teams. This of course, does not deny the responsibility of management and leadership. It simply means that managers cannot expect people to do as they are told just because they say so. The organisation works because everyone in it makes it work. The power to make it work is no longer vested in the managers. They certainly have very strong responsibilities, but telling people what to do is rapidly going out of fashion!

A fundamental tenet of Corporate Internal Marketing is that awareness is vital to the acceptance of a piece of communication, be it verbal or written. This also holds true of external marketing. The consumer has a right to know about the products and services that they are buying.

The last few years have seen an explosion in the information about products and services. This includes, for example, the food revolution, with its colourings and additives, and even the medical profession is being hit by patients not prepared to lie back and take whatever is thrown at them, just because the person pronouncing on them is called Doctor.

The same is now true internally, although in some older industries with older workforces they may have a few years of grace before they actually have to explain to their people why they are doing things!

The same was the case for the deregulated local bus companies that were previously subsidised by local authorities. Suddenly they faced this thing called 'competition'. The management teams of large and small organisations had to learn the skills that would make them profitable. Companies like Greater Manchester Bus, and Oxford Bus Company were suddenly having to consider things like 'branding' and 'customer service'. They had to impact on the internal market with mission statements, training programmes, communication exercises, etc. The ability of people at all levels in these types of organisations is a key factor in the training and internal marketing plans.

In Europe, the issues brought about by 1992 have also raised the question of ability. Not just in learning new languages (and for

Britain this is a major problem) but also in learning to deal with the different cultures, with the different markets, with the different manufacturing and distribution systems and methods. All of these become crucial to the success of organisations.

Add to this the globalisation of markets, the new philosophies of such systems as Just In Time, Quality, Throughput Accounting and the massive advances in Information Technology. The net result is a workforce that is sorely in need of increased ability, yet painfully lacking in the awareness of what is about to hit, and consequently harbouring low levels of positive attitudes.

Ability

The skills needed to do a job are becoming more and more unique – for almost every job you can think of. Rapid change means that the simplest of tasks in many organisations may be undertaken manually one day and the next day the self-same employee could be working as part of an integrated advanced manufacturing system with a computer sat in front of him. Previously simple tasks, like pressing till buttons, are being supplemented with often demanding selling and inter-personal skills. No one is safe!

At the other end of the scale, the worlds of finance and technology are spawning a new breed called 'knowledge workers'. These 'knowledge workers' are filling ever increasingly sophisticated niches with their services that are very much in demand one day and may be totally useless the next.

The massive changes brought about in other sectors produce similar situations. For example, does a manager in a public company or government body, with no experience of, say, the cut-throat world of competition and tendering, have the skills, i.e. the ability, to be able to deal with the requirements and pressures put on them?

To take an example, Gardner Merchant, the international industrial, health and educational catering part of Trusthouse Forte, used its sales and marketing skills and operational expertise to attack the rapidly deregulating catering contracts in the Health Service. These skills were not necessary, or not as necessary in the monopoly situation within the Health Service.

The only way to improve the competitiveness of any organisations is to improve the three A's – Attitude, Awareness, Ability

Corporate Internal Marketing identifies these by using whatever medium is appropriate . 'Hold on,' I hear the trainers say, 'training does that.' Yes of course it does: for the section of the issues which require training. Training cannot, for example, tackle the introduction of mission statements, or the attitudes to IT, or the marketing of strategic and tactical plans. Training cannot tackle the creation of integrated approaches to communicating pay and reward structures. Training cannot tackle the associated actions and plans needed to be produced by the individuals to meet their targets. Training cannot tackle the strategic changes necessary to ensure that communication takes place in rapidly altering global markets; communication to often vastly overburdened people, who have little enough time to 'do their own job, never mind spend time talking to others' (a cry I hear time and time again). Training is, however, tackling many of the issues that are raised by Corporate Internal Marketing. The two disciplines are inextricably linked. As will be seen later, it is one of the key products and services that Corporate Internal Marketing can support in its tough fight to get into the internal market place.

To recapitulate, through improved Attitude, Awareness and Ability brought about by improved communication and training, every individual is capable of giving greatly increased Added Value. This can be measured. More organisations are calculating Added Value and marketing the results to shareholders and others, by producing statistics such as profit per employee and added value per employee.

Tactics from below: meeting customer requirements

We have already dealt with 'strategy from below'. However, it is not just strategy that is being communicated. There will be many tactical issues raised that will provide the organisation with a wealth of principles and practices. If these were practised everywhere they would lead to significant improvements throughout the organisation. These practices are often called 'standards' in many organisations, and are sometimes more affectionately referred to as 'best principles and best practices'.

By gathering them in a structured way, as a result of the research methodologies used by Corporate Internal Marketing, the organisation stands to benefit from the might of the collective brain power of its people. If the principles and practices can then be disseminated in a way that encourages 'ownership' the organisation will benefit. Everyone will be less precious about taking up new and improved internal product or service. It is when these new and improved products and services lie around with no one to pick them up that the individuals who know their worth get very demotivated. It is when they are picked up and others will not buy into them because of poor internal marketing that they can also get very demotivated. By the same token, if the people who are using existing methodologies are not sold the new ideas in an effective way they will fail to 'take them on board'. They will also be demotivated if they know they are using methods which are recognised as inferior.

The task of Corporate Internal Marketing is two-fold when it comes to 'tactics from below'. These can be summed up by a lovely phrase which I heard from Robert Crawford, Service Circle Co-ordinator of the Royal Bank Of Scotland. His role, in essence, is to collect the best principles and practices and to disseminate these throughout the bank. They come from the work and ideas of each branch and departmental team charged with collecting and generating ideas locally. He calls it: 'The gathering and sharing of the wisdom of the people'.

Many organisations have gone down the route of having teams of people who get together to improve the methods and practices. The processes for doing this are discussed under the heading 'Innovation from all' (see page 76.) Once the ideas are generated, the main issue for the organisation is ensuring that their use is maximised. In order that this can happen the ideas have to be gathered. This is not only true of teams of people coming up with new ideas, it is true of individuals as well.

Even more fundamental than dreaming up new ideas is identifying whether the internal or external customer has a need for them.

If no one wants a better mouse trap then a lot of time can be wasted inventing and launching it!

This is called research! It may be either qualitative or quantitative research. The skills can be taught. They often only require a simple process of using structured, 'open' or 'closed' questions.

Taking the example of Gardner Merchant again, the company trained its managers to use a series of customer questionnaires. This forced the managers to discover the customer requirements before they attempted to introduce any new ideas. The temptation of people put in the position of being able to recommend or introduce new ideas is to put forward their own hobby horse. The danger then is that the new idea or improved standard does not produce the results expected, and the people responsible may feel reluctant to expose themselves to further failure.

The same holds true of the introduction of best practices to improve the output of people. These need to be researched prior to attempting to introduce them. A further benefit of doing this is that it can then be said that the introduction of ideas was as a 'response' to a need, not an imposition.

The strengths of using the recognised techniques of research in Corporate Internal Marketing further enhance the transference of best practices and principles. It is recognised that the process has validity in the external marketing of products and services. No one in their right mind launches a product today without the need being established and the likely take-up being estimated. Both of these are highlighted in the research.

This process is given further credence by the assumption in 'quality programmes' that everyone is part of a customer supplier chain. So the first thing that needs to be done is to 'establish the customer's requirements'. Yet, the connection with research has not been made. Crosby, in his book *Quality is Free*, writes of the fundamental definition of quality as 'conformance to requirements', and goes on to say that 'measurements' must then be continually taken to 'determine conformance to those requirements'. This is absolutely valid, but the system and language used bears no relation to that used and practised externally. Research does exactly the same thing. So now the organisation has an internal language of 'quality', and an external language of 'marketing'.

The internal customer supplier chain

It is the recognition that everyone is a customer which should set off the Corporate Internal Marketing process. This process happens whenever the issue of conformance to customer requirement is raised. In essence, a quality programme by its own definition, must be a marketing programme. It will be seen later that the marketing steps taken to bring a product to the external market place, are just as applicable to any individual or team attempting to have their ideas bought into by the internal market place.

Clearly, a tremendous amount of work has been done at a technical level in terms of systems and measurements in quality. I am not suggesting that the 'baby gets thrown out with the bath-water'. If the basic premise is that quality is all about customers, this means that marketing principles must apply. Indeed, with much of the interaction being on a one-to-one basis between individuals, then the setting of requirements and agreeing the terms is more likely to be that of a sales transaction.

Organisations spend large sums of money training and retraining sales people. Their job is to constantly service customers' needs and constantly monitor feedback. They then pass that feedback to the marketing people who can respond to problems and opportunities. This requires a high degree of skill.

The same could also be said of the skills needed by each internal customer in assessing and delivering against their customers' needs. The first step taken by people when getting together as part of a quality programme is effectively a sales process – it must be, if they are all customers. Corporate Internal Marketing will improve this process by ensuring the following:

- The tactical execution of any strategy will focus on the gathering of data via structured research.
- The needs of the internal customer on a one-to-one basis will be

met by the recognised use of selling techniques that ensure they want and get the right products and services.

- The distribution of the best of the products and services being provided internally will be done by the use of targeted marketing.
- The constantly updated needs of the market place will be measured in terms of the ultimate aim of both internal marketing and external marketing, i.e. profit.
- The language used to inspire the individuals will be one of marketing and selling. This allows every individual to use tried and tested techniques on their own customers.
- The focus is on customers' needs and meeting them, in a positive and exciting way.
- The training of a marketing-based approach will provide the hooks – new skills and personal development. This will be of benefit to those people who have been trained in the technical aspects of this type of programme.

Does this sound like a takeover of quality programmes? It isn't. The point is that the nature of any type of programme will require the awareness and use of Corporate Internal Marketing. Indeed, as the workforce become more and more sophisticated in their needs and desires, and better trained to handle the people aspects involved in all jobs, there will be a need for even greater use of the sophisticated external marketing techniques.

This is backed up, albeit perhaps unwittingly, by Crosby as he writes about the fourteen steps of quality in *Quality is Free*.

Step One: Management Commitment

Action. Discuss the need for quality improvement with management, emphasising the need for defect prevention.

(*Sell them the idea that providing the right products and services to internal and external customers is a good idea. Also target the message on one of the features of the programme.*)

There are plenty of films, visual aids, and other material available to support this communication.

(*There is a target market who are unlikely to be sold the ideas by unskilled sales people. The hearts and minds of these people will only be won over by sophisticated marketing techniques.*)

and later . . .

Step Five

Action. It is now time to share with employees the measurements of what non-quality is costing. This is done by training super-visors to orient employees
(*sell them the ideas as well*)
and by providing visible evidence of the concern for quality improvement
(*i.e. meet customer needs*)
through communication
(*i.e. marketing*)
material such as booklets, films, and posters
(*although no mention is given of the need to ensure that the 'quality' of this material meets the customer requirements!*).

Don't confuse this with some get-motivated-quick scheme.
(*These marketing people are only capable of short-term hype not long-term strategic campaigns!*)

It is a sharing process, and does not involve manipulating people.
(*So why the need for all the flash marketing material, and the selling process at senior level and 'orienting employees'? Of course it involves manipulating people, people love to be sold to, they love to be persuaded to buy into things they might not have considered before. Marketing and selling are not dishonourable professions; there is nothing wrong with using the skills – but don't overuse them and pressurise people into short-term decisions that will later affect their long-term buying. Most market-ing and sales people do want long-term customers. It makes a lot of sense, as the most expensive customers to reach are those who have not bought the product before.*)

THIS (sharing with employees) IS AN IMPORTANT STEP. IT MAY BE THE MOST IMPORTANT STEP OF ALL.

(*'Quality' is just like every other product or service which requires people to buy. As a product and service being provided by the organisation, it needs internal marketing and selling. In addition to this, the product must meet customer requirements – and that to the external world is the function of marketing.*)

Service and administrative people should be included, just like everybody else.

(*There are other target markets who must be considered – whether or not they should be seen as 'just like everybody else' would be a function of the research into their needs and requirements, and their acceptance of the creative approach used.*)

and finally . . .

Step Fourteen

Repetition makes the programme perpetual and thus 'part of the woodwork'. If quality isn't ingrained in the organisation, it will never happen.

(*This is a people orientated, long-term, on-going programme – or in marketing terms – an internal customer targeted, strategic campaign, aimed at turning non-users into users, who, through constant advertising and promotion are encouraged to perform repeat purchases.*)

The difference isn't just in the words, it is a whole mind set. Corporate Internal Marketing has the ability to provide supporting professional skills. These will ensure that customers' requirements are met. It is through Corporate Internal Marketing that the tactics needed to gather and share the best principles and practices of the organisation are instilled in every individual, and the commitment to continue is driven by consistent targeted messages.

Quality programmes are all about generating tactics from below; constant improvement through constant input of everyone. This will come about when the processes and techniques of Corporate Internal Marketing are used by everyone, when they are all able to market and sell their ideas.

The picture becomes more clear

The language of marketing applied internally creates a comfort zone for those who have already got used to it externally. The focus is on customers in almost every aspect of the terminology used, e.g. Target Market, Research, Product, Services, Branding, etc.

The feature of corporate internal marketing is that it relies not only on the power of marketing but also on the fundamental practices of human resource development to bring about change.

Those with closest contact with the customer are the front-line individuals. They can usually see just as clearly as anyone the way forward for the organisation. Techniques such as Research (MBWA!) will reveal the strategies from below.

'Added Value' from the improved contribution of every individual happens by providing internal products and services, such as training. These products and services simply have to affect the three 'As': Attitude, Awareness, Ability.

The results of 'Quality' programmes are just one example of the tactical improvements that every individual can make to the organisation. Quality and corporate internal marketing are inextricably linked through internal and external customers.

4 | *The benefits*

Empowerment at all levels

One of the biggest problems that managers used to face in an organisation was the feeling of being unable to act and make decisions. This may have been a result of fear of the consequences of 'sticking their neck out'; or it may have been the constraints placed upon them by their superiors. This is exemplified by some very low levels of expenditure authority vested in some very highly paid people.

Much of this has changed. There is also a new desire for it to be changed; but the vestiges of the past are steeped in many cultures. The speed of decision making that is required today is unlike anything that people have previously encountered. The levels of bureaucracy that have been removed in incredibly short time scales have forced a greater need for decisions on fewer and fewer individuals. Yet the self-same individuals have not been given the support and skills that they feel they need to be able to respond to the new challenges facing them.

These needs naturally involve the management skills and techniques which are trainable. These are, for example, problem solving, decision making, planning, leadership skills and team skills. They are also the technical skills needed to deal with a changing environment that boasts whole new methodologies in the workplace. In addition to these skills there is a whole new organisational environment and culture in which they have to operate. A large part of this environment is generated by the one certainty that does exist in business today, summed up by saying, 'Nothing is as certain as tremendous change'. Additionally, the other certainty is that as the structures get 'flatter' the pressures get greater. What are these pressures?

- Greater demands on time.
- Greater demands on effectiveness.
- Greater demands from the people in and around the team to meet their needs, and share their concerns.
- Greater demands from home.
- Greater personal demands on improved quality of life.
- Greater demands from customers.
- Greater demands from 'above'.
- Greater demands to produce and increase profitability.

And so the list goes on. Yet this list is a new one, added to the list that was talked about earlier that creates fear in individuals – for their position, their status, their security, their job.

The net result is a tremendous strain, especially at middle management level. The easiest way out of this, for those who are in the unfortunate position where the organisation does not invest in the training, development and the communication processes, is to retreat to a 'safe position', where they believe they cannot be harmed. It is one where they put a squeeze on just about everything, to prevent or delay decisions being made. This is classically referred to as applying 'control'.

This is best exemplified by what I describe as the 'egg timer effect' (see Figure 4.1). It may not have any basis in qualitatively re-searched data, but the power of its message has been attested to in the many organisations that have had this theory presented to them.

In essence, the net result of this middle management 'squeeze' is to produce an amazingly powerful counter to the attempts at opening up the communication channels. The squeeze prevents the internal marketing of ideas, products and services. This can be to, or from, those individuals who are on either side of the internal chain of command. In turn, it prevents not only the individual concerned from making decisions, but also restricts and prevents those above or below from making decisions, because the information that allows this to happen is not flowing.

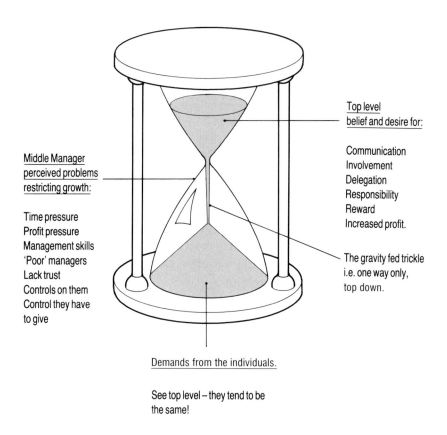

Top level
belief and desire for:

Communication
Involvement
Delegation
Responsibility
Reward
Increased profit.

Middle Manager
perceived problems
restricting growth:

Time pressure
Profit pressure
Management skills
'Poor' managers
Lack trust
Controls on them
Control they have
to give

The gravity fed trickle
i.e. one way only,
top down.

Demands from the individuals.

See top level – they tend to be
the same!

Figure 4.1.   The bottleneck to growth.

The interesting thing about the 'egg timer effect' is that it shows that the hopes and desires of those above and those below the individual who is controlling the squeeze are almost always the same. It is not until the squeeze is opened out that the start of empowering all the individuals in the organisation will happen. The second characteristic of the 'egg timer' itself, which makes this model so pertinent, is that the flow (in this case of information), is always downwards.

In one organisation this downward 'cascade' of information was described in one qualitative research group as being 'from that shower at head office'! Too often people believe that information is something to be handed down, from decision makers to the people at the lower levels. This is embodied in the methodology of the 'briefing group'; almost a military style 'tell' session, with a concession to the people after they have been 'briefed' to say what they think. Having been presented with a *fait accompli*, it is often not wise to say what you think! In addition to this, the flow of locally targeted information often dries up. This is because it comes from managers who are controlling and squeezing information. They do this in a bid to retain their authority. It often leads to only two or three briefing groups being held, and because they soon dry up, they lose their credibility. The attempt at communication is seen to have failed. This of course puts the squeezing manager back in a strong position. They are then the sole source of information transfer. They no longer have to expose themselves to groups. The process moves back to a one-to-one basis. And so they return to the old practice of 'divide and rule'.

Yet the pressure is on. Not for less responsibility but for more. People want to use their brains. The Esso research by MORI highlighted that people want involvement. Once they get involved, they will be able to take responsibility.

It is through the targeting of key information to all levels that the individuals will start to demand greater and greater autonomy. This does not mean that a reduction in 'leadership' is required – people need and want strong leaders. What is needed is a lessening of the levels of control orientated management.

The key issue for individuals in the organisation becomes the responsiveness of those around them to the decisions that they are making. These people – either above, below, or colleagues – become the customers who benefit or otherwise from the decisions. The opening up of communication will ensure that the speed of response allows the decison maker to know very quickly if they have made the right decision or not. By opening up the communication the people feel that if the information being targeted at them meets their needs they will increasingly demand to be taken into account.

The employee revolution has begun

Revolutions are about empowering the people: this revolution is perhaps the largest ever to be experienced in the history of man. As this is being written, the East European nation states are going through exactly the same process.

The needs of the people are gaining in strength as their affluence grows. Their needs are growing in their level of sophistication as the world moves through a technical and economic revolution.

People's wants and desires move up Maslow's *Hierarchy of Needs*. They move from basic to social needs, and onwards toward the self-interested need called 'Self Actualisation'. Now, whatever level of need is being appealed to, the methods of getting through to people in the internal market must meet the same levels of sophistication that they are used to, in their role as external customers.

If people will not put up with a state which tells them what to do, then they are certainly not going to put up with an organisation – or even less an uncommunicative boss – who tries to do the same.

The opposite side of the coin is that the organisation needs them to be making decisions. It is doing everything in its power to ensure that they have the local information needed to make their decisions. The current demands of customers wanting better 'quality' and value for money, financiers demanding higher interest, shareholders demanding higher returns all mean one thing in this high-risk society – profit. The hierarchical days of layers of managers contributing little to the good of the organisation or community are on their way out.

The people want empowerment

The way to empower people is to meet their needs with the internal products and services. These must then allow them to have what is becoming a stronger and stronger cry – freedom! This cry was typified by a pub manager in the Tetley Walker chain, and was heard at an Issues Group.

To fill in a little background to this, it was felt that the intended introduction of a cultural change might advantageously be heralded by a new incentive scheme. However, in order to assuage the anxiety among senior managers and show them that the likelihood would be that the needs of managers would be released from the 'egg timer effect', two days of highly structured qualitative research were held. These Issue Groups are designed to inject all the strategic issues into the discussion to test the validity of internal perceptions.

And so to the 'freedom' cry of managers and staff in organisations throughout the land. It did not take long for it to come. As the very first manager walked into the room he said, 'I hope we are not here to talk about incentive schemes. The only incentive I need is to run my pub.'

A note about the power of the unions

If it is accepted that the key need of employees who are looking to achieve independence in this revolution is to be left to get on with it, and the leaders of the organisation are doing all in their power to ensure this happens, then the great 'us and them' divide will disappear. The self-same pub manager in the research group informed the team (of colleagues and managers) that once they were left to do all the things that they knew they were capable of, and middle management stopped interfering, then the need for the unions would disappear. This was an interesting observation, to which he added, 'I am a union representative, so I have nothing against unions. It is just that, up until now, they have been the only way to communicate around the middle managers and get to the top. Once they let us manage, which is after all what we are paid to do, then the need for us to skirt around them will disappear.'

So, the flatter the structures, the greater the levels of communication and Corporate Internal Marketing, all help towards empowering the individuals. The need disappears to leave this power in the hands of a few people, who may be perceived to be using it in a way not acceptable to the individual, i.e. politically.

Empowering the people does not mean a socialist revolution in the workplace. It means everyone accepting greater levels of responsibility to assist the organisation and themselves to fulfil their needs.

These changes are not only desirable, they are vital, if the organisation is to survive. What the pub manager was actually saying was summed up in the view held by the group. What was required was not a boss/subordinate relationship (especially when the area manager was hardly ever seen, as they were kept extremely busy), but a 'partnership based on trust'.

This element of 'trust' is the next strategic change which Corporate Internal Marketing brings about.

Trust

There is a new wave of morality that is sweeping through organisations as they move down the paths of 'Excellence' and 'Quality'. Very few people have recognised it yet, but the more popular term for it would be 'religion'.

The work being done by consultants, human resource specialists and the like, is almost akin to that of missionaries. They go into the organisation and 'spread the word'. They provide the basis for their 'high priests' to be trained, often called 'champions'; they leave their 'bibles', often called manuals, with the converts. They tell their parables of other 'good Samaritans' doing excellent things all over the world – these Samaritans often seem to have mysterious foreign-sounding names to add to the spice of the story – like IBM (perhaps it's short for Ibraham?).

They can now also create the impression of immortality by appearing on the everlasting medium of a training video. They are called 'gurus' by their disciples. Finally, people are prepared to travel great distances to hear their words of wisdom; or in the case of Tom Peters to be harangued about their corporate sins (like not putting the janitor's name under his photograph when the CEO is named under *his* photograph!).

Is this going too far? With the demise of the Church, especially in the UK, it is perhaps a good thing that someone is taking up the role of provider of spiritual guidance.

Read this set of values from my organisation. To produce these words, a tremendous amount of soul searching went on; and a great deal of debate took place, all of which ended up with perhaps the fastest change in some people's outlooks that they had ever experienced. Not everyone was hit by the fervour created, but there was a fundamental recognition that the ways of the past would not be tolerated.

We value: recognition of individual contribution.

We value: teamwork

We value: honesty and integrity

We value: a source of social responsibility

We value: mutual respect and integrity

These attitudinal shifts occur as a direct result of people interacting with others in a structured way. The debates and discussions are even provided in 'company time', so that unlike Church, the individual does not have to invest his own time. Attitudes towards the organisation, customers and colleagues are discussed effectively in the context of more 'honourable' methods of making a profit, through improving internal and external relationships. The individual must therefore consider both his personal and work ethics. To give two simple examples, customers should never be looked down on in any way, such as calling them 'punters'. Secondly, colleagues' needs should be respected, e.g. no smoking at work, even in the unlikely event of being in the majority.

What has religion got to do with Corporate Internal Marketing? A great deal. Without being in any way sacrilegious, religion provides an interesting parallel. For centuries it has been one of the best sold and marketed 'products and services' the world has ever seen. What is happening now is that the same type of messages are suddenly becoming increasingly important in the workplace. In fact the fervour created by strong belief is exactly that desired by most organisations. Look at what is happening in Japan. It is not the methods and practices (like Just In Time) etc. which ensure that the levels of quality and cost are almost unbeatable, it is the people's total commitment to these technological and production 'gods' that guarantees their total domination in so many markets.

Much of the work by the Western 'experts' in these areas is little more than an attempt to verbalise the actions required, rather than translating through Corporate Internal Marketing techniques the deep rooted beliefs necessary to make them work.

Unfortunately, this perception is made worse by business programmes on TV. Examples of this ability to create in-built trust, loyalty, commitment, enthusiasm, etc. usually involve British workers in Japanese owned factories in some far flung new town in the UK. They are either doing physical jerks at some ungodly hour in the morning or sitting in groups in the 'uni-level' canteen having a pep talk or sitting in 'quality circles'. This does little to create a desire for change in others. It is not decrying the validity of what is happening in these organisations. The point is that the message being given to these employees is coming from a different source than before. They are more likely to be disposed to buying-in to this message because they are effectively in a foreign environment. The old adage applies, otherwise they would not have gone for the job in the first place – 'When in Japan do as the Japanese do.'!

This same employee commitment is desired by Western organisations. However, they cannot change the culture without changing the deep-rooted beliefs of everybody. In a telephone poll survey of British companies who had tried to introduce JIT, 90% failed in the first three months. Why? The answer lies firstly in the quality of the marketing in the launch, and secondly in the trust placed by the individuals being asked to change their ways. If the target market lacks the basic trust in the organisation and its motives, then nothing will move them to buy the new products and services being offered.

The needs of the individual at a basic emotional level are for those often reiterated virtues that are heard in church – trust, integrity, respect, etc. Consider then the possible objectives of a customer service campaign. These are not definitive, but serve to show the close proximity of religious teachings.

1 To provide your customer with a level of service that you would expect when you are buying products and services.
   (*Do unto others as you would have done to you.*)

2 To ensure that the customer is treated with the utmost respect even when it appears that they are being 'awkward'.
   (*Turn the other cheek.*)

3 Deal with complaints in a tolerant, friendly way.
   (*Let he who is without sin cast the first stone.*)

4 Welcome the customer in a polite friendly way.
   (*Be a good Samaritan to these total strangers that you are being asked to deal with.*)

5 Ensure that our children's policy is adhered to, as they are important customers today and in the future.
   (*Suffer little children to come unto me.*)

It is the targeting of these messages into the heart and soul of the individual that forms part of the brief in this, and many other internal marketing campaigns. Trust is produced when Corporate Internal Marketing is practised. It is through the organisation having to change to prove to the individual that it means what it says that this benefit is created.

The individual will not, for example, practise any new technique or skill for long if the manager does not practise it. The individual will not give of his best if all he is doing is being taken advantage of. The individual will not respond to greater amounts of responsibility being thrust on him if the respect for his contribution is not forthcoming. So, what can be expected with greater levels of effective Corporate Internal Marketing?

1 Greater levels of research and simple 'listening', backed up by response, leads to greater levels of trust.
   (This is not to be taken lightly, e.g. the trust placed in the brand and its values by the external customer is dearly bought.)

2 Better targeted messages homing in on specific needs leads to greater commitment to the organisation.
   (This is the same as external marketing finding the hooks that make the customer eager to buy.)

3 More and improved information means the individual will be more loyal. The mushroom theory of 'keeping everyone in the dark and feeding them rubbish' *is* rubbish.
   (External marketeers who fail to keep their products and services in front of the consumer will, owing to their short term and fickle nature, soon end up with a dead product.)

4 Pride develops when an individual knows that he is trusted, and that this recognition is demonstrated to others.
   (The new car in the driveway is a powerful testimony to pride, and how people will go out of their way to seek and to demonstrate it.)

5 Finally, the biggest buzzword in human resource development circles today is 'ownership'. This is created through the very processes of Corporate Internal Marketing which serve to show individuals that they are just that, i.e. individuals. It demonstrates that their needs are being met by research both present and future needs. It shows that they will then deliver what is expected of them, if they are trusted.
   (In external marketing, the process of involving customers is far less critical – ownership comes when they have bought the products and services and are 'delighted' with them.)

Innovation from all

The one demand that is placed on the external marketing department, above all else, is providing the customer with something NEW, NEW, NEW!!

This may be in the products and services themselves, in the

advertising, the promotion, or, for the salesforce, it may be in the form of new markets, conference themes, incentive schemes, or in the packaging, branding or corporate identity. There are always demands for things that are new.

The pace of change itself has created an almost insatiable beast demanding the 'new'. If it isn't 'new and improved', then there must be something wrong with it!

There are one or two products and services which don't appear to change, but on closer inspection they are moving as rapidly as the latest piece of information technology – well almost. For example, Fairy Liquid appear to have used the same advertisements for 25 years, and indeed the basic story of parent, child and bubbles at the sink has not changed (with the odd foray into other creative ideas on the way) but the production techniques are as up to date as you would expect, and – shock! horror! – we now even see a man at the sink!

The external customer is literally assailed by everything new, every day. The same is now happening in the workplace. The latest advance in IT is new one day and obsolete the next. People management techniques and practices change every time someone brings out the latest management best seller. The individuals at the sharp end experience a constant stream of new messages.

How do they respond?

Added to all this, everyone in the organisation is now being viewed as a vital cog in the wheel of improving quality. They are also expected to contribute to the creative input, and to be immediately capable of handling the process of innovation to bringing these ideas to the market place. Finally, they play a crucial part in turning in increasingly tough profit targets.

Without wishing to beat the marketing drum too hard, it is the techniques of those two key skills of creativity and innovation that rest with this function. Marketing spends its entire existence in managing these, in order to satisfy the external customer. More importantly, it must be recognised by everyone in the organisation that both quality and innovation are only meaningful if they are placed in the context of customers and their needs. Hence, the other marketing skills such as research design and testing also come into play.

There are further skills which are also vital in this process of improving quality and managing information. These have been touched on elsewhere under the general headings of problem solving (sometimes referred to as problem prevention), planning and decision making. This is where human resource skills are invaluable.

And so to the definitions again. Oxford Dictionary – Create: Bring into existence, give rise to, originate.

Perhaps it is worth mentioning the part of the definition which is sometimes used by other non-creative people in the organisation, if their cosy world is shattered by the goings-on of the creative individuals who are forever challenging the order of things, and looking to replace, renew, restructure, and reject things with their new ideas, viz. Create: Make a fuss!

Or to quote Tom Peters who quotes Quinn:

> Most corporations fail to tolerate the creative fanatic who has been the driving force behind most major innovations. Innovations, being far removed from the mainstream of the business, show little promise in the early stages of development. Moreover, the champion is obnoxious, impatient, egoistic, and perhaps a bit irrational in organisational terms. As a consequence, he is not hired. If he is hired, he is not promoted or rewarded. He is regarded as 'not a serious person', 'embarrassing', or 'disruptive'.

Oxford Dictionary – INNOVATE: Bring in novelties; make new.

The difference is that creativity brings ideas into existence, innovation turns them into products and services. Corporate Internal Marketing puts the two into context by establishing a number of things within an organisation.

1 If customers want NEW, NEW, NEW, then we must ensure we give it to them.
2 If it takes an 'upsetting of the (internal) apple cart' to get new ideas into the system to replace the things that customers no

longer want, so be it. It is not the creators and innovators that we ought to be coaching and counselling about their pushing and shoving of others (and generally in the process dulling their desires to be at the leading edge), it is the ones who are getting upset. These are the people who are, in fact, not the holders of 'all that is right'; they are the ones who will let the competitor overtake you.

3 Failure is success. If you have failed then you have tried. Something like 95% of all new products fail in the first two years. It is a good job that the innovators of these did not give up and go home because we wouldn't have the other 5%!

4 Most creativity and innovation rely on everybody in the organisation to contribute; therefore everybody should receive the training to assist the organisation to meet its overwhelming need to improve quality and innovate.

5 Most creativity and innovation are stifled by the attitude of the creators, e.g. worry/fear that it won't succeed, and the attitude of the others involved, e.g. worry/fear that it will succeed and highlight their inadequacy. The introduction of a process which ensures that does not happen will help alleviate the biggest stumbling block to both processes.

The only problem here is that while everyone has got hung up, quite rightly, on Jan Carlzon and the 1000 × 1% improvements, there appears to be very little evidence of the skills training to enable the process to happen. Where it does happen, the tendency is for there to be a concentration on improvements in quality of existing products, services and internal procedures and practices, rather than creating and innovating.

One excellent example of this element, in a quality improvement programme, together with a strong slant on innovation, is in the Royal Bank of Scotland. The entire programme they are running, called 'Where People Matter', began as an internal campaign to focus on customer needs. As a consequence of its success, the programme's theme was carried into the external marketing. The power achieved from both an internal and external marketing campaign is ultimately what can be aimed for in most organisations.

The individual branches and departments in the Royal Bank of Scotland have two elements operating under the title of 'Service Circles'. The first of these, called 'Doing it Right', is the activity which 'looks at the services we provide for both internal and external customers. It looks at what we do and how we do it. . . . This activity will establish the standards of performance that our services need to meet. It will also identify the problems that prevent us from meeting the required standards and develop ideas to overcome them.' To do this, there are 10 steps in the process. Of these, the three key steps that are effectively marketing orientated are:

- Identify customers (*The target market*)
- Establish the requirements of the customer (*Research needs*)
- Communicate the actions (*Advertise the improved products and services*)

The second activity in the programme allows the individuals at branch and department level to concentrate on the major area of innovation under their control, i.e. the service they give. While ideas for new products and services for the whole bank are gathered and put into practice, the framework of existing products at any given time in most organisations leaves little room at local level for major innovation, specifically on product. This is not to say that a great deal can and should be done at local level to meet and surpass the needs of customers. It is in this 'surpassing' of the needs of customers that the process of innovation takes place. It assumes that the innovation brings with it a level of service that is neither expected nor even requested. Hence the title the bank has given this process: 'Surprising the Customer'.

'This activity is intended to examine our *means* of communication with our customers, internal or external, to ensure that we are using them most effectively. If we are to gain a reputation for being more effective and more personal in the services we provide, our means of communication must be looked at closely.'

Once again there are three key marketing orientated steps, which are exactly the same as those previously stated. Whether looking at 'new' or just 'improved', the customer requirements are paramount. And so, back to the central premise, that if customers are involved, then so should the role of Corporate Internal Marketing. Where it is involved, it will keep that focus paramount simply by its language and its processes, and innovation will be fundamental to what everyone recognises of the soap powder syndrome – 'New and Improved': in other words keeping up with, and ahead of the customer.

Innovation is therefore one of the greatest benefits of Corporate Internal Marketing. Together with empowerment at all levels, and 'trust', they achieve the key needs of the organisation and the individual – the desire to get on with the job, the environment that lets them do it, and the ability/opportunity to continually improve.

The benefits shine through

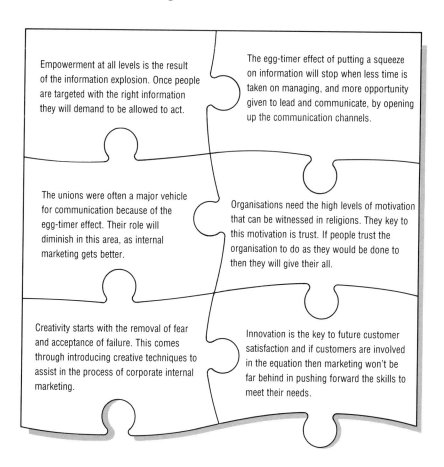

Empowerment at all levels is the result of the information explosion. Once people are targeted with the right information they will demand to be allowed to act.

The egg-timer effect of putting a squeeze on information will stop when less time is taken on managing, and more opportunity given to lead and communicate, by opening up the communication channels.

The unions were often a major vehicle for communication because of the egg-timer effect. Their role will diminish in this area, as internal marketing gets better.

Organisations need the high levels of motivation that can be witnessed in religions. They key to this motivation is trust. If people trust the organisation to do as they would be done to then they will give their all.

Creativity starts with the removal of fear and acceptance of failure. This comes through introducing creative techniques to assist in the process of corporate internal marketing.

Innovation is the key to future customer satisfaction and if customers are involved in the equation then marketing won't be far behind in pushing forward the skills to meet their needs.

5 | *The model*

Introduction

Too often models are complicated. They are there to provide a number of benefits. Simplifying the understanding of complicated processes should be one of them. The other benefits are worth stating here, before getting into the inter-related aspects of Corporate Internal Marketing depicted by this model. The reason for looking at this is that when transferring the knowledge of Corporate Internal Marketing to others, it is through using and understanding the model that it can be done most effectively and simply. An understanding of how to use the model is essential.

1 **A big picture from little details**
   Having shown people the model in its entirety without explanation, it can be guaranteed that very few people are likely to appreciate it.

2 **Understanding grows through debate**
   The absorption of the facts will be best achieved as each individual element is debated. If the model is put forward as a basis for this debate, rather than as a *fait accompli*, then the person trying to 'internalise' this new method of seeing the internal corporate world will not be threatened by the new order: they are being asked to consider it, not forced to accept it.

3 **Acceptance comes at varying speeds**
   The build-up of the picture, the facts, and reasoning behind it, has

taken the author many years of working in this field. Acceptance of the reasoning behind this model will be at a speed determined by the individual.

4 **Not everyone wants to buy the product**

Having tested this model on numerous occasions on individuals in many large and small organisations, I can say that I have come across only one or two people who do not believe that the Employee Revolution is here, or, that organisations need to meet the challenge with Corporate Internal Marketing. They always had a vested interest in the established order of things. Surprisingly, they were usually involved in one of the areas in Corporate Internal Marketing such as the company newspaper, but recognised the very diminished role that was being suggested by the new philosophy. Naturally enough the reaction in this situation is highly defensive, usually manifesting itself in all-out attack!

Using a model allows the arguments to build up rationally and logically. The rejection comes with the realisation that the big picture places the individual in a less important role. The arguments that then follow are usually emotional and illogical. The nice thing about this is that when it occurs in a group situation, it serves to reinforce the validity and understanding to the rest of the group.

The counter arguments actually run something like this: 'But what you are saying is that if they have got a boring job, then everything should be done to ensure that they stay. Well clearly, from my experience they leave anyway, so why bother!'

In a group discussion, others can criticise this type of comment, strengthening their own acceptance of new ideas.

The basis of Corporate Internal Marketing strategy

The model is, therefore, a very useful tool. One of its main benefits is evident when it is used by the whole organisation. Once the Chief Executive accepts it as the basis of a communications policy, i.e. an internal marketing policy, then a number of things start to happen.

Structured approach to the business

First and foremost, if the CEO is using a model, then by definition, he is approaching the business in a totally structured way. Perhaps for the first time the complexities of the business can be expressed in a way that allows everyone in the business to understand what the CEO, and indeed everyone else, is attempting to do, and the methods of trying to do it.

The best previous models of organisational structure were those of the departmental splits of the functions. Thus, previously, everyone realised that in order to succeed it was necessary to have a board, a marketing function, a personnel function, an accounting function, etc. These functions then each did their own specialised thing, and the business progressed or otherwise.

The problem is, the approach is not holistic. It simply demonstrates that there are a number of things that are necessary to allow the business to function. It is also divisive in many organisations, where an 'us and them' attitude builds up, as well as localised, parochial perceptions of what the organisation is trying to achieve.

To overcome this functional split of the organisation, it is then further necessary to attempt to provide an 'overview' of the business, e.g. its direction, results, etc. through using inadequate and inappropriate vehicles of communication such as the company newspaper, or briefing groups. If anything, these tend to further intensify the functional split of the business through their focus on departmental activities.

The 'one piece of paper' approach

The Corporate Internal Marketing model puts down, *on one piece of paper*, the interfaces of all the elements of the business. It does so in such a way as to stress the importance of the individuals in the organisation, at every level, and also the inputs and outputs of the organisation, without specifying the functions or departments.

The 'one piece of paper' approach enables everyone to relate to what is going on in the business in a simple way. It does this through showing its activities, rather than its specialised areas of operation. The nice thing about this is that a previously very confusing array of inter-relationships becomes very clear.

Communication defined

'Communication' in its narrowest sense (of allowing individuals at the very least to understand and be able to repeat what they have heard) can only truly happen if the subject matter is placed in context.

The Corporate Internal Marketing model places all the elements of the business and of the need to be communicated into a framework that generates a reasoned understanding of what needs to happen to make the business operate. In short, the model paints a picture of the business that defines the elements of that business. These elements then define the areas in which the individuals can expect to be informed, consulted, and instructed.

All too often, however, the array of communication that occurs is thrown into the organisation without any form of context. Individuals are totally confused as to what is happening, why it is happening, and who thinks what is important.

COMMON UNDERSTANDING

The model, in essence, paints a picture. Therefore, if everyone sees what the picture looks like, there will be common understanding. Most people in organisations today have only a very hazy view of their own role in that organisation, never mind anyone else's role. In addition, there is often very little understanding of the overall mission, the strategy and its structures. This often happens it seems, even after they have been explained.

There is a morass of issues in every organisation which have no apparent formal place in its structure. The methods and variety of putting things across and the apparent complexity of the messages that are sent and received create further confusion.

MUCH ABOUT THE ORGANISATION IS MADE TOO COMPLEX

The purpose of having a model which is simple is that everyone can understand it. Once this common understanding is achieved, then the individuals can get on with running the business, rather than being impeded and frustrated in their attempts at finding solutions to problems resulting from a lack of communication.

Lynette Royle, head of Public Relations at Guinness (post Ernest Saunders), says simply of communications, 'In the end, every problem in business can be traced back to one of communications.'

If the organisation does not produce this common understanding today, then there is likely to be a great deal more time spent remedying the resulting problems. These are usually brought on by a simple lack of clarity and understanding about what is being communicated and why.

The external elements–customers

```
EXTERNAL CUSTOMERS
WHO WE ARE AIMING AT
```

If there is one single thread running throughout the whole plethora of management books on improving one's business, it must be, it has to be, it should be, it can only be – CUSTOMERS.

There are a number of jargon words that have been put before organisations to indicate this focus, two of which are 'Excellence' and 'Quality'. These may not help clarify what is required, and can often obscure the simplicity of the situation, i.e. that people need to understand that they are there simply to meet customers' needs. It is worth exploring this, as the Corporate Internal Marketing model puts 'CUSTOMERS' at the very top.

To give some examples of the words used to create the new focus in organisations:

1 **Excellence** The word itself does inspire, and has done a tremen- dous amount to goad people to aspire to reach the giddy heights

achieved by the almost innumerable case studies and examples cited in the various books. However, the four secrets of 'Excellence' are, in the end, only ways of satisfying internal and external customers, viz:

- superior service;
- constant innovation;
- full use of internal people;
- leadership by MBWA.

Perhaps the link with marketing might have been made earlier if the titles of the books produced by Peters *et al.* had been as follows: *In Search of Customers; A Passion for Customers; Thriving on Customers; The Customer Streak.*

2. **Quality** The introduction into the language of 'Quality', of the concept of the customer/supplier chain, has done wonders to make people realise that internal people are not just corporate assets but are vital links in a chain which can so easily be broken. I wonder though, if the focus of 'Quality' as a word, has led to yet another search for an intangible holy grail. In fact the definition of 'Quality' itself places it in a context most people can relate to, i.e. quality is meeting *customer* requirements, now and in the future.

3. **Purpose** To quote some exciting work being done in ICI Agro-Chemicals Division, the 'Purpose' is 'To help farmers feed the world'. Put in simpler terms where customers are the single focus, 'To help our *customers* feed the world'.

The word 'Purpose' is as emotive as 'Excellence', but my only comment would simply be that the top down driven 'purpose' of any organisation must be to meet its direct customers' needs – however laudable the 'purpose' of its indirect customers.

So, three emotive words all saying the same thing, which is not quite as emotive but is perhaps more focused. If it is more focused, and hence easier for everyone in the organisation to relate to, then the recommendation would be to stick with the simplicity of the word 'customers'. You will soon see why this must be the case. The intention is for everyone in the organisation to concentrate on the skills and techniques of marketing applied internally, as they have been accepted and recognised and applied externally.

Products and services

Marketing history is all about customers, products and services. It looks something like that delineated below and is described in the book *Le Marketing Interne*. Roughly translated from French, this is 'Internal Marketing'! (The subject is well under discussion in the European Community. In fact I had the pleasure, if not surprise, to be the only British speaker, in two days of speakers, at an international conference in Madrid in 1987. Virtually every country in the Community was represented by a speaker talking on one of a large number of issues centred on Corporate Internal Marketing. This was at a time when very few people in the UK were even aware of the subject.)

THE POST WAR HISTORY OF ENTERPRISE (adapted, updated and added to from *Marketing Interne: et Management des Hommes* by Levionnois (Les Editions d'Organisation, 1987))

1950–1960 THE PRODUCTION ECONOMY

A period where demand exceeded supply and all the producers had to do was to concern themselves with the process of production, and process of sales.

1960–1970 THE DISTRIBUTION ECONOMY

A period where supply and demand were roughly equal. In order to survive, the key became the success gained in establishing geographic markets and servicing the needs of those markets. In other words, the battle between manufacturers was supply based.

1970–1980 THE MARKETING ECONOMY

The consumer (but not yet individual customer) becomes king. In a European and global economy the reversal of the situation of supply and demand occurs to oust the factory, sales, and distribution-led organisations. Supply now exceeds demand and the consumer is faced with an increasingly sophisticated and diverse choice of products and services, all vying for their money. The way is open for the marketing professional to meet and create the needs for their particular products and services.

Competition becomes fierce and new skills are needed to meet the rapidly changing needs of the external customer. However, without organisations realising it, this self-same external consumer has also become the sophisticated internal employee, who, for the moment, mainly requires being better managed and better paid.

1980–1990 THE ENVIRONMENTAL ECONOMY

Better described as the 'Economy of change'. Nothing is now certain. From petrol crisis in the early 1980s to environmental crisis in the late 1980s. From increasing co-operation in the European Economy as 1992 approaches and beyond, to amazing destabilisation in the Communist bloc under Gorbachev. From massive mainframe computing power in the early 1980s to massive desk-top and lap-top power in the late 1980s. From a focus on export potential to a realisation that we are entering a marketing-driven age of the global market. From derison and fright about Far Eastern products and services to the manufacture of them on 'home soil', as they infiltrate Western economies.

All of these environmental, economic, competitive, technological, psychological and consumer based changes have fuelled a management revolution. This revolution has been channelled in the West by a desire to be as good as the Japanese, and been led by the gurus talked about elsewhere in this book, not least of them Peters and Crosby.

It must be noted before going further into the 1990s that the 1980s were still not the era of the external 'individual customer'. The focus on individuals each making up the target markets – rather than mass marketing techniques – was only just being realised. It was preached in popular terms with the advent of *In Search of Excellence* by Peters and Waterman (Harper & Row, 1982). This of course, was not revolutionary in itself, being based on observation of the too few organisations practising it.

1990 – THE INTERNAL AND EXTERNAL CUSTOMER ECONOMY

We now part company from *Le Marketing Interne.* The focus has now firmly shifted to the very specific needs of the individual external customer. 'Change' has become the norm. The speed of change has become the issue facing people in and out of the workplace. The forces of change, such as technology, politics, global concerns, family and community isolation, poverty, social concerns, wars, have all become the elements creating the tensions and stresses. Communication has created a well informed society.

What has happened is that the power, upbringing, and awareness that individuals have of their external rights and influence over the producer of products and services (and indeed governments and ideologies) are now transferring internally. Before moving on to the essence of Corporate Internal Marketing, the external focus of the model needs to be strongly fixed in place.

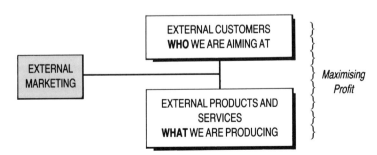

Meeting the needs of the external customer

The word 'meeting', as already discussed in the phrase 'meeting the needs of the external customer', has been chosen very carefully. It has been used to describe the primary function of external marketing. Essentially the external customer really is 'king'. They have ultimate power not only over their own buying decisions but also of others – how many others was only slowly realised with the advent of consumerist power. This was manifested in all sorts of ways (from TV programmes to loud complaints in shops).

The function of marketing, however pro-active, is therefore a subservient one to meet the needs of the external customer. The external marketeer in a free society cannot force the customer to do anything. The customer can, and does make choices based on all kinds of criteria, many, if not most of them, being anything but rational or logical.

The needs of the customer must therefore be identified. They must be specified in terms of the exact type of products and services that are required. A complete and on-going process of getting those products and services to the market place must be established. This process has been defined and, in all but the most backward of organisations, has been accepted under the banner of 'Marketing'. It is not the intention of this book to add to the wealth of material on this subject. All that is necessary is to place marketing in the context of the instigator, creator, generator, communicator, persuader and executioner of the process that uses its skills and techniques to bring in a profit. Using a well-known epithet, it does this by 'meeting the needs of the customer with the right products and services at the right time in the right place at the right price'.

The question is: Why have so few people realised that marketing internally can have the same power as externally?

The answer is: No one has recognised that they have had to!

The new focus is one of the most exciting and difficult challenges yet to face organisations. With the massive amounts of change affecting the organisation and its people, the process of communication and the art and science of turning that into marketed messages will be vital. No organisation will be immune to the needs of its customers – both internal and external.

Maximising relations

Split the business in two!

Wouldn't it be nice if everyone in the business could see that it isn't as complex as they thought? The answer to complexity is to reduce it to its component parts. In business there need be only two component parts.

These are the *Relationships* that are created whenever people are put together (willingly or unwillingly) and the *Resources* that are needed to allow the people to operate and produce the goods and services that the organisation provides.

Two areas need to be put together to make an organisation tick. Is this too simple? I believe that to make the model more complicated is not only counter-productive, especially in terms of a model aimed at ensuring understanding of 'communication', but it is also unnecessary. The alternative, which appears to be the norm in most organisations, is not to have a model, and to assume that the business is too complex to put across to the individuals in it.

If the business can be split into these two key areas, the task faced by everyone in the organisation is to maximise these, both separately and together. So, maximising relationships, maximising resources and maximising the two working together can be the simple titles given to complex processes – but at least the individual can now put a name to what is necessary. Once something has a name, then it can start to be catalogued and defined.

The basic process of maximising relationships is, fundamentally, one that can be tackled and improved by utilising training and human resource development skills. The process of maximising resources is based on the disciplines that have evolved from operating the organisation. The message being preached is that Corporate Internal Marketing not only tackles the process of merging relationships and resources, but it also enhances the individual processes.

For example, the people will be far better equipped to maximise their personal relationships with selling skills: in addition, the organisation will function more smoothly if the distribution channels of information relating to its resources are correctly structured, that is if individual departmental plans point in the same direction as the organisation's overall strategic plans. This only occurs if the channels and priorities are recognised.

By having a model against which to work, and to be able to 'see' the priorities, the interactions, the channels, etc. the individuals in the organisation are able to recognise the contributions that they are making. These contributions may range from the provision of strong leadership from the Chief Executive to any of the basic skills provided by the individuals, but everyone becomes confident of the vital role they play. It may sound like platitudes, but this must become the objective and belief of all organisations. Few appear to have made the transition from theory to practice. The Japanese have succeeded. If the 'culture' is analysed in Corporate Internal Marketing terms, I suspect that at the heart of the many myths surrounding the methods, for example Just In Time, Quality, etc., is an ability to say the right things at the right time to the right individuals. This provides the bedrock of their success. What is said, and who it is said to will be totally different in Western organisations. The timing of the messages may also be alien to the Western way of thinking, but the underlying process will be the same.

This raises the interesting point that Western management may be no less skilled at recognising the needs of the business (do they really not know that high stocks are a bad idea?); it is just that they are less skilled at internal marketing, and being able to maximise the resources and relationships together.

6 | *The employee revolution*

And so to the title of the book. The heart and soul of the concept of Corporate Internal Marketing has been born out of The Employee Revolution. It is a revolution in the truest sense of the word. An uprising of the employee population demanding and achieving changes to areas of their life in work and the methods and practices that surround them. Very few would have predicted it would be so powerful.

Out of this revolution that the 'employee' has created, the same results, if different words, have been achieved as with its counterpart in France 200 years ago. The French Revolution changed the status of the peasant class to 'Citizens': the result of The Employee Revolution has been to change the status of 'Employee' to internal 'Customer'. The similarities are striking.

Thus, for example, within a very short time span, organisations have changed from an autocratic culture where the hierarchy and pecking order produced an elite who were (and in some places still are) called 'Sir', to an open egalitarian society where everyone is on first name terms. Some of the practices, like named spaces in the car park being replaced by a 'first come first served' rule may take a little longer (even in the most forward companies), but it won't take long for the upward pressure and disgust at unnecessary privilege being manifested in further changes!

This does not mean that the organisation goes soft, to pander to the whims of individuals. The opposite is becoming the norm: organisations are toughening up and demanding more. The key

is that this is acceptable to the employee if they give more, not just money, but the things that the individual perceives as important to them, in order to fulfil their function and be recognised in the role that they play.

The Employee Revolution may be a quiet one but its strength must not be underestimated. The effects can be increasingly seen in every aspect of organisational life, e.g. in the way that they are attempting to market themselves to attract new recruits into its society. The image makers and builders of advertising and design are beginning to regard recruitment as a product that needs to be marketed carefully to attract the right 'Customer' to buy.

The Employee Revolution has probably produced the phenomenon of MBWA and has demanded good leadership, rather than good leaders suddenly deciding, or being told, to focus internally. If the need wasn't there to see and hear the leaders face to face, then the 'product' would not have been bought!

The Employee Revolution is producing the demands for more involvement in the jobs being done. The pride people feel in the things they do may have been stifled by management's lack of concern over quality as they strove for more and more profit. Therefore 'Quality' programmes would not be bought if there wasn't a perceived need for them, or belief in them.

The revolution begins

As already stated, 200 years ago, the French Revolution saw an uprising that had at its heart the change of status of the 'people'. They changed from being peasant classes to being equal 'citizens' – well, that was the idea! Now 200 years later history is still having to repeat itself. Is the analogy fair?

Let me ask two questions which will ultimately lead to discovering the answer: How many employees are there in your organisation?

Please tick the appropriate box: 100 ☐;

200 ☐;

300 ☐;
500+ ☐;
1000+ ☐;
5000+ ☐.

Now identify what was wrong with this question.

Answer: As long as you and everyone else in your organisation thinks of them as 'employees' then you will have, and continue to have, a major problem.

Turn the phrase around from the 'Employee Revolution' to something less complimentary but in essence saying the same thing, 'The employees are revolting'! and the *double entendre*, while humorous, neatly sums up the aim of this book – to help bring about the realisation that as long as the term 'employee' is used, it will continue to have a lot of hidden meanings creating the mis-understandings which feed the internal communication problems.

The Employees are Revolting! The second question is: Why?

The term 'employee' has a wealth of meaning that creates the following perceptions in organisations. Some of these have been heard too often to be coincidence, and have been taken from a survey of over 2000 managers and staff in a retail organisation facing problems in recruiting new 'employees':

1 Employees are 'paid' people, therefore they can be told what to do.

Wrong They now leave and cost a fortune to replace.

2 Employees are underlings. I am the manager, they will automati-cally have to respect the authority vested in me.

Wrong They are too much in demand from other organisations in areas of low unemployment, and otherwise too independent minded to take 'nonsense' from anybody these days. (I remember one research group in which a very insecure manager said that he thought that to move away from the formal title of Mr was a 'bad move', as it might reduce the respect that his employees had for him!)

3 Employees are a homogeneous group of people who work for the organisation.

Wrong Just like the outside world, you would be hard pushed, in any collection of people numbering more than a few, to come across a more disparate, fundamentally different group of individuals. The problem that the untrained person has is that they all tend to look 'pretty much the same'. It is therefore very easy to assume that the common term 'employee' can be applied.

4 Employees work in departments, the factory, the office, etc.

Wrong 'Individuals' work in these places. It is like a marketeer saying for example that 'Yorkshire is a target market'. Yorkshire is a county, an arbitrary area that has individuals who happen to live there. These individuals can be subdivided into target markets, but any marketeer who tries to target a geographic area without further defining exactly what or who he is aiming at, will soon be out of a job. Not to put too fine a point on it, it is like assuming that America, to take a big example, is a target market. And yet one bank manager told me that his 'machine room' was a target market.

This fundamentally ignores the fact that it is people that buy products and services. It would be extremely dangerous to target a 'machine room' in which there were two pregnant women, with a message aimed at convincing people about the wonders and joys of information technology, when they had just read an article about the dangers to unborn babies. This in fact did happen!

This perception only arises because the word 'employee' is seen to reduce everyone to the same status – unless of course you are a 'manager' or a 'board director' and then you are of a different, often seen as much better, status.

5 Employees are looking mainly for good pay and conditions.

Wrong The products and services that they are now looking for from the organisation are not just money and perks.

6 Employees are not people with characteristics like honesty and

integrity. These qualities are difficult to find when recruiting, especially in hourly paid staff.

Wrong There are very few cut-throats and thieves in society!

7 Employees with characteristics, for example like the desire to be involved in their jobs, are not needed to fill what the manager perceives as boring jobs.

Wrong The definition of a 'boring job' is not decided by the manager, it is decided by the individual. The feature of both internal and external marketing is that 'beauty is in the eye of the beholder'. The manager who leaps to conclusions and undersells what may be, for example, the most exciting opportunity that an individual has ever had, will be doing himself a great injustice, and wasting a lot of money. All too frequently, this is the perception of managers when advertising positions. Indeed, in the excitement stakes, the term 'job' is on a par with the term 'employee' when it comes to expressive terminology! You only have to look at the rows of dull, factual, and often off-putting job advertisements to realise that most of the people marketing these positions perceive the readers to be dull people looking for boring jobs.

So, we have a term used to describe all the amazingly complex and varied internal target markets, which creates a perception something akin to the term peasant. Unfortunately, perception is all. If this is to change with 'the employee revolution', then the easiest way to do it is for the term to change. The word 'employee' must disappear and be replaced by a term which creates different perceptions, placing the importance on the individuality of the people in the organisation and those who it is hoped will be attracted to join it. It must also reflect the need to apply internal marketing techniques, when attempting to market or sell products and services, and attempting to match the needs of the individual to that of the organisation. The term should be 'internal target market'.

The revolution will have truly begun when, in the French Revolution style, the change from 'peasant to citizen' is matched by the change from employee to internal target market. The fact that a lot has happened in 200 years to make the ensuing change more beneficial to the individual is one interesting difference between the two periods. At the same time, it is both amazing and sad that in the 1990s there are still people who view others as lesser beings.

The Employee Revolution is forcing a rethink in the attitudes and practices of the leaders and managers, not those of the internal customer. *They* know what they want. It is up to Corporate Internal Marketing to provide for their needs. The way to do that is against a consistent model.

The jigsaw becomes easier

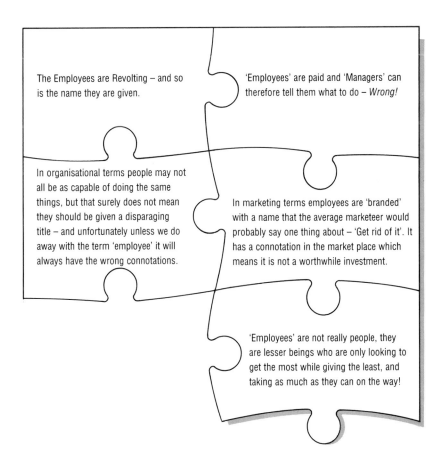

The Employees are Revolting – and so is the name they are given.

'Employees' are paid and 'Managers' can therefore tell them what to do – *Wrong!*

In organisational terms people may not all be as capable of doing the same things, but that surely does not mean they should be given a disparaging title – and unfortunately unless we do away with the term 'employee' it will always have the wrong connotations.

In marketing terms employees are 'branded' with a name that the average marketeer would probably say one thing about – 'Get rid of it'. It has a connotation in the market place which means it is not a worthwhile investment.

'Employees' are not really people, they are lesser beings who are only looking to get the most while giving the least, and taking as much as they can on the way!

7 | *Internal markets*

The people issues – Individuals

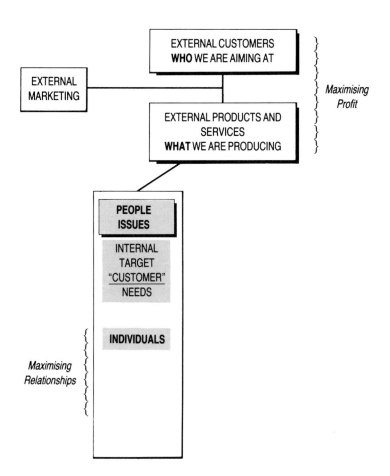

So, to the biggest mental hurdle yet in changing the perceptions within an organisation. If you believe that the term 'employee' is no longer acceptable then the next step must be to replace it with something that is!

To a marketeer there can be only one term used to describe people in large numbers, and that is 'target markets'. A target market has a number of characteristics. These have similarities allowing them all to be put into one group which can be targeted with the same type and style of marketing message.

Clearly, within an organisation the number of times that an attempt will be made to target them all will be very limited. Even with a 'sheep dip' type campaign, i.e. one with the broadest of messages such as customer care, it must be recognised that the very breadth of the target market makes it not really a target market. The consequential watering down of the message to cater for all tastes means that in the truest sense of the word, all the employees in an organisation cannot be classed as a single target market. Life would be too easy if that were the case.

Added to this, because external marketing has moved such a long way since its true emergence in the 1960s, the internal marketeer is going to have to cope with a much more sophisticated set of people. These people are now used to the quality and quantity of marketing messages that they are hit with every day. This is true not only of the common perception of what marketing is all about, i.e. advertising; it is true of all the other disciplines in marketing, viz., the design, the packaging, the branding, the promotion, the PR, and so on. These have yet to be truly practised in the internal market, but they are already so well established in the external market place that there is a lot of catching up to do! It also means that the impact of well-produced internal campaigns is likely to be a lot less strong than might have been the case a decade or two ago. This situation is not alleviated by a symptom of internal marketing which creates more demand for better quality and quantity of the internal marketing itself and also the products that the individual demands. This is what I call the 'Oliver Syndrome' – but more of that later (no pun intended!).

Some organisations are still in the Stone Age when it comes to the techniques that are being used to target and reach their internal target markets. The rest of the world has moved along. In fact, while the view is that external marketing is now light years ahead of the internal marketing of most organisations, times are definitely changing internally as well.

The comparisons that now exist are that some 'employees' are being told what to do via messages as subtle as a Stone Age club, while in other organisations individual target markets are being hit with messages transmitted by the latest in technology (such as interactive video) sent by internal marketing departments. The message becomes very clear to someone looking for a new job, or looking for a move!

The 'people' in an organisation are therefore not a mass market, they are a many and varied collection of individual niche target markets. The realisation and recognition of this will in itself create the biggest change in attitude, as managers begin to see that they can no longer hide behind traditional methods of 'managing'. Having begun to strongly suspect these methods are not working, managers will now start to recognise that internal target markets need as much caution in approach as external markets. They will realise that the internal world is changing and that the role they traditionally played in filtering, syphoning, stopping and distorting information is one which they can no longer afford to play. The methods of transferring information these days allow the internal target markets to be reached by working around the blockages if necessary. If managers are to survive and grow with an organisation then they will have to adapt to the new demands being placed on them. The biggest of these is using all their skills and the techniques of Corporate Internal Marketing to create people who are ready, willing and able to carry out the enormous demands that are being placed on them.

This pressure is part and parcel of the trade-off in organisations.

The trade-off which says that while we are placing demands on you as an individual we will do our utmost to provide you with the products and services that you need from us as an organisation.

In order that this can happen there needs to be a clearly described methodology in defining the internal target markets – the next stage of the internal marketing process. There is still a long way to go, in terms of the level of sophistication, but a start has to be made somewhere!

What do individuals want in *your organisation?*

Without the benefit of having all the data on individuals that was referred to earlier, such as ACORN, analysis, etc., where to start? I believe that the KISS (Keep It Simple, Stupid) principle is best. Having accepted that people can no longer be seen as 'employees' then the next move would simply be to see them as *'individuals'*. Everyone in the organisation would then be seen as having a unique set of characteristics that need to be taken into account whenever they are on the receiving end of Corporate Internal Marketing. The picture can be built up from there as necessary.

Once the organisation buys into the new language and philosophy that individuals actually are different from employees, and that they cannot be told what to do, the questions will be asked, 'What skills do I need to be able to deal with individuals? How can I, as a manager, and they as people with their own needs and desires, get what we both want?'

To answer the first question, it is necessary to define the needs and desires of the individual. In other words, before a marketeer decides, for example, what shape the advertising campaign might take, he needs to find out what people want and therefore what they might buy. So, it is essential to do your homework before attempting to answer the questions set. In this case, the homework is 'Research'. Before going any further, it may be wise to point out that many an ill-informed manager believes (too often for comfort) that they always know what their 'employees' want. The list would probably look something like this:

- good pay;
- good conditions;
- good holidays;
- free lunches;
- good pension;
- good hours;
- nice colleagues;
- good prospects;
- perks;
- good annual review.

The permutations may be slightly different, but essentially all of these are the classic ingredients of the standard job advert. The amazing thing is, that there is nothing there that is remotely connected to the quality of the work, the quality of the leadership, or the input that the organisation will give to the individual to become effective in what they can, or might be able, to do.

What do individuals want from *your organisation?*

So you think you might have included 'good training' in the above list. Well here's the challenge. Place their requirements in order of importance. Create a Top Ten for your individuals:

1	6
2	7
3	8
4	9
5	10

The skills required to help you complete the list are in Chapter 10 (pp. 146–65). The products and services they require are provided by the organisation. Both are covered later.

Teams

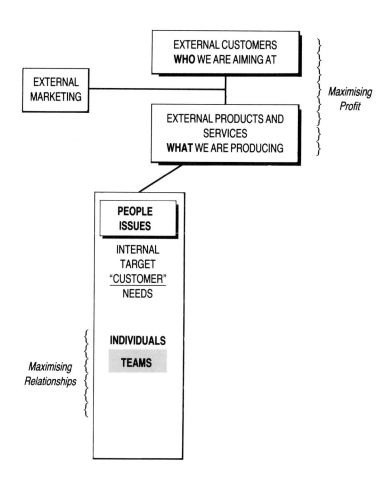

Enough has been written by training experts and psychologists on the subject of teams in terms of their composition, their dynamics and the 'how to', when it comes to being part of them. What is unique to the marketeer is that he does not usually have to target his message to more than one, or at most two people. Even in a family situation there is usually one key decision maker.

The dynamics of team-based environments are such that even the decision maker is likely to be heavily influenced on a permanent basis by the team. The politics, jockeying for position, the posturing, the emotions, the styles, the back stabbing, will all play a part. In short, the Attitudes, Awareness, and Abilities of the individuals will impact on each other.

The requirements of the team to produce, so that all the inputs of the individuals will influence the outcome, often mean they are effectively performing as one unit.

The problem is: How to market to a group of disparate individuals with one consistent message that will be targeted to them all?

Additionally, the problem is intensified by the changing nature of business. The flatter structures, the looser hierarchies, the fast responses required today are all producing more and more teams. By their nature they are less formal, they come together very quickly and disband again, they are issue orientated and rely on very effective communication processes. These processes also need to be effective with the rest of the organisation. A classic example of this would be the Service Circle/Quality Circle. Their importance has not yet been recognised nor exploited in the UK, in comparison to Japan. Neither has the critical nature of 'gathering and sharing the wisdom' of these teams been recognised.

To give an example of how this gathering and sharing of the wisdom might occur, see the centre page spreads featuring the *Good Ideas Book* of Gardner Merchant.

There is a long way to go in terms of the data needed to build pictures of teams, and hence to be able to produce effective internal marketing. A good deal of time, effort and money are often wrongly spent on creating competition between teams. Sales targets forming the method of motivating groups of individuals, e.g. branches or departments. However, the basic needs of individuals must be met, otherwise incentives will not work. In external marketing terms, there is no point in promoting a product nobody wants.

Managers

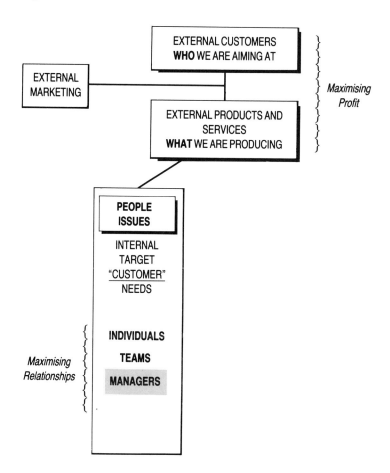

Plenty has been written about teams and even more has been written about managers. In the context of Corporate Internal Marketing, managers make an interesting internal target market. The only reason that they can justify being an internal target market is their position, which creates a set of characteristics sufficient to allow the overriding position of these people to produce a target group. This is a similar classification to the one of 'Leader', in that the position is itself the deciding factor of their targeting. There is one big difference however, as will be explained.

This is like saying that the position of, say, 'father' or 'mother' provides a target market. Of course there are products and services that these people will have to buy that are pertinent to their position, but to suggest that it is the positions themselves and not the people who occupy them will lead to producing generalisations and a situation where no further progress could be made. Thus, for example, a father or mother living in a high-rise flat with 10 children and no income will be a totally different proposition from a father or mother whose children have left home and who are enjoying the benefits of no mortgage and high incomes.

This may seem an obvious comparison, but having suggested that 'managers' can be seen as internal target markets, leaving it at that would be to consent that the classification is perceived as valid.

In the absence of effective research, and a great deal more work on the classification of people in management positions, the use of 'manager' as a term for target markets will have to suffice for the present.

Why is this classification important? It is only necessary to think of the myriad pieces of information and 'communication' that flow at this internal target market to realise that the classification already exists in people's minds. What doesn't exist is the realisation that the recipients of this deluge are not just 'managers' – it is only their title! They are people who effectively can be put in their own classifications. These would have then become target markets and therefore have similar needs, desires and likes and dislikes in terms of the design and style of messages. They would also need to be marketed to with a piece of communication targeted at them.

Leaders

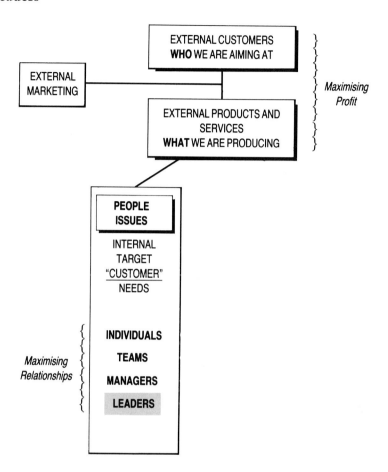

Does the same apply to the term 'leader' as applied to the term 'manager'? Is it classifying the position? Yes, but the one important difference is that the 'leaders' of an organisation do not have to be in formal positions of authority. They can be anywhere in the organisation, holding any position. They will tend to be leaders as a result of their personality, charisma and strength of character. It is therefore more likely that there will be more similarities between them, in comparison to the much wider group of 'managers'. Once again, however, the classification is really only one of immediate convenience until more accurate targeting can be done.

A note about the four internal target groups:

The interesting thing about this set of internal target markets i.e. individuals, teams, managers, leaders, is that this is reminiscent of the (now out of date) socio-economic groupings ABC.

It is necessary at this stage of the development of Corporate Internal Marketing not to invent new groupings, classifications or titles. The conceptual leap of recognising that internal customers are, in reality, internal target markets is sufficient. This will create the realisation that if 'communication' is to get better, the only way to do it is for the 'communicators' to recognise that they must become internal marketeers.

If at this stage, people are comfortable perceiving that there are only four internal target markets, and that these correspond to their present conception of the structure, then, in fact, the internal target marketing has been effective.

Experience, using the classifications to date, indicates that people are very comfortable with them. If from here, the level of sophistication can grow, then the process should not take too long.

The nice thing is that the quality and quantity of the internal marketing material is likely to improve at the same pace as both the target markets' demands and the discipline of Corporate Internal Marketing itself.

8 | *Maximising resources*

The apparent complexity of organisations is enough to create confusion in the best of corporate planners. So what chance does the average individual stand when it comes to knowing what the organisation can give to them, and expect from them?

Each day people turn up for work and things just happen to be there. Someone somewhere is always responsible for having produced or organised things, and in general terms it is pretty obvious why they are there – or is it?

We have previously dealt with the internal target markets in order to establish the existence of classifications of people in the organisation. We shall now look at doing the same for the organisation itself. The starting point is in taking the next conceptual leap, necessary to put everything that the organisation does into context. It is the next step in the process of The Employee Revolution, started by the concepts of 'Quality', where everyone internally is perceived as a customer. If this is the case, and customer requirements are established as being a valid concept, can they be put into the language of marketing? Yes! There are only two more steps to go!

Step One

If you accept that the people in the organisation are internal target markets, then the next step is to recognise that these markets buy internal products and services.

Step Two

If internal products and services can be viewed as the requirements that the organisation provides in order to allow the people to fulfil their function, then suddenly a whole new light is cast on the way that the organisational issues are put across to the people. The effective way is via Corporate Internal Marketing in order that the resources provided are maximised.

In external marketing terms the concepts are plain. If someone says or does something to assist you to achieve a desired result, it is called a 'service'. If someone provides you with a physical article that is designed to meet specific needs, then it is a product. In internal marketing, the service is generally of a consultancy nature. It is what most managers and leaders spend a lot of their time doing. They provide consultancy, on behalf of the organisation, in order to facilitate the processes necessary for producing the product. The output of this consultancy, be it a method, solution, etc., is the service.

The internal products provided can be anything physical which the individuals can utilise to help them achieve the goals they are set. Thus, a training manual is a 'product', as is a staff room, notice board, meals at work, a car park, a pension, etc.

Having gone to all the trouble to produce these products and services the methodology of Corporate Internal Marketing ensures that their use is maximised. It does this by using the external marketing techniques which have been devised and honed to bring external products and services to external target markets. These are all documented later, and include research, development of products and services, creative techniques, design, branding, packaging, test marketing, internal distribution, internal selling skills, internal promotion and re-appraisal and re-launch.

Vision, Mission and Values

In order to build up the organisational model it is more logical to do it 'bottom up'. The whole essence of this model is to put the leaders at the base of the organisation (as will be discussed under 'Structure'). If the leaders are at the base of the model then the key service that they provide is also in the same position. In short, the core service that the organisation has to provide for the internal target markets is one of 'direction'. It is on this issue that all else sits. To mix metaphors, it is the bedrock of the structure and provides the goal that the people will strive toward (see diagram below).

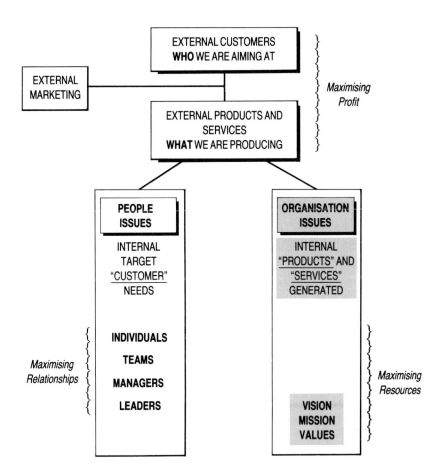

It is not the purpose of this book to attempt to discuss the actual products and services themselves in any great depth. The role of Corporate Internal Marketing is to take those products and services and ensure that they meet the requirements of the organisation and the individuals.

What is interesting about the way in which vision, mission and values are internally marketed is that they are probably among the worst examples of Corporate Internal Marketing to be found. A great many CEOs and the boards of virtually all organisations would be upset to think that their key output is not being at the very least transmitted, and at best bought into.

The key problem is recognising the difference between 'absorption' and 'impact' of the message. The net result is that the key decision makers in organisations spend many hours in debate to produce the future direction. They have had the benefit of this debate, i.e. absorption, while the rest of the organisation is left to change their thinking or otherwise from at worst, a paragraph or two on the wall, and at best, a front page spread on the company newspaper, i.e. impact.

> **When CEOs recognise that the discipline of external marketing must also be used internally, then the organisation will start to move – in the direction that they want! When CEOs also start to recognise that what is good for them is also good for the rest of the organisation, then the rest of the organisation may become as committed and capable as they are in their own sphere of 'Excellence'. So why should the individuals not have the benefit of constructive debate, well thought out presentations, sound logic and reasoning behind all the proposals being put forward?**

Unfortunately, even if the people responsible for putting them across believe in the messages, if they have not been trained in how effectively to market and sell them internally, then the process breaks down.

If this is true of apparently simple things like mission statements, (which when boiled down can be one or two sentences long) then what chance a more complicated issue? Add to this the problem of leaders themselves showing only temporary commitment to the internal service they provide, and it is no wonder that there is a great deal of cynicism about it. It is like a salesman selling something which neither he nor you really believe does the job required. Alternatively, the product may have taken lots of preparation and launching, but if it is then forgotten for something new, or left to others less qualified to champion, then once again it will fail.

The other side of the coin is that if marketed correctly, the vision of the leader, the mission of the organisation and the values of its people, to others and the organisation itself, will provide an almost unstoppable momentum for the future direction.

Definitions: Vision/Mission/Values

As a marketeer it is extremely difficult not to try to simplify things. In everything undertaken – from pack design to advertisements – the customer must be able to comprehend what is being said. To make things more complicated for the marketeer, the average attention span of the customer has been reduced by the very process itself. Whereas a 90-second TV commercial was considered accept-able to get over the concepts of even simple products, this is now too long for the attention span of many consumers. The way around this has been to turn the slots into mini soap operas. Indeed, some of these have become classics in themselves. We are living in a very fast-paced society which is used to everything in 'bite sized chunks'.

It makes sense to give the terms 'vision', 'mission' and 'values' a simple and short set of definitions that can precede the marketing of these concepts as they apply to the organisation. It may be interest-ing to research the words themselves within the organisation, as I suspect that to the averge person, their elitist terminology would be somewhat esoteric sounding – in short, off-putting!

VISION – THE FUTURE

Whoever is perceived to be able to see into the future will almost always find followers. It almost doesn't matter whether it is good or bad! The often quoted examples at two ends of the spectrum are Jesus Christ and Adolf Hitler. Within organisations people expect the CEO to be able to see into the future and to chart a way forward for the rest of the organisation.

The problem with the word 'vision' is that its mystical over-

tones may or may not help get the simple message across, e.g., 'This is what I think the market will look like in two years' time'.

MISSION: THE GOAL; THE SENSE OF PURPOSE

Is it to be biggest, best, most respected, most caring, most innovative, etc? These may be sub-sets of the goal, but according to Eli Goldrat in *The Goal* it is to make money, and according to the Chartered Institute of Marketing it's more simple than that – to make a profit. The size of that profit will in turn be affected by the 'values' held by the organisation, and how much is invested in upholding those values.

The problem with a goal like making money is that individuals look to having a bigger share than they can either have, or can justify. Individuals also need something more than just money as a focus.

A mission statement creates an almost quasi religious sense of purpose. It enables the organisation to work to achieving its place in the future, i.e. it is held within the vision of the CEO.

This sense of purpose is as vital to the followers of the leader with the vision as the vision itself. The way it is internally marketed and kept fresh in the eyes of the organisation is of the utmost importance.

VALUES: THINGS HELD DEAR TO OUR HEARTS

The values of an organisation fall into two categories, people and organisational values. Both of which could have numerous statements of intent. They will all begin with something like, 'The things we hold dear are . . . ' The critical part of this is the use of the pronoun *we*. There is no point in just some of the people in the organisation working towards a new morality (for that is what it is) if there are those who do not subscribe to it.

As already mentioned, organisations seem to be taking the place of religious instruction. There is, however, one difference that is not very subtle. The objective of creating the new morality is not just for the individual, it is to produce a commonality of spirit. This in turn drives all the individuals to work and give their best. Indeed the work ethic is usually instilled in the values! These values could include the following (taken from the Handley Walker Group, Mission and Values Statement).

People values

We value: RECOGNITION OF INDIVIDUAL CONTRIBUTION.

Each employee has a potential that should be recognised, and their contribution should be appreciated and rewarded. We place particular value on individual qualities of self-motivation, initiative and the understanding and acceptance of responsibility.

We value: CONSULTANCY AS A CAREER.

We want to provide an environment which supports the development of each individual's professional capability and encourages career progression and long service relationships.

We value: TEAMWORK.

An environment of teamwork and mutual trust encourages respect for other individuals' contributions, needs and viewpoints.

We value: HONESTY AND INTEGRITY

We want open communications between individuals and between individuals and the company, conducted with honesty, integrity and a recognition of the dignity of the individual.

We value: A FRIENDLY ENVIRONMENT.

A friendly working environment helps us to maintain a business in which people are happy to work.

We value: LOYALTY.

We expect individuals to show loyalty to the business's success, through involvement and support for decisions. In return, the individual has the right to expect loyalty from the company.

We value: OUR SUPPLIERS.

External suppliers are also people and are an important part of our team. They should be subject to the same standards of honesty, integrity and respect as are our own staff.

Customer values

We value: OUR REPUTATION.

We seek continually to reinforce our reputation and credibility with customers, as simply 'the best'.

We value: MUTUAL RESPECT AND INTEGRITY.

We seek to maintain mutual trust and respect between our customers and ourselves, by demonstrating integrity and honesty in all our dealings.

We value: TOP QUALITY WORK

Our aim is to maintain the highest standards of work, emphasising quality, providing value for money and based on individual pride in achievement.

We value: COMMUNICATIONS.

Only through continuing communications with our customers can we ensure that our services meet their requirements and provide the benefits they want.

We value: LIFETIME CUSTOMER CARE.

We seek to build long term relationships with our customers, extending beyond current project commitments.

Innovation values

We value: AN INNOVATIVE ENVIRONMENT.

We want an environment which constantly stimulates new ideas and employee innovation.

We value: OWNERSHIP.

The feeling of ownership is a powerful force in the realisation of selective innovation of selected innovative ideas.

We value: THE ENTREPRENEURIAL SPIRIT.

In summary the Vision, Mission and Values are the *raison d'être* of the organisation and (mixing languages!) the *modus operandi* of its organisation and people. Although new ideas must be considered from a commercial viewpoint, fear of failure must not deter future innovation.

Structure

The structure of an organisation used to be, and in many cases still is, one of the key reasons why politics is played. It is used by some leaders as a way of focusing the attention of people, simply by restructuring. It is the status producer of hierarchies, so beloved and at the same time hated by the status conscious – depending on 'how well they did in the last round of promotions'.

Restructuring within organisations is given validity by the changes in government, cabinet, etc. The career ladder is perceived to be a great motivator. The structure exists to provide future opportunity. It is often now used to link in with performance-related pay.

Structures are vital to allow the organisation to exist. Does this seem reasonable? Are these the types of comment and debate that might happen if the word 'structure' gets thrown into the corporate conversation?

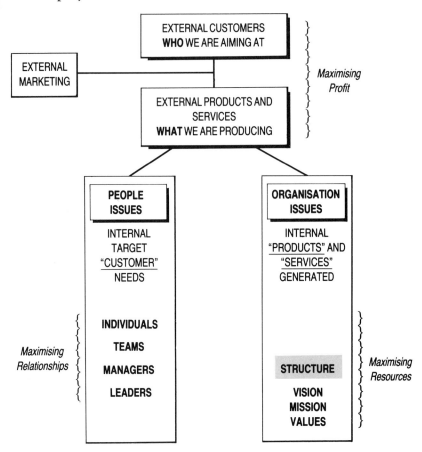

There is another view beginning to emerge about structures:

In essence, structures only exist to enable the process of 'communication' to work. The more senior the person the more responsibility they have ensuring that the process occurs. Does it therefore follow that Corporate Internal Marketing drives structures and not the other way around?

It can be argued that as a result of enhanced technological communication, and the recognition of the ineffectiveness of numerous layers of management, structures have been flattened, almost, it seems, at a stroke. This massive change in organisations provides the QED to the statement that structures are there to serve the communication process – not the other way around!

The flattened structures have in themselves demonstrably improved the communication process. With the benefit of hindsight it is now painfully obvious that the taller structures simply created poor communication, requiring a need for more people to sort it out.

If this is accepted, then the next quantum leap that organisations should be taking is to establish what their internal marketing processes and procedures are. Then they should build formal structures based on the requirements set by Corporate Internal Marketing!

Each individual in the structure is then viewed as an internal marketeer responsible for producing and providing the right goods and services, at the right time, to the right people, at the right price! In fact, this once again is no different to what Crosby is saying. Given the right skills, internal marketeers will set up their own channels of research and distribution, without the need for formal channels being imposed on an ever changing internal world.

So, what should the new corporate structure look like if it is to be bolted on to an internal market? The fact is, the structure has already been determined by the needs of Corporate Internal Marketing when deciding on the model against which it should operate. At the top of the model are customers – nobody can argue with that. The individuals in the business who produce the products and services that are sold to the customers must be the next most important people, hence they come at the top of the internal target market 'box'. Then come teams, managers, and finally leaders.

The concept is similar to that described as the 'upside down pyramid'. If the width of the 'box' were to reflect the number of people in it, then the two concepts would be identical, save for the idea of having teams as a formal part of the structure (see Figure).

This structure is not just a whimsical view of the internal corporate world. Why? There are some very strong arguments in favour of this philosophy.

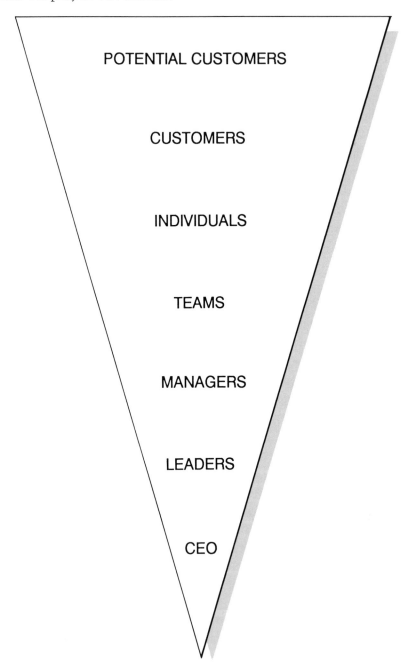

Figure 8.3 The inverted organisational pyramid

Customers at the top   Only by the leaders believing that customers are at the top of the list when considering every action will the individuals in the organisation believe it as well.

Individuals run the business   Only by letting the individuals focus 'upwards' – towards customers – and letting them get on with servicing their needs, will organisations lose the inward facing cultures that exist where the focus is upwards towards the boss. Additionally, and as importantly, who wants to be at the *bottom* of the organisation? Every corporate structure I have seen, every divisional one, every departmental one, has one person at the top – the boss.

Why? Because it makes him feel important. Well, there are more people at the 'bottom', so turning the pyramid on its head produces more satisfied internal customers. Having become boss, the person who is responsible should no longer need their ego puffing up. It is the new recruit, the person having to do the work, the person having to face the external customer who has the toughest job of all. They should be recognised for that, not made to feel lowly and insignificant.

Teams provide the matrix   No individuals can hope to do it all themselves. The use of both formal and informal teams is becoming a feature of organisations that previously had the fatter structures. These teams are put together and disbanded in rapid succession, to solve specific issues as they occur. Levels of authority become almost meaningless in this type of co-operative environment. The importance and status of teams should be recognised in the structure, and they should be a fundamental part of the Corporate Internal Marketing process.

Managers open the channels   The function of managers is to manage, but manage what, or who? The answer is invariably that they manage people. All they have to enable them to do this is their mind and their mouth. The good manager uses both. But what is it that they actually do? Considerable effort goes into some training schemes but, mostly, managers learn by their mistakes. But what do they learn? To say the right thing at the right time to the right person. Their output is a consultancy service in the truest sense of the word. They don't actually make or do anything. Their role is one of enabling, so it must follow that, if they are providing a service to internal customers, it needs to be marketed. Moreover, the manager is almost always a conduit for information, ideas, decisions, etc. Their importance in the distribution process of Corporate Internal Marketing is vital. That is why good training programmes rely on the manager to at least champion them, and at best train them in. Thus their use of Corporate Internal Marketing is vital. The Corporate Internal Marketing words for this would be to 'sell' them in.

Leaders support the spinning top   For CEOs, to be told that they should be at the bottom of the pyramid can present problems. The answer to that is that their role is one of a pivot.

Looking at the upside-down pyramid, the structure is not best described as being 'two-dimensional'. It can be given a far more 'solid' look by making it three-dimensional. The best analogy would be that of a spinning top.

The role of CEO now really starts to come into its own. This tiny point at the bottom of the spinning top will decide in which direction to go. The smallest movement over rough ground will judder the whole organisation (e.g. the cry, 'I want those figures on my desk tomorrow with an explanation' will often affect the whole organisation as it stirs into action).

> **The role of the CEO is vital. It is to support the weight of the organisation and keep the momentum going. Only by the leaders perceiving that they are there to provide this supportive role from below, not playing an autocratic part from above, will they get the most out of the talented people that actually produce the products and services.**

Corporate Internal Marketing produces the 'spin'   If a top is going to stay upright it needs to spin. The dynamic nature of this analogy is much stronger than that of a static pyramid. Is the top moving forward or all over the place? Is it staying upright pointed up to its customers, or is it leaning toward certain sections of them? Will the lean become too much and make it topple over?

These analagous questions provide a marketing-based look at an organisation both internally and externally. It is the *internal* marketing process which will maintain the momentum.

Plans – who needs them?

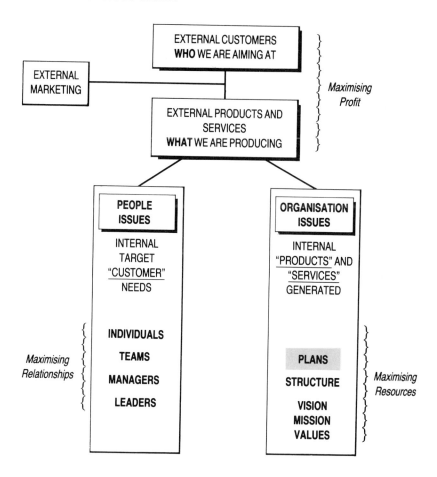

Personal observation would suggest that the old business adage about 'people doing the urgent rather than the important', holds true, especially in the fast paced environment people live in today. It is especially applicable to the planning process. The 'day-to-day' crisis style of management allows the manager to do what he is best at (or at least what he thinks he is best at) and that is, solving problems. Effective planning prevents the problems occurring, but then the manager may feel he is not as important.

All of this may be happening at subliminal level, but it does nevertheless seem to point to the conclusion that, either planning *per se* is not a 'service' that people are capable of undertaking, or that there is a degree of difficulty in the internal marketing of those plans.

In the first instance – the capability of producing plans – there appears to be a distinct lack of training in this area of business. Very few organisations put those responsible for planning (i.e. most managers/supervisors) on training programmes to look at the 'process skills' of management problem prevention and decision making.

In the second instance, it may seem to most managers that, having spent time on the plans, there is a distinct lack of enthusiasm for carrying them out. Questions that may arise from this are, is it the plan, or the quality of the presentation, the willingness of the target market to want to take them on, the ongoing promotion, or the ideas and information, or some other factor affecting the acceptance of this service?

In both cases, the training not being carried out and the plans not being accepted, the root problem is highly likely to be the quality of the internal marketing.

Now – and forever more!

So, once again we have a 'service' provided by the internal producers, and it must be internally marketed to enable the business to function. What if the plans are badly marketed? The internal customers may be able to stumble on, from day to day. But this leads to frustration, and with The Employee Revolution gathering momentum they are becoming more disposed to leaving. They want to find an organisation which will provide them with the way forward in achieving the mission that has been set by the leaders.

If the mission has been effectively marketed internally, the demand for good planning at every level of the business is going to be high. But how far forward looking do the plans have to be focused? Until recently, it was highly acceptable to think in strategic terms of five years. Many a five-year marketing plan has been produced, with often detailed projections. In today's marketplace, the speed of change, the constant threat from new products, new competitors and many other unpredictable circumstances, often only allow for two- to three-year strategic plans. Tactical planning is now a continuous process, whereas in the past, it could often be done on a six-monthly or yearly basis.

This constant revision of plans – both tactical and strategic, means that they will require constant Corporate Internal Marketing if the people in the business are to know 'what the hell is going on'.

The sense of bewilderment that exists in many organisations through lack of awareness is made worse by the increasing demands of the individuals today to know more of what is going on. It is not good enough, therefore, to be seen to be lumbering on from crisis to crisis, or to have inadequate or conflicting plans.

What has changed is that, previously, plans were prepared essentially for the benefit of the organisation. Today the internal market place demands a service that meets individuals' needs. Increasingly, these needs are for awareness, involvement and belief in the future of the organisation.

The belief will come when the individuals are convinced about the capability of those responsible for ensuring the organisation's survival in a tough market place. Those responsible, therefore, need to be skilled, not only in the planning process but in being able to internally market those plans.

Plans, what plans?

No department is safe! Everyone must work to a plan, therefore everyone in the organisation should have the benefit of knowing what they are working to, and why.

The people who should be best at internally marketing their plans should be the marketing department. Too often, however, the perception within marketing is that their function is an external one. If they get involved internally, it is likely to be, for example, with new product launches in order to ensure that 'sales' people make their products successful, i.e. a somewhat selfish reason. Is this unfair? Having 'been there' I have to admit to this from a personal point of view. If any external marketeers have wandered down the corridor recently to chat to the human resource development specialists about the needs of the internal market place then I suspect they are few and far between.

If the external marketing people are not well versed in internally marketing the strategic and tactical plans of the business, what chance have the accountants, works people, and even the strategic planners themselves?

Practices

The practices of the organisation are the actions that the individuals take in carrying out the functions they perform. Every one of those practices needs to be conveyed to the individuals in a way that tackles their attitude, awareness, and their ability. Every one of these practices has to be conveyed in a way that allows the methods to be transferable to a number of individuals. The way to do this is to view them as products, which then have to be marketed, or sold to the internal target markets.

Traditionally, the practices of the organisation have been referred to as 'standards' or 'systems' or 'working methods'. The way of getting them across has been to write them down in heavy tomes, called manuals. The people responsible for the production of these

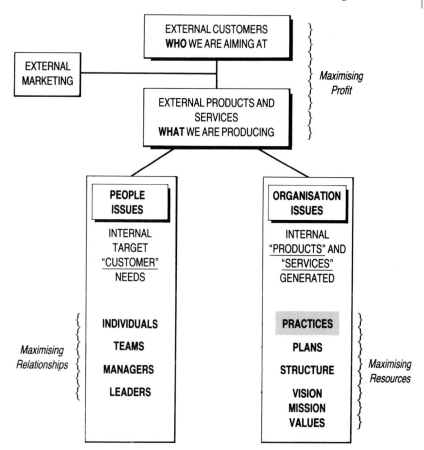

tomes have often not been the people responsible for the work itself; it was usually reserved for the 'experts' at writing manuals, i.e. administrative or training people.

The net result of many of these manuals on the 'standards of practice' may or may not have been good: the problem is that no one wanted to buy the product. The targeting, the creativity, the packaging, the incentives and rewards were all either ignored or at best handled by untrained people. It all leads us back to where we started, with the people issues. The people who were supposed to read manuals were 'employees' who were paid to do as they were told, and acting according to the book was one of the things that they were told to do!

Along comes the period of massive change that we are now experiencing and the book is constantly being rewritten. The amount of information that people are supposed to read, and the number of functions and responsibilities that they are supposed to perform, means that there is always a valid reason why people are not paying the attention to certain things that they should.

Now Jan Carlzon, Philip Crosby and Tom Peters all appear, and tell everyone that what is now important is rewriting the book every day! Then along come the Japanese, who prove that the constant attention to making things better, i.e. creating new standards which everyone should be performing against, can hit people at the rate of millions per annum. In some major Japanese organisations, the reported rate of suggestions in the 'suggestion scheme' varies from 4,000,000 to 6,000,000 per annum. In one UK organisation, with approximately 50,000 employees, the number of reported suggestions in the 'suggestion scheme' numbered approximately 5000!

Yet, two suggestions per week on how to improve the business or new ideas that might be tried from each individual is not a lot to ask. Indeed, if you were to listen carefully, this is probably happening now, and there may be many more than two suggestions per week. With 50,000 employees that is equivalent to 5,000,000 per annum.

The point is, that if the business is going to be improved from 'above' (note that the direction has now changed to match the inverted top structure!) the transferral of the information to enable everyone to benefit is going to be vital.

But are all these actions to be seen as the 'practices'? Is it simply a matter of detailing out every single action that is necessary to enable the organisation to function? The answer is that individually 'they are too numerous to lump together'. In marketing terms, there need to be discrete 'products that the market place wants to buy'.

Internal products

These internal products are no more or less than you might expect. What may surprise you (as it has done a number of organisations) is the order in which your employees place their demands for these products.

The 'products' are very much like Top Ten tunes which are played because they are what people want to hear. In approximate order of time frame from joining an organisation these products are: recruitment, induction, leadership, training, development, career, future, involvement in the job, pay (reward and recognition), information. The interesting time is when individuals' needs for these products are researched. The organisation is then able to respond with the right products, at the right time, to the right people. That is when the benefits falling through to the bottom line really start to be highlighted.

When the organisation can then go even one stage further in order to anticipate the demands of the individuals, it will get a reputation, both internally and externally, about the quality of its care for the people who work within it.

The most famous example of this must surely be Marks and Spencer. Long before other organisations were even thinking about 'staff care' (let alone customer care), Marks and Spencer had introduced staff policies and internal products and services that had people talking about it, and queuing to join. Even down to providing hairdressing facilities, the needs of the individuals were considered vital to the organisation.

Gardner Merchant, the contract catering arm of Trusthouse Forte, has built a multi-million pound business through organisations investing in the welfare of their individuals. Providing a good three-course meal may be a legacy from the past, when the need was to supplement the employees' diet, but today it is a 'perk', i.e. a 'product' that is intended to enhance the other main products that the organisation provides.

Yet, unless these products are put into a context that builds an overall image of the organisation, all the investment in internal product development and launching and sustaining the products may not be maximised.

- Maximising the resources of the organisation is one of the fundamental goals of Corporate Internal Marketing.
- It can help all those who operate within it and who produce the internal products and services.
- It will help to ensure the products and services are being introduced and sustained as effectively as possible.

The organisation slots into place

If the 'people' in the organisation are internal target markets then it follows that the organisation would be best to structure itself so that the things it produces internally are treated as 'internal products and services'.In this way the issues become clear and they should be dealt with through corporate internal marketing.

Vision, Mission and Values provide the overview of the future of an organisation and the way it will operate. They provide a consultancy service by the leaders to give depth and meaning to the individuals in the organisation.

Vision, Mission and Values allow people to follow the leaders, who are providing the service with the foresight required.

The Structure of an organisation is like that of a spinning top.

The key individuals are those interacting with the customer at the top.

The Plans of an organisation are a consultancy service which provides the strategy and tactics. Like any service it needs to be marketed.

The CEO is the pivot at the bottom providing stability and direction.

The Practices of an organisation result in the internal products it produces and internally markets.

9 | *The internal marketing mix*

Meeting the needs of internal customers

The reasoning so far about the use of marketing skills to meet the needs of internal customers brings us to the last two elements of the model. There is, however, one big difference between external marketing and Corporate Internal Marketing that needs to be explored before looking into the heart of the model.

It has been said that the skills of external marketing are to 'meet' the needs of the customer with the products and services that are being demanded, and are expected to be in demand. It is, of course, also possible to create demand with innovative ideas that people do not even know exist.

The main proviso that the external marketeer must work to, is that if customers fundamentally do not want, or cannot afford, his products and services, there is no point – in the short term at least – in trying to persuade them otherwise.

The role of an external marketeer is clearly based on 'meeting' the needs of the customer, who may have to be persuaded that the products and services on offer are better than the competition. This is where the skills of marketing and selling come into play. The customer does however, have the last word in the matter.

In the internal world of an organisation things are different. To

CORPORATE INTERNAL MARKETING

THE HOLISTIC MODEL
SHOWING THE STATEGIC IMPORTANCE
OF THE INTERNAL MARKETING MIX

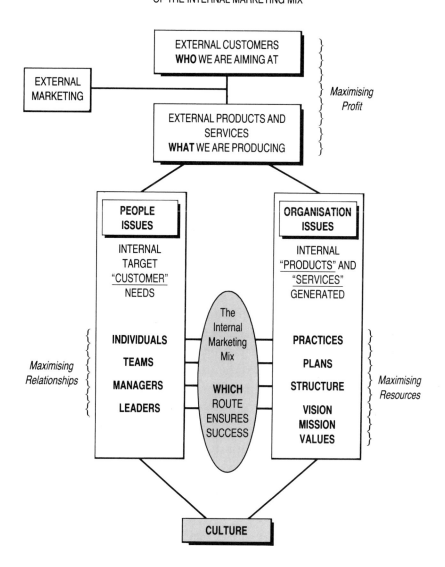

take an extreme example to make the point: if 'meeting' the needs of the internal customer was the objective of the internal marketeer, then the organisation would soon be out of business! For example, to 'meet' the needs of an individual within the organisation it might be necessary to pay them a million pounds a year! Clearly, this does not 'meet' the needs of the organisation.

This relates back to the flaw that organisations found when they tried to introduce McGregor's X and Y theory. The internal customer, if treated totally as 'king', is highly likely to take advantage of the situation to the detriment of the other shareholders in the organisation and therefore the organisation itself.

- The needs of the organisation, and the needs of the individual will inevitably be different.
- The role of Corporate Internal Marketing cannot be to 'meet' the needs of one to the detriment of the other.
- The key element in the whole process will be to 'match' the needs of both the organisation and the individuals.

Clearly, there will be times when there will be direct conflict, but in the main, the recognition of individuals in any organisation will be that they cannot allow its downfall through unreasonable demands to satisfy needs that cannot be met. It may be necessary through Corporate Internal Marketing to create the awareness and acceptance that their need must be 'matched', and if this is unacceptable, the inevitable result is either compromise or confrontation.

The reason for much of the confrontation in the past has been that individuals in organisations have not perceived there to have been a 'matching' of needs, far less an attempt to 'meet' their needs.

For the organisation that actually starts to practise marketing its internal products and services in a way that creates recognition of the strength of commitment to the individual, then the payback can be tremendous. Many organisations are doing a great job of matching the needs of the people who work in them, yet if you were to ask the individuals about the internal products and services on offer, there would be little perception of a co-ordinated policy.

How many organisations can claim that they have an internal image as strong as Marks and Spencer? Or, to take a specific example, how many individuals feel that the 'free' catering they get is really part of a package, or is it more a right? Apart from recruitment, virtually nothing is done to put together a totally co-ordinated package, targeted at the person, once they have joined the organisation.

One excellent example of this total approach to Corporate Internal Marketing is that of Trusthouse Forte's Catering Division. The interesting aspect of this programme, called 'Winners', is that it is run by someone who is, I believe, Britain's first internal brand manager. Robin Turner works within the marketing department, yet his remit is, in current parlance, human resource development.

This title and position is the first of many. David Young heads up an internal marketing department within Midland Bank. Once again, his position is within the marketing department and not personnel, although it is clearly recognised that the role of human resource development is vital in producing many of the internal products and services.

The same brief, previously held by Personnel, is now held by Malcolm Nicholls, the Marketing Director of Tetley Walker, the north-western based brewery and pub chain of Allied Lyons.

The Butlin's Holiday World's 'People Development Programme' already quoted, is another example of a total approach to matching the needs of the organisation to the individuals.

The Royal Mail is about to undertake one of the UK's largest Corporate Internal Marketing programmes. One of the items at the top of the list of issues to tackle is to enable everyone in the organisation to be able to 'communicate'. This will be done by transferring the skills to the key internal target market – the managers.

Knowingly or unknowingly, other organisations that are looking at this area now are many of the large and respected market leaders.

There are also many small organisations – size has very little to do with the need.

This highlights the growing realisation that the importance of running a range of internal products and services for thousands of internal customers will soon be recognised by more and more organisations.

The first practical move that an organisation can make is to ensure that the introduction and ongoing success of Corporate Internal Marketing is held strategically by someone, or indeed a department. They fulfil a 'gate-keeping' role and at the same time are responsible for transferring the tactical skills to the individuals in the organisation.

In other words, the role is not to build up a large team of (costly) people as a power base. The internal marketeer, like his external counterpart, does not need to actually do the physical production and carrying out of internal marketing. The role is fundamentally strategic, and the internal people who fulfil it should use the internal and external experts to carry out the tasks necessary to make it happen at a tactical level.

So just as the external marketing department plays a liaison role with the internal departments, and the external agencies, the same will happen with internal marketing. For the external marketing departments these agencies include advertising, PR, sales promotion, direct mail, etc. For the internal marketeer the likelihood is that the outside skills will come from a number of sources such as the aforementioned agencies plus a number of others. They will all have, at some time, assisted people internally. Not surprisingly, moves are afoot among all of these companies to look to exploiting this new business opportunity, and to winning the potentially large accounts.

The agencies that are moving, or have moved into this area, include an array of companies. They specialise both in external marketing support, and those which have been involved in particular aspects of internal services and are listed later in this chapter. All will have particular strengths, but most of them will have one weakness; they do not have the combination of *both* external marketing *and* internal human resource development skills.

Beware of those who only bolt the skills that they know already onto this very complex area. I have seen large sums of money being squandered that need not have been spent. For example, on incentive schemes, one organisation is spending £4 million on what they describe as a 'Beast' that they have created, and it needs feeding even greater amounts of money. If the products and services that the individuals want, like training, are sufficient to motivate them, why is it deemed necessary to throw money at them as well? Alternatively, in external marketing terms, there is no point in going out with money-off promotions on a product which the market does not have confidence in, e.g. an incentive scheme to motivate, when the leadership provided doesn't inspire people.

And so to some of the fundamental misconceptions about Corporate Internal Marketing. The same kind of misconceptions existed in the days when the Institute of Marketing was having difficulty in being recognised. Indeed it is true to say that it was only in 1988 that it was granted a Royal Charter.

Corporate Internal Marketing is not about sexy campaigns, creative-looking training manuals, multi-screen conferences, etc. It is about maximising relationships, maximising resources and matching the needs of the organisation and the individuals. The achievement of these goals may require any or all of the above techniques of getting the products and services to the internal market place; but that is the result, not the actual process and responsibility of the role.

So, beware internal detractors who may have a vested interest in attempting to say that the practice of Corporate Internal Marketing trivialises the complex nature of business. If this criticism were levelled now at external marketing, the cry would be 'Luddite'!

Beware also the external agency that has a vested interest in pushing their product, which may simply be a 'sexy' campaign but will not fit the job in hand. I remember one external marketeer who used to go into his advertising agency briefings and say of their approach, 'The answer is that you have to spend lots on television advertising, what is the question?' The strength of the response generally suggested that the cap fitted!

Having said that, there is a growing band of experienced professionals who are looking for long-term relationships and who will provide both the strategic direction and back-up support to the internal marketeer. These include:

1 **Human resource development organisations** Having worked for and with all the people on this list my personal inclination would be to find one of this type of organisation that has merged marketing skills with a fundamental understanding and practice in human resource development. By accident or design many of the large-scale training programmes that have been introduced into organisations do have many of the elements of Corporate Internal Marketing.

2 **Below-the-line agencies – sales promotion** Many of these agencies are involved in promotions and incentives and have experience of dealing with 'on the road' sales forces. Added to this skill, they have then moved into 'employee incentive schemes'.

My natural inclination is to say that 'nothing kills a bad product better than good marketing'. If the fundamental internal products and services are not right then throwing prizes and money at people is a short-term solution likely to lead to long-term problems.

On top of an incentive base, many of the below-the-line agencies offer video production, which has also prompted them to move into the area of training.

3 **Video production companies** 'The answer is a video-based programme – what is the question?' Video is an excellent medium – for two key reasons. One, it depicts lifelike simulations which create interest and generate what is really important – the debate. Two, it provides support to the person responsible for stimulating the debate in a way they may be unable to. It is therefore an excellent tool. It is not, however, a solution to all the issues that

need to be introduced by Corporate Internal Marketing.

There are other good uses for video. However, for an internal marketeer to go to a production company to advise on anything but the production, would be like saying to an external marketeer to forget about the Saatchi and Saatchis of this world and head straight to Wardour Street, the home of many video production companies, for all your advertising needs. You may save yourself the agency costs, and you may get a very nice advert, but is it the *right* advert?

4 **Advertising agencies** As I write, Saatchi and Saatchi are not only pulling out of the consultancy business (who are heavily into human resource development), they are also facing a tough time with advertising budgets being cut. The natural reaction of Saatchis and many other advertising agencies will be to look to this new area as it is one that potentially offers the largest opportunity for growth in marketing services in the world. The problem arises as a result of their believing that their specialist skills in external marketing can be transferred into internal marketing.

In the sphere of external marketing, while the advertising agency will get involved in strategy, their major role is to assist organisations to advertise. To do this, the solution will invariably be a combination of a number of media, e.g. TV, newspapers, magazines, posters.

The one thing that can be guaranteed about each of these media is that what is transmitted gets to the final customer as intended. There is nothing in the way to alter the message. The TV set or newspaper delivers a consistent message to every individual.

Additionally, the 'message' that they are skilled at putting across can usually be contained within, at most, 90 seconds of a TV commercial, or a double page spread. This means that the advert is not only consistent – it is short and simple.

It calls for one main skill. It is this skill that external marketeers go to advertising agencies to produce. It is why they change agencies if they do not succeed in creating demand for the product. This skill is *creativity*, which can reduce the 'essence' of the message into just a few words and designs. The most successful of these are often winning awards and have massive target market recall for their endurance and brilliance. Take for example:

HEINEKEN REFRESHES THE PARTS OTHER BEERS
CANNOT REACH

A MARS A DAY HELPS YOU WORK REST AND PLAY

COKE IS IT!

MILD GREEN FAIRY LIQUID

All of these are brilliantly simple – but the simplicity of the product and its benefits lie behind the advertising message, and this forms the main work of the agency.

In the world of Corporate Internal Marketing the message is invariably not only more complex, it will almost inevitably be best transmitted via a chain of people. These people (usually at management and supervisory level) will, almost without exception, either wittingly or otherwise be 'translating' it to suit their own needs.

In other words, the distribution channels of Corporate Internal Marketing messages are not static, and cannot be guaranteed to be totally relied upon to maintain a level of impartiality. To the advertiser, the distribution channels are just TV sets, or pieces of paper. The internal distribution channels are 'warm and breathing' and can be totally unreliable when it comes even to sticking to the message. Worse still, they may not be trained to deliver the message in a consistent way, even if they do not want to change it.

Additionally, the messages that need to be transmitted are highly unlikely to be able to be put across in 90 seconds or less. At the very least, one of the three 'As', but most often all of them, will need tackling when it comes to getting any message across to

The Power of
Corporate Internal Marketing

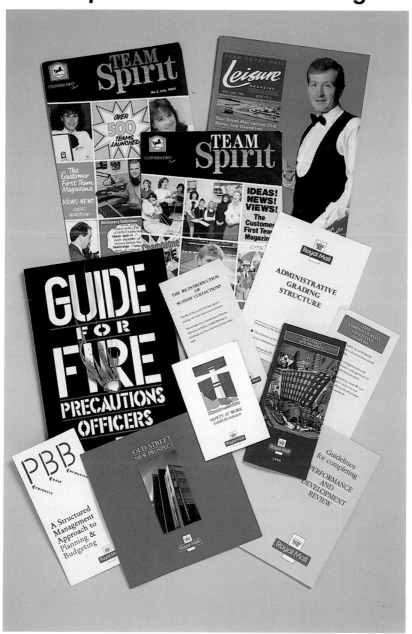

GARDNER MERCHANT - TRUSTHOUSE FORTE

Cultural Change Through A Focus on One Key Issue

What's it all about

The Gardner Merchant campaign has been a long term strategic approach to internal marketing in the business. It has been run to create an environment that is focused on customers needs rather than one based on producing meals.

The message has been the merchandising of products and generating sales through trained and motivated people.

How was it done

The campaign has run through a number of tactical executions including video based training; a guide about researching and fulfilling customers needs; and a method of training managers and individual team members about the power of effective merchandising via a game. The game explains more effectively the complexities of this area in a couple of hours what would ordinarily require a couple of days.

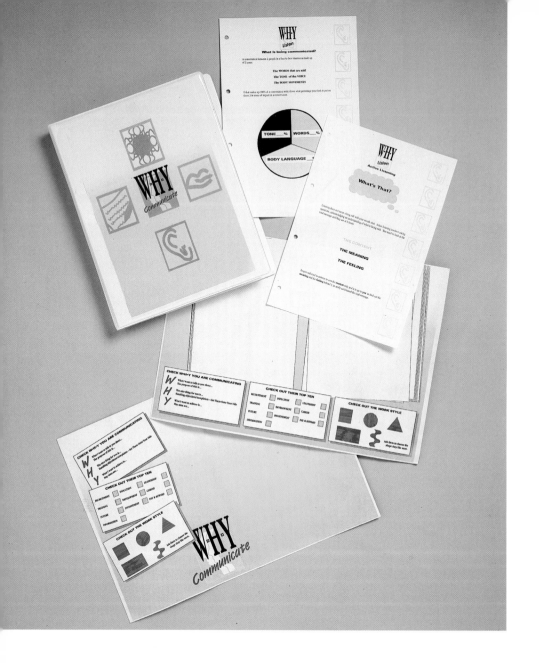

The Royal Mail · Rough visuals for testing

Before pressing any buttons on creative work it is always best to research the appeal of the designs. Just as in advertising, the days are over when things were passed if the MD's wife liked them, the same is true in internal marketing. If the training manager thinks they look OK, that is not a recipe for guaranteeing that the Internal Target Market will like them.

These designs were created for a programme with the Royal Mail. In fact the research groups didn't like the yellow and found some of the designs were not to their taste. The final design sprang out of one of the designs that was liked. Design is all a matter of taste, so the evolution of something that is liked may take a lot of hard work and testing. Too often, however, trainers see this vital area as 'the sizzle' and not the sausage – the question is, who wants to eat uncooked sausages?

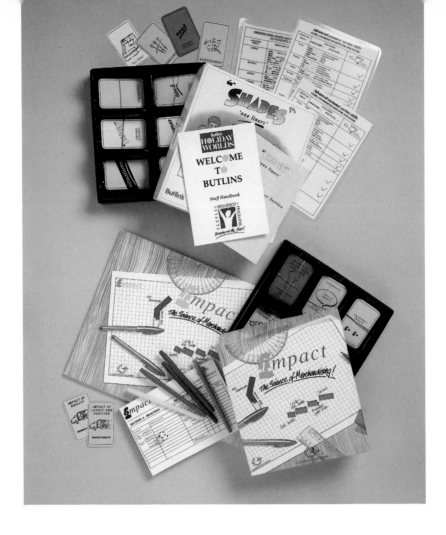

Butlins Holiday Worlds · Training and developing people should be fun

Shades – One Liners · Learning sales techniques by playing a game!

This innovative method of reaching the target market was initially for Butlins Holiday Worlds. It is now being targetted in a different format for financial and other organisations. The concept makes role play less threatening by using a game. Often used in management training to liven up long courses, the simplicity of games and their universal appeal makes them ideal for everyone. The speed of learning and the ease of illustrating the often complex interplay of various elements involved in the training situation make them an ideal vehicle for delivering messages.

Esso · Top of the top ten

Recruitment · Induction · Leadership

Internal marketing really comes into its own in large widespread organisations. The need for the targetted distribution of often long and detailed messages needs careful internal marketing, from 'creative' through to the timing of the launch and the follow up.

Too often the answer to many training and development needs has been to send out long boring tomes, usually in small type, printed in one colour. Compare this to any external magazine, such as *Cosmopolitan* or even the trade press, and the answer to why they are not read is obvious!

With the demographic time bomb hitting the UK and Europe the recruitment, induction and retention of good people has to be done by managers. The key to making them realise the way to do this is by getting them to see 'employees' as 'target markets'. Finding the hooks that appeal to them is the first stage in training them to become internal marketeers.

The Midland Bank · Corporate internal marketing

The holistic model in practice

Midland Bank in the UK are going down a route of very strong product branding born out of customer segmentation. This is obviously not a tactical move but part of a carefully constructed long term strategy.

Crucial to the resulting levels of specialism needed both for understanding customer needs and for product knowledge comes the need for everyone in the organisation to be given the right information at the right time in the right way. The targeting of information must allow them to absorb it and feel motivated to act.

'Building on Success' is the long term strategic campaign designed to provide the internal products and services to the internal target markets – it is driven by the Internal Marketing Department who act as producers and gatekeepers of the messages. The leading edge external marketing by the bank and their emphasis on corporate internal marketing, makes this one of the most holistic approaches to corporate strategy in the UK.

the internal market place. Whether the issue cuts across attitude, awareness or ability the complexity of the internal products and services means that it is not enough just to advertise the idea.

There is, however, one very important message that the advertising world can teach the internal market, that is the power of a campaign. All too often, for example, it is felt that a one-off training course will change people. They are often subjected to what amounts to a one, two, or more days' 'launch', then left to sustain the impetus on their own. The situation can actually be made worse by high-quality trainers who, just like good salespeople, are able to create tremendous enthusiasm, lots of awareness and terrific course *critiques*. With nothing to support and sustain the high impact of the launch, the individual is then left, unable to fulfil the built-up expectations.

The same is true of training courses and any other type of transfer of information, idea or action required of the individual. In the external world the number of OTS (opportunities to see) a commercial is a vital factor in determining its impact on the uptake of the products and services that are being advertised. The repetition of a message is just as important internally. One-off courses, meetings, etc. are often not enough.

5 **Design Houses** The amount of money spent on corporate design by large organisations is almost legendary. Millions of pounds have been poured into the identities and logo designs of the likes of ICI, BP, British Airways. Where the battle for the customers' cash is at its most fierce, in retail, even more is spent on design, layout, signage, etc. This has happened with virtually all of the high street retailers and financial institutions, like Midland Bank, Barclays, Debenhams, Woolworth, Marks and Spencer, Tesco, Sainsbury, plus of course the smaller niche retailers like Sock Shop, Tie Rack, etc.

What is said by the design houses about corporate designs is yet another example of the same issues being raised by Corporate Internal Marketing. They are however, coming at it by a different route. This issue is that the internal image of an organisation should be reflected in its outward presentation to the market place. If the image is, for example, to be one of caring for its customers, or of an innovative company, or one that looks to providing high levels of added value, then it must deliver what it promises. In order for that to happen, the internal target market must be aware of the goals and expectations that the customers will have.

The result is that the design company will start to explore many of the areas that have already been discussed. Through research and internal debate about the design issues, they will attempt to match the internal actions of the individuals with the external demands of the customer.

In terms of the 'Attitude' of the organisation, this approach is as valid as any other. If all the relevant disciplines are involved, then each will have their input as to how the organisation needs to be changed. This change will be brought about to meet the requirements set for the designers. Ultimately, these must be agreed by the CEO as the holder of the vision and the mission.

The one restriction that is created with the sole use of the design route is that just like external marketing, the corporate branding process is only one part of a much larger whole. Designers may help to create the visual imagery of a brand or even corporate logo. To do this, it is vital that the designer has a thorough understanding and 'feel' for the product or organisation. There is however, nothing to suggest that they have the internal skills to change the perceptions of the people affected.

So, there are a number of routes to choose from in order to achieve the required level of professionalism in implementing internal marketing. Having now put the skeleton in place, the next step is really to get down to the meat of what needs to be done. Before doing that, a summary via a jigsaw page may help put this last section into context.

Putting the picture into context

External marketing 'meets' the needs of customers who need not buy what is on offer. Internal marketing must 'match' the needs of the organisation to the people in it who may have to buy what is on offer. This creates a new set of rules from those of external marketing.

The skills of human resource development are also needed to facilitate this matching process, e.g. coaching the individual who cannot or does not want to buy into a new way of doing things.

External advertising is based on simplifying often basically simple product benefits. Internal marketing may be about putting across complex issues that are inter-related to many other areas of the business.

The plethora of external marketing support agencies may not have the skills or experience to handle the issues. Nor will they have the products, such as training packages necessary to meet the demands of the internal marketplace.

10 | *Researching the needs of the individuals*

The three A's soon become four!

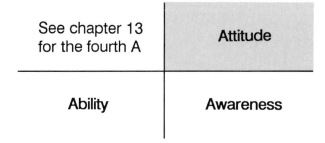

See chapter 13 for the fourth A	Attitude
Ability	Awareness

Figure 10.1 Four cornerstones of internal market research

Before making any decisions about the type of products and services that are going to be put into the internal marketing mix, the needs of the internal target markets must be established. Again, any model that is going to be transferred to everyone in the organisation must be simple if it is going to be used and understood. I have written about the three A's in strategic terms; now to use them tactically.

They will form a fundamental part of the background data on which decisions will be made. What is helpful to any form of internal marketing is if the internal target markets themselves understand which elements of their needs are being addressed. By keeping it simple, i.e. KISS, then everyone is aware of what is being attempted. In addition, the apparent mysteries of internal marketing are laid bare for all to see.

The three A's, just to remind you, are Attitude, Awareness and Ability. In everyday terms these are 'how you feel about something'; 'why you do the things that you do'; 'what you have to do to successfully complete the task'.

Simply classified, they are the feelings, the knowledge, and the skills. The beauty of such a readily understood classification is that it provides people with neat boxes in which to put what would otherwise be a very complicated picture. Of course they are all intertwined, and nothing is ever that simple; but for a system to be workable, it has to be understood. Questions then arise about what these three classifications comprise. Their composition must form the basis for the research data.

It has already been said that the order of importance of the three A's is Attitude, Awareness and Ability. Again this is a general statement giving a guideline as to what to tackle in overall terms. As with external marketing, there is no one single answer to what is required, every situation is different and needs analysing. The only way of approaching this issue professionally is through research. The nice thing is that preconceived notions, which may or may not be right, now have to be checked. The discipline of Corporate Internal Marketing does not allow for the assumption (often arrogant) that the originator of the products and services knows what the people want or how they want to see those products and services presented.

The 12 Attitudinal factors

Personnel experts will tell you that when it comes to interviewing people or doing an appraisal, there is one technique that allows you to get into the real psyche of a person. It is not by asking them what they do, or what they know (i.e. ability and awareness), it is by asking them what they feel about something. Most people will be able to look at a situation and give a personal view of their concerns, will be able to express their likes and dislikes, and talk about their other emotions. They may not be able to tell you why they did something, they may not be able to tell you what should be done about something, but they will generally 'feel' something – even if it is indifference!

It is people's attitudes, which, when positive, will open up the possibilities discussed under the strategic changes of Corporate Internal Marketing, e.g. strategy from below. Negative attitudes are invariably the demise of the organisation, or the departments, or individuals within it.

Unfortunately, individuals' attitudes are the trickiest area for any untrained, or even trained person to try to alter – as evidenced by every psychologist on emotional problems, or by the external marketeer when trying to alter perceptions about their products and services. The lessons learned by external advertising demonstrate that logic just does not apply. The eternal cry of Mr Spock that 'It's just not logical Captain', unfortunately, but excitingly holds true in Corporate Internal Marketing.

To try to put any products and services into the internal market without first being aware of the attitudinal factors is to court disaster. Having said that, the internal trend has been only to look at attitude surveys. But, just by tackling how people feel, and by making them feel warm and cuddly toward your internal products and services, the campaign will soon die a death if they don't know why they are doing things, or what they are supposed to do. This is why so many 'smile campaigns' fail.

So, to get into the individual psyche, and from there, into the team or organisational psyche, an attitudinal survey, as part of a wider reaching approach, is important. It is, however, only a part. There are 12 attitudes to research and consider in internal marketing. The first of these *must* be people's attitude to themselves!

1 Attitude to yourself

This is not the place to delve into the mysteries of the human ego. Neither is it the place to start to recommend solutions to motivation and morale. There is, however, a growing recognition that people's attitudes to themselves is the starting point for many training programmes. If individuals are not confident about their own personality, skills, social standing, etc. then to try to create something new will be perceived as a threat to their own model of themselves. These deep-seated perceptions can, however, be very sympathetically and empathetically tackled in the individuals' training and development. The level and extent of this attitude can be carefully set through research. This will ensure that the right emphasis and message is delivered, to the right people at the right time.

People's attitudes to themselves must also be tackled continuously through Corporate Internal Marketing. The organisation must provide strong and consistent messages to the individuals, that say that it believes that they are 'winners'. This is the title and consistent message in the Trusthouse Forte Motorway Division's Corporate Internal Marketing campaigns. If the confidence in people is demonstrated, then it will be reflected back.

2 Attitude to external customers

A variety of words and phrases used in an organisation can betray its attitude to external customers. These are all quotes:

> 'Punters';
>
> 'Awkward';
>
> 'Unreasonable';
>
> 'Those bloody idiots that keep asking for . . . ';
>
> 'If only we didn't have them';
>
> 'They always want what you haven't got';
>
> 'They get on my nerves';
>
> 'I hate looking after customers, they always . . . '.

Does this sound like the script from your last customer service film? Do the phrases sound a bit trite? They may to you, but are these attitudes not alive and kicking in your organisation today?

They may be watered down after your expensive customer service campaign, but to what extent? Do you know how much more work still needs to be done? In fact the job of changing attitudes is never ending. That is why, for example, in external marketing after 25 years or so, we are still seeing the same type of advert for Fairy Liquid.

The need for massive internal attitudinal shifts, for example to customer service, will always exist. The nature of the job, as all professional on-the-road sales trainers know, is such that continually awkward customers will erode the 'goodwill towards all men' type of attitude that is generated in customer service training programmes. This is in addition to rubbing away the knowledge of how to handle customers, and ultimately the individuals' skills and techniques. No amount of training will ever compensate for the previously gained lifeskill experience.

So, decision makers, beware: if you think that you have done your bit to improve attitudes towards customers with that big campaign back in 1980 something, then think again. This is the reason why most organisations have a very strong ongoing Corporate Internal Marketing policy for its professional salespeople, which includes constant training, motivation, leadership and reward. Yet the same Attitudes, Awareness and Ability are needed by virtually everyone in the organisation dealing with customers, including internal customers. However, it is left to one-off campaigns to tackle them, or 20 minute sessions every now and again, when sales are flagging. Is it any wonder that the attitudes to external customers leave a lot to be desired! When this poor attitude is combined with the high levels of awareness and ability required to handle today's more sophisticated customers, it is instantly recognised that the three A's need constant internal marketing.

3 Attitude to external products and services

How does the individual in the organisation feel about the products and services that they are spending all their energies trying to provide? They don't think much of them? They can't relate to them? They never see the end product in use? They think the customer is being ripped off?

If any one of these is the case, then you may have a major problem on your hands. But, you might ask, do they have to feel good about the external products and services? Of course they do. They have their pride, their respect, and their genuine interest in what they do. The research will determine what attitudes people hold, and how many people hold them.

The McGregor theory of the X and Y organisations applies here. McGregor states that the 'fundamental strength of the human side of enterprise' (as his book was called) enables an organisation to know, because of the internal strength of feeling, how far it will have to move to achieve acceptable levels of performance. As stated before, however, this human side of the business is not the panacea for all ills, it is only one aspect of the 'matching' process of the needs of the individuals to the needs of the organisation.

There are a number of organisations where poor morale could be attributed to the perceived negative attributes of the product. In one organisation, which will remain nameless, the attitude of the staff was even more negative because both they and the customers knew they were being 'ripped off'. There was nothing that the individuals working there could do about it, apart from leave. The virtual monopoly that the company enjoyed meant that the customers could not do much about it either. One individual in one of the research groups, set up to analyse the best way forward, complained that she was 'embarrassed and very reluctant' to divulge who she worked for whenever she was in a social situation.

The net result for the organisation was that morale was low, customer contact was avoided, and the level of service did not even have to be researched because it was often appalling. All that was measured was the level of complaints. The happy ending to this story was that the ownership of the sites changed, and the investment in the fabric and the products and services that were provided was massive. The customers were delighted with the new quality, i.e. it met their expectations. The staff were targeted with a big Corporate Internal Marketing campaign. This restored their confidence in the product and in themselves. Within two years individual members of staff were featured in an external advertising campaign. This succeeded in reversing the perceptions of both internal and external customers.

4 Attitude to the leadership you are given

The 1990s will see a massive change in what is required by internal target markets. They are no longer likely to be content with the type of close day-to-day supervision, checking and guidance that has traditionally been the prerogative of the manager. Indeed, the manager, with his vastly increased workload, and fewer moments in the day to spend watching over people, is forced to 'let them get on with it'.

The role of the 'manager' therefore, is now moving rapidly, by default and demand, to being one of a leader. The attitude of the individuals towards the immediate leader is going to determine their effectiveness in the job. This will be as a direct result of the amount of respect they feel, and the quality of the input, guidance and other leadership traits that the leader possesses.

The days of being closely managed have to be over, as neither the time nor the investment can be justified. At the same time, if individuals are pushed beyond the stage of coping with their role (i.e. the Peter Principle takes hold) then neither they nor the organisation is benefiting.

The attitude to the leader, responsible for creating in them the self-motivation to produce the goods, is much more important than the old style manager who had the time to closely oversee individuals. They were protected in their inefficiency by large numbers in the organisation. Those days are gone. The 'leaner and fitter' organisations of today have to provide a new breed of leader who will take people with them.

In short, if the leaders and leadership they provide are not respected, then once again, individuals' attitudes will be affected and will suggest a lowering in the level of motivation, output, effectiveness, etc.

The attitude of individuals to the leadership they are given is another element that needs researching. The interesting thing about this element of the Corporate Internal Marketing mix is that often it is not so much the quality and strength of the decisions that individuals have a problem with, it is the way they are put across, or often, not put across. Researching the attitudes to leadership and to the leaders themselves will give a strong indication of the quality and strength of the Corporate Internal Marketing. If leaders are not perceived to be very good, it is likely that their image is not being projected effectively.

5 The attitude to internal products and services

Having spent some time getting to the point where the individual sees that what the organisation provides are 'products and services' (as per the Corporate Internal Marketing model), then it would make sense to test the attitudes of the individuals to these products and services. Just as in external marketing, the starting point must be with the attitudes of the customer to the products and services. The same must be true internally, these products and services being the Vision, Mission and Values; the Structure; the Plans; and the Practices.

Specifically, the most fundamental of all are the products which allow the individuals to produce the outputs they are responsible for. These are the 'Practices', and are the bulk of the outputs of the organisation.

Any attitude survey, and any internal development of an organisation's products and services, will require a close look at how the individuals in the organisation feel about the existing products and services, and the proposed output and any changes.

Does this sound like a lot of hard work and expense? Once established, with a level of base data, the ongoing research is much quicker, faster and cheaper than the bigger and more detailed initial surveys. The difference between internal surveys in most organisations and the research in external marketing is frequency. The former are usually one-off, and then consigned to the bottom drawer; the latter are constantly used and monitored to continually improve the level of understanding about customers' needs. Internal research will have more impact when internal marketing is fully established. This will happen when the discipline of Corporate Internal Marketing is recognised for being able to provide greater returns on the investment than other competing demands on limited resources. The 'catch 22' situation is that the only way to prove this is through research!

6 Attitude to the internal customer

The employee revolution will have begun when organisations really perceive that employees are not employees. They are individuals who collectively make up internal target markets. This is best explained by the concept that individuals are provided with products and services by other individuals, just as they in turn provide products and services. Or, 'everyone is everyone else's customer'.

This concept already exists in many organisations through Crosby and other Quality programmes. The only way that the parochial and divisive nature of inter-departmental, inter-divisional and branch and head office splits is ever likely to turn to positive and helpful service, is through the recognition and acceptance of the 'internal customer'.

In many organisations this concept has yet to take hold. Even where it has, the attitude of the individuals may not have reached sufficient numbers to be considered significant. As it is the attitudes to the internal customer which are a crucial part of a quality programme, then these must be researched. Again, this must be done before putting the product into the internal market place. Before deciding the specific needs of the individuals, it is more sensible, more cost effective, and ultimately more likely to be successful, if the feelings of the internal target markets have been effectively researched.

7 Attitudes to financial goals

This is a fascinating area within organisations. It is the one where the individuals and the organisation can come into serious conflict. The traditional round of wage bargaining is often based upon the organisation pleading poverty or the need to invest, and the individuals or their representatives pointing to the profits. If the profits don't exist, they point to the level of inflation which they must keep up with, or ultimately, to the value of their contribution and levels of efficiency that they have put into the organisation.

The individuals on the one hand want the most out of the organisation that they can reasonably expect, yet on the other hand, the dichotomy comes popping out about the financial goals of the organisation itself. Many individuals have a fundamental lack of awareness about the financial aspects of an organisation, and about the impact they themselves have upon it. This is hardly surprising, as the effectiveness per person, in terms of the value they add to the output, is often not measured in total, far less individually. Nor is the individuals' effect on profitability.

Worse still, in many organisations it is felt unnecessary to inform individuals about *any* financial data. This not only includes the year-on-year figures (which often only serve to create illusions of 'Oh, they can afford to pay me more') but also the daily sales, costs and other statistics.

Is it any wonder that if individuals have a poor attitude to the revenue, costs and profit of an organisation, they do not particularly care about their impact on its financial position? It does not mean that they need to have the Profit and Loss account read to them on a regular basis. It does mean, however, that their attitude may improve if they are involved and are aware of financial implications of the part they play. To give an example: the campaign to improve sales and merchandising in Gardner Merchant contract catering establishments introduced a very simple measure of financial success. The measure could be quickly and easily produced on a daily or weekly basis.

Most importantly, it was internally marketed to every individual via a graph put on a notice board. The fact that the managing director had a copy of all of these graphs sent in on a weekly basis, and personally phoned the managers to congratulate or ask what went wrong, had a massive impact on the campaign. But at individual level, for the first time in many instances, they were being made aware of the financial effect their efforts were having on the business. The results were dramatic, both on the revenue and on the attitudes of the individuals to selling products. They had traditionally believed that their role was to produce the products, not to merchandise or sell them.

To motivate people, it is not enough to say, as is so often the case in many campaigns, words to the effect that, 'If you don't pull your finger out then you won't have a job'; or the opposite type of platitude, 'If you work hard then there could be a lot in it for you'. This will do very little to affect the attitude of the individual. The motivation level that people may have in working to improve the financial position of the organisation will only improve if they are involved and informed.

Traditionally, it is the manager who believes that information is power and is fearful about sharing any financial information who will have major problems with his team. This will be exposed in any survey on attitudes to finance.

8 Attitude to your career and future

An individual may have an excellent career path ahead of him but may feel that his future does not lie with the organisation. The two are, of course, closely linked, but it is worth highlighting the difference.

The career path of an individual should not be perceived in terms of those who are destined for the 'top' (or the bottom as it should now be!) Unfortunately, most of the concentration is placed here by many organisations. Given that the vast majority of individuals will stay within a fairly restricted income band, why is it that in terms of recognition and title they cannot progress?

The work done by Butlin's Holiday Worlds, part of the Rank Organisation, in which they are working hard to improve the status of all individuals, categorically stated that the attitudes of seasonal and part-time individuals towards their career in the organisation was such that they wanted to know that they could progress, and be recognised for it.

The simplest case of a career structure for non-managerial individuals is one that is being used worldwide in McDonalds, the hamburger chain. The company is extremely demanding of people in the work place. The speed at which they have to move is above and beyond many other jobs, and the demand on them from the managers and the customers is incessant. The 'career structure' used provides some of the motivation to act and is visibly demonstrated by the five-star system of badges. Every individual knows exactly where he or she is on the success ladder. The stars themselves are a recognisable sign of achievement.

Why shouldn't all those individuals who are apparently 'stuck' at a level or grade, perceive that there is more to the grade than meets the eye? If the career opportunities in an organisation are seen to be limited, then again, perception is all, and if something positive is done about it, motivation is more likely to increase.

The attitude of the individual to his career is one well worth including in any research programme.

9 Attitude to your involvement in improving product quality

'Why didn't you tell me that it needed fixing?'
'It's not my place to do that, is it?'

'Just change this here, it should work much better now.'
'I've been saying that ever since I started this job.'

'Well why didn't you say something?'
'Nobody asked my opinion, so I didn't think that it was my place to volunteer it.'

'Can I move this filing cabinet, everyone keeps knocking into it?'
'Why are you asking me? You could quite easily have gone ahead and done it.'
'I thought that bosses liked to make all the decisions.'

These are typical conversations. Typical of the range of attitudes that people have toward improving the quality of the things they are doing wrong or see as wrong.

It is estimated that it takes around 10 years for an organisation to be able to turn this core attitudinal problem around. In essence, this is the aim of all 'Quality' programmes.

To take an example: British Airways are in year six of a 12-year commitment. What they have established, from a very heavy research programme, is that there are two key elements to customer satisfaction. The vital statistic they discovered is that only approximately one-third of satisfaction is reliant on the quality of the product. If you think about it, you don't expect the plane to set off late, to stall in mid-Atlantic, to be dirty, to have toilets that don't work, to have torn seats, to arrive late, etc.

These aspects of product quality are often termed 'hygiene factors'. Customers today *expect* a level of quality of product well beyond the levels of only a few years ago. The problem may be that the organisation may not have caught up with them, in what they deliver. The expectation level of the quality of product and the overall quality of life is as high as we find in the latest glossy advert, TV soap, or designer shop we visit. Organisations *must* therefore deliver product quality to provide a minimum degree of satisfaction.

This leaves, in the case of British Airways, and probably most other organisations, a massive two-thirds of the level of customer satisfaction coming from the quality of the service. Unlike product quality, there is a low expectation of the quality of service that may be given. This in turn, however, leads to a correspondingly high degree of satisfaction when good service is delivered! In order that an organisation can succeed, the attitudes of employees in wanting to improve both these aspects of quality are vital.

British Airways have a huge programme running which has resulted in a remarkable and well documented turn-around. The Corporate Internal Marketing programme is well known by its customers, as customer service features strongly in the external marketing campaign.

It is about the power of harnessing the strength of feeling of individuals in the organisation. Not only can you become the 'world's favourite organisation', you can, as British Airways has recently achieved in its sector, become among the most profitable. The only way to do this is to get people involved. This level of involvement needs to be constantly measured to assess the successes of the past and the direction for the future.

10 Attitude to your involvement in innovation

The logical extension to improving the quality of existing products and services is to look to introducing new ones.

> **The difference that exists in attitudinal terms between improving quality and introducing innovation is that many individuals think they are not creative or clever enough to come up with new ideas.**

This is a basic mind set. In their book *The Creative Manager*, Evans and Russell talk about the creative process: 'Learning to work with the creative process is not about learning new techniques; it is learning to trust the creativity that is already within us all. It is a simple enough idea, but the consequences of this shift in perception are immense. It means that we can and should see ourselves as our own greatest resource. We do not have to wait for someone to 'put' something into us. Nor need we write ourselves off as not belonging to the creative few.'

If seeing yourself as creative is the ideal state for everyone, the question in your organisation is how far away are you? Having been heavily involved in the creative process in internal and external marketing I can vouch that it is people's own attitude that stifles creativity. Additionally, it is often jealousy and the fear of new ideas that stifle the innovative process. Do individuals in your organisation shy away from new ideas? Do they mistrust the people who are not afraid to say their piece? Do they criticise those who are more likely to both come up with new ideas, and be in the forefront of putting them into practice?

It is the processes of creativity and innovation which bring new products and services into both the internal and external markets. The attitudes that people have about them are crucial.

Tom Peters, in *A Passion for Excellence*, has some questions which could well do with being included in any attitudinal research programme:

Are you and your colleagues 'hero creators'?

Do you, even when it makes you grit your teeth a bit, hail the pain-in-the-neck champion?

Do you focus on modest heroism (i.e. lots of mini heroism)?

Do you reserve your top plaudits for the pragmatist champion, the person(s) *not* involved in the dramatic part of the project, but whose obsession with the nuts and bolts phases may have cut the cycle time most significantly?

How (and how regularly), very specifically, do you 'post' such acts of heroism?

Is everyone, at all levels and in all functions, aware of exactly what you think heoism is?

Is your definition of innovation limited in any way?

Of creativity?

Do you consider a minor procedural invention by the receptionist to be true creativity?

These attitudinal questions to innovation and creativity are ones that will paint the true picture of an organisation and the individuals in it.

11 Attitude to reward and pay

It's all very well asking for the people in your organisation to adapt to the tremendous changes that are happening, and to ask them to contribute to the success that you are hoping for. As a result of this, you intend to be leaner, fitter, more pro-active, more creative, more innovative and therefore ultimately more profitable, i.e. make more money. The obvious question is: How do people feel about the rewards and pay they receive?

However, this does not mean that people need constant reward, albeit that there is a constant demand for increased income. It is a self-fulfilling situation that if you accept a certain level of pay, you are not going to move significantly outside it unless you are promoted. It does mean that people will have certain expectation levels of reward. What are these? How well are they being met? How much does this job, the people or the leadership provide the reward they require?

Thus, in addition to the financial benefits, how much satisfaction are they getting from the job, i.e. is it personally rewarding? How much do they feel rewarded from their involvement with customers, colleagues and bosses?

How much would the organisation save if the attitudes of its individuals to the reward, pay and recognition were as high as might be expected?

The difficulty once again, with a new discipline, is that until norms are set, both within an organisation and for outside comparison, it is difficult to know what can be expected, especially of soft data. The main thing is to start collecting the information.

One excellent example of the perception of individuals about their involvement in the job and hence how well they feel they are getting personal reward, is from a recent survey Esso undertook with MORI. In addition to the data collected for Esso, MORI has comparative data from other organisations.

In the survey, 64% of Esso forecourt staff (employed by individual operators) 'are interested in the job they do and already feel involved'. This compares to the MORI norm of only 20% of employees who are interested and already involved. A further 27% of Esso forecourt staff feel interested in the job and are seeking greater levels of involvement. The normal MORI findings are that 45% want more involvement.

The great news for Esso was that in total, '91% of your people are ready and willing to continue, or start making a more effective contribution to your business'.

'Compared with MORI's average, your staff are over three times more likely to feel really involved with their jobs.'

In total, Esso only had 1% who saw it as 'just a job' – compared to the MORI average of 9%. Only 8% don't want involvement – compared to 26%.

These statistics show that individuals not only care about the job they are doing and want to be involved; they indicate that if this involvement is not forthcoming, they would look elsewhere.

So what Tom Peters argues is a 'nice to have', may soon become a 'vital to have'. People want to be involved in their work, and that means helping improve what exists and introducing new ideas of their own.

One additional piece of information worth noting from the Esso survey relates further to the attitudinal issue of pay. It shows that pay is often a major issue only when other things are wrong. The highly involved and motivated workforce among the independent dealers led to the following statistics in the summary of the findings:

'Pay is always an issue, but of the 13% of employees seeking alternative employment, only one-third of them, i.e. 4%, say that they are leaving because of it.'

In other organisations where qualitative research has been carried out, this can be summed up by saying that in those departments where managers are poor, pay is a major issue; in those departments with good managers, it is not. Where there is a motivation problem, it is usual to find that the poor managers blame the organisation, and its pay and reward system. Naturally, they can't blame themselves! This links back to those who feel involved being more satisfied.

The Esso survey also measured this total satisfaction. The results showed an incredible 93% of people get real satisfaction from their jobs. The interesting statistics produced by this survey lead on to the next attitudinal factor, the attitude to Corporate Internal Marketing.

12 Attitude to Corporate Internal Marketing

The information that came back from the individuals within each of the service stations was excellent news for Esso. It also surprised the dealers. Because they didn't feel it was necessary to answer the questions themselves, they had almost entirely different views on what they thought the individual cashiers, etc. wanted. As a result of their misconceptions about what people got out of working for Esso, the external marketing in the recruitment of people was based on wrong assumptions. This led to some totally wrong approaches being taken to attracting new people. Once employed, it then led to wrong approaches to keeping good people. In short, the individuals got a lot out of working in the service stations, while the managers thought they saw it as just another job. This being the case, managers saw no reason for getting them involved, or to want to find people who liked responsibility, or to ultimately praise and reward people who did contribute.

The recruitment advertising almost apologised for the job and showed none of the 'benefits' of involvement, etc. The interviewing by the managers stressed the down side of the jobs. The induction centred on task orientated training to get the job done to the managers' satisfaction, rather than building up the responsibility of the individuals. The on-going motivation was not centred on initiative but on the adherence to standards laid down by the manager. The net result was that the Corporate Internal Marketing was, in many instances, fundamentally lacking at site level, while at corporate level, large budgets were being spent to address the needs and demands of individuals.

An intensive training, development and reward scheme for cashiers was introduced under the banner 'You make the difference'. It was necessary to create the right attitude among managers, and then to increase awareness and ability to put the internal marketing plans into practice.

A programme and campaign called 'The Right People Programme' was developed. It provided the managers with the MORI research to help start altering their attitudes. This was done by developing awareness of the needs of the people working on the sites. The main conclusion was that a gap existed between the management's perception of what was needed and what the people (both new and potential recruits) wanted. This was summed up in the introduction to the programme as follows:

Welcome to 'The Right People'. Today we face a problem. Attracting and keeping good people is very difficult. Quite simply, people are more selective about the jobs they do, and increasingly, they're selecting work that offers stimulation and personal satisfaction, in addition to wages. If we are going to compete in this challenging new market, we need to offer more than ever before. That doesn't just mean money – leadership, training, support and motivation are all vital factors that we must be *seen* to provide. In simple terms, a good manager will attract and keep staff even when other employers in the area are paying more.

'The Right People' recognises this. It's a complete programme designed to help *you* become more competitive in the employment market. In it, you'll find practical advice and information on the kind of people to look for, how to attract them, how to recruit them and, most importantly, how to keep them.

This illustrates how the attitudes of people in an organisation will impact on the way they do things. It shows how marketing terms, the messages and the style of presentation used to put them across, will affect attitudes.

It is by continually checking, not just on the products and services that are on offer in the organisation, but on how they are marketed that the organisation will ensure a total approach is taken to providing for the needs of the individual.

'Nothing kills a bad product better than good marketing.' The reverse is also true: 'Nothing kills a good product better than bad marketing'.

Conclusion

How people feel is vital. Marketing forces you to measure people's strength of feeling. The emphasis placed on the issues will tell you where you need to concentrate your efforts. The nature of the feedback on how well you are approaching Corporate Internal Marketing will tell you if you are getting the style of the communication correct. The changes in the data will indicate your levels of success.

The picture emerges about how you feel

To yourself: Do you like yourself? If not, how can you like anything or anyone else?

To external customers: Are they punters?

To external products and services: Are you proud of what the organisation produces?

To the leadership you are given: Are you all fired up?

To the internal products and services, i.e. mission/structure/plans/practices: Do you believe in them?

To internal customers: Are they customers or political rivals?

To the financial goals: Is money and profit healthy – or just a way to demand more pay?

To your career and future: Are you stuck – and do you want to stay anyway?

To your involvement in improving quality: Who asked you to stick your nose in?

To your involvement in innovation: Are you criticised if you come up with something new?

To reward and pay: Is it a major issue? Then something is wrong!

To corporate internal marketing: Is it effective in getting through to you?

II | *The second A – Awareness*

See chapter 13 for the fourth A	Attitude
Ability	Awareness

The recognition among managers is beginning to dawn that it isn't enough just to tell people what to do: they also want to know why. That may or may not be the case in your organisation, but how do you really know that the managers and leaders feel inclined to say *why* things happen? How much do the individuals feel that they have been told what they want to know? Additionally, what are the main issues that they are interested in, or might be interested in?

Once again, the list of issues raised in this section is not intended to be definitive, nor is it in any sort of order. We are beginning to move into uncharted water here. At least with attitude surveys, research has been going on for some time. Some of these may well have included information about how people 'feel' about the reasons why they were doing things; but this is not an awareness issue. Individuals' awareness of organisational issues is determinable by the factual data that can be gathered on their knowledge of the subject. It is also important to know how much information it is *necessary* to give them, and how much they can cope with.

This can be put into the research, and analysed and compared.

AWARENESS OF WHY THINGS ARE DONE

Awareness will invariably centre mainly around facts and figures. It will provide the background and the information on which individuals will base their decisions. However, in addition to the simple scenario of providing individuals with the type of general information that may be available within a department, the advent of Information Technology has produced two other needs. Unfortunately, this creates almost conflicting situations. On the one hand there is now an abundance, indeed an over-abundance, of information. On the other hand, the degree of specialisation of the information has meant that it is of use to only a limited number of people, often at more 'junior' levels in the organisation. What then becomes important is that they are aware of the things that they have the authority to act on. Hence, a teller in a bank will soon be able to tell at a glance your credit worthiness, and whether to suggest a loan for that new car they overheard you mention.

So, in many cases, lack of information is not the problem. The time to be able to devote to reading and absorbing information is the problem. The deluge of information is such that putting priorities on it is almost impossible. The quality of the internal marketing of the information is such that it either does not get read or there is a scale of absorption ranging from 'instantly forgotten' to 'excellent news'.

In an era of IT an organisation can and, from my observations, does have major problems with the levels of awareness of individuals. This is definitely a problem when it affects the motivation of the individual, e.g. when they want the information for their own purposes and don't know how to find it or use it. It is a major headache when the organisation needs the individual to know the reasons and explanations for something in order to drive the business forward, and it is unavailable or buried in a mass of other data.

Take banks. Just over a decade ago there were three products that a cashier had to know about – current, deposit and business accounts. Today, there is not only a super abundance of individual types of current and savings accounts, but banks are selling the same products as building societies, insurance companies and investment houses.

Product knowledge becomes vital. But then other kinds of information become important, such as which products should be sold in order to be successful in this month's award scheme. In addition, more information is needed on how well the individual and the team are doing against its quarterly target. And, for example, why there are pushes on things which were not even submitted for acceptance in last month's scheme. If target setting is recognised as a good idea, the awareness of why they are set may well be important to the individuals, especially if their income is dependent upon it.

Here then, are the four main issues to address with awareness. Without getting too deeply into the exact questions which may need asking on any particular issue, there is a very simple set of guidelines to follow to ensure that 'all the angles are covered' on any one topic.

The guidelines were set by no less a person than Rudyard Kipling who identified, long before the current terminology of 'open questions' was coined, that there are six key words. Experience shows these are the words on the lips of increasingly more individuals in organisations today. So why not be pro-active and answer the questions before they are asked? Kipling had a rhyme which went:

> I keep six honest serving men
> They taught me all I knew
> Their names are what and why and how,
> And when and where and who.

These words can be applied to the following:

1 Organisational goals

What are they? Do you hear people say, 'What is this one-page thing called a mission statement; this doesn't really tell me anything!'

Why are they being pursued? Is the vision really enough, or is there scope for allowing employees an insight into the financial and other considerations?

How are they going to be enacted? Is it by mergers, acquisitions, etc. and, for example, how will it affect me?

When are things going to happen? If you don't really know, then tell me, don't keep me in the dark and let me read it in the newspapers.

Where will things happen? We live in a global market, and the rapid events going on everywhere make my little corner of the world more vulnerable than I might like.

Who will be affected? I know that change is the order of the day but all these 'flatter structures, leaner and fitter organisations and takeovers', etc. always seem to come down to the individuals being moved on or out.

Do these seem like reasonable enough requests that individuals might ask of an organisation? The view up to now has been that it is easy to satisfy the requests. If the mission statement isn't enough then they can always have a look at the annual report and accounts!

Let's look at one organisation where everyone was aware of what was going on – it was splashed all over the newspapers: the seemingly never ending saga of Ernest Saunders and the Guinness and Distillers affair. I have no intention of talking about the case, but will comment on the way the organisation tackled the massive motivational problem that existed as a result of it.

The biggest problem they faced was in providing the information and data on the future of the organisation that would satisfy the individuals on the six awareness issues. The route taken was to be completely honest about the plans, strategies, etc. In addition, a wonderfully simple way of encouraging people to listen followed. It was to offer them a stake in the future of the organisation. Here was an apparently troubled company being positive and proactive. What better way to gain the confidence of the people!

So, in the summer of 1987, every employee was issued with a document entitled 'The Guinness Employee Share Opportunity'. It formed the start of a major initiative, providing the answers to the 'Kiplings' on the organisation's goals.

I quote in its entirety the letter from the Group Chief Executive, as I believe it is an excellent example of a response to the needs of the internal target market.

Dear Colleague

It gives me great pleasure to introduce this latest initiative in our programme of encouraging wider employee share ownership throughout the Guinness Group.

The Board of Guinness PLC places a high value on employee share ownership because it offers you the opportunity to share in the Group's success.

This portfolio has been prepared to provide you with a convenient means of retaining information on share ownership and the Guinness share schemes, and to enable you to keep secure the papers, certificates and correspondence you will receive which relate to them.

The Guinness Employee Share Opportunity is a continuing programme in support of your Company's commitment to employee share ownership. You will receive regular updates, information and further offers to participate from time to time.

The Group's long-term strategy is aimed at continuing development and, other things being equal, this should reflect positively in the share price, though, as you know, stock markets can fluctuate and your personal financial planning should take that into account.

I hope as many of you as possible will take up the opportunities offered by the schemes described in this folder. If, like me, you have confidence in your company and we continue on the road to success, your reward should be the increasing value of your shares and the security of knowing you have a steadily growing stake in the company in the future.

Yours sincerely,

A.J. Tennant
Group Chief Executive

Here is a selection of some of the other information included in the 'Factfile', all aimed at encouraging share ownership, which in turn generates interest, involvement and commitment.

Contents

- A summary of Guinness performance.
- A graph showing the performance of the shares at six monthly intervals between 1981 and 1986.
- Graphs for you to maintain your own records of monthly share price movement in 1987/88, and . . .
- An extract from the *Financial Times* showing where and how to find the current price of your shares.

The following is a list of some of the questions to which well targeted replies were given:

1 What exactly is the Guinness Sharesave Scheme?
2 Am I eligible to join?
3 When can I join?
4 How can I join?
5 What happens when I join?
6 How much can I save under the Sharesave Scheme?

etc.

Every shareholder of course then receives an annual report. The 1989 report featured the following paragraph in the Chairman's Statement:

> Within Guinness we have two major assets – our brands and our employees. As I have travelled around the company, visiting plants and offices, I have been most impressed by the ability, enthusiasm and commitment of our employees in continuing to sell our brands. I would like to thank everyone in the company for their loyalty and support since I became Chairman. I have been greatly heartened by the will and the wish of everyone to restore the morale and the reputation of this marvellous business.
>
> Sir Norman Macfarlane

In addition to this there is an ongoing commitment within Guinness for a presentation to be made to every single individual in the organisation, by a main board director every six months. This features the strategic aims of the organisation (e.g. to concentrate on the Far Eastern markets) and allows full and frank discussions about the health of the company and anything else that people want to raise.

If this can be done in an organisation which has had more than its share of problems, and can generate a high level of motivation, then imagine doing the same in an organisation which has not had to suffer from such debilitating episodes.

2 Team goals

These are simply a microcosm of the organisational goals, or at least they should be. If the team understands the organisation's goals then they are more likely to ensure that the team goals will fit.

How often though, even at the simplest level, do individuals have no idea of the 'Kiplings' behind the work that they do?

3 Individual goals

A considerable amount of work has been done to establish the best ways of creating the understanding of what an individual should be attempting to achieve, and how to measure those achievements. One of the methods is by objective setting, i.e. MBO – Management By Objectives. Another, similar, method is by KRAs – Key Result Areas.

This is not the place to debate the basic 'product' or the features and benefits. But, suffice it to say that individuals are beginning to demand this sort of internal product to provide them with the sense of direction that they need.

The cascade (i.e. launch) of KRAs in an organisation and the subsequent Corporate Internal Marketing of the successes, is one of the ways of matching the needs of the individuals to the needs of the organisation.

Is 'measurement' an important part of Corporate Internal Marketing? Peter Hazzard, Food Services Director of Gardner Merchant, has a saying which goes something like this: 'People work against three main criteria:

- what they like doing;
- what they are good at;
- what they get measured on.

They must therefore know what they are being measured on, and why.'

4 Awareness of customer needs

It is not enough to have good product knowledge. All the product knowledge in the world won't help if you don't know what the customer wants, why they want it, and when they want it. This applies internally as well as externally.

Does this sound like a statement of the obvious? Why bother researching it? All that is needed, surely, is letting people know what customers want! If this is the case, then why do organisations spend so much time and money on external marketing, helping the customer to clarify what they want. What chance does the individual in an organisation have?

And it gets worse. How, for example, does a 22-year-old female cashier, living in a bedsit, relate to serving the 60-year-old male executive, with his half-a-million a year income. Sure, she can be nice to him, but what does he really need in terms of the financial services the organisation can supply?

The organisations that get this right, and get closest to their customers, will have the biggest edge in the quality of their service. The external marketing department will have plenty of customer information; all they need to do is to share it by creating awareness that helps individuals in the organisation to understand why they are doing what they are doing.

12 | *The third A – Ability*

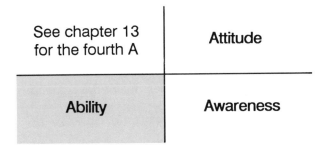

See chapter 13 for the fourth A	**Attitude**
Ability	**Awareness**

Now we are moving into the sphere of skills training. Provided that people feel good about what they are doing, provided that they feel comfortable and confident that they know why they are doing it, then all that is left is the skill required to do it, i.e. Ability.

Things can get really interesting here for the internal marketeer; this is where the traditional training department comes into its own. There are various methods of delivering training, but they boil down to three:

1 On the job – with a trainer (even if it is Nellie)
2 Off the job – with a trainer (even if it is a computer)
3 Self-teach – without a trainer (on or off the job)

In simple terms, to the marketeer, the first two are delivery of a product through word of mouth to small groups, i.e. selling; the third is delivery of a product by audio/visual communication to large, remote groups, i.e. marketing. This is not to say that the training element is redundant, far from it. It *is* to say that internal marketing is a vital part of delivering Ability. It is the internal marketeer who will hold the information about the individuals and their needs and who is so well situated to determine methods of design style and distribution of the product.

Ability to do the job required

The training and other messages that need to get through are competing in a very tough internal and external environment. This includes not only the better quality of the Corporate Internal Marketing being provided but other factors being placed on the individual. In today's environment the main areas are stress and pressure. Evans and Russell devote a chapter to this in *The Creative Manager* – after all, creativity is now one of the demands placed on individuals of their ability to do the job:

> The very situations in which we most need to draw upon our creative resources are frequently those situations where we experience pressure. These may be the pressures of deadlines, of responsibilities, of other people's expectations, financial worries, domestic problems or the difficulties of coping with a young family. Whatever their cause, their effect is usually one of making us feel fatigued and dull rather than relaxed and open. As a result creativity suffers, just when we need it most.

And so does the impact of Corporate Internal Marketing. The internal target markets are not in front of the television holding a beer and absorbing the latest message about new 'Whizzo'; they are at work. They are being trained in new skills. They are under pressure to perform. At work, their ability to learn new skills is limited. It is, for example, far removed from learning a new hobby at home.

In addition, the quality of the internal marketing of training products suffers from small budgets and lack of expertise. Compare this to the quality of external marketing!

It is their ability, involving the fundamental skills, which will allow each individual to do the job. The advances in this area are tremendous, for example in technology-based training and open learning. If only these advances were being matched by the attitudes of organisations to investing in people and developing them. There is still too much lip service paid to training. The move in human resource development is away from imposed off-the-shelf training solutions which are forced on the individuals, whatever their own particular needs. Instead, many organisations are recognising that the individuals themselves need to take responsibility for their own training and personal development.

There are two car manufacturers at the forefront of this. One is the Rover Group, who are aiming to turn the whole organisation from one that 'teaches' its employees to becoming 'the learning organisation'. The other is Ford, who have launched a major campaign to allow its people to develop themselves in non-work activity called the Employee Development Assistance Programme. Over £2 million is being spent to assist individuals to realise their potential in whatever area they choose. Of course, this personal development is aimed at the organisation gaining as well. Midland Bank have also heavily invested in a self-development programme for all its people called 'LEAP'.

The ability or skill that people need must come from training or development. The biggest hurdles to overcome now are the two main areas of how best to market the training products and what level of budgetary investment is needed to succeed. The former issue of internal marketing is only just being addressed; the latter issue of budgets is one that is increasingly being recognised, but not necessarily being acted upon. If times are going to be tough, it takes a brave CEO to pump money into people development when the focus is on the bottom line.

13 | *The fourth A – Actual*

Actual	**Attitude**
Ability	**Awareness**

In marketing terms, it would be a complete waste of time knowing how someone felt about your product if they could not afford to purchase it. Hence, the simple classification of ABC allows you to target to the people who *can* afford your product. It also shows that they are in the type of group who have a continuing need to purchase. More detailed information allows better targeting in, for example, address, income, debts, age, marital status, etc.

In other words, factual or (to stick to a word beginning with A) actual data or information. This type of information was provided in the 1981 census and linked to purchasing research data to provide ACORN.

The same need for information must be true of the internal market place. It isn't enough to know, for example, that 35% of individuals don't feel that they are being informed of events and have to rely on the grapevine. Which departments are affected? Which level of individual? Which age group? What training have the 'bosses' had?

At present the information available is pretty crude, and is mainly for use in a 'buckshot' type approach to large-scale programmes. But what happens when the quality of Corporate Internal Marketing has to be better? What happens when the broad issues have been put across and the individuals start to look ever more to their own specialised needs? The type of actual data that can be usefully used to target employees in rifle-shot type internal marketing will have to be much more sophisticated than that used now.

For example, the same type of data that is being collected in terms of psychological tests can be used by the organisation as a whole. It can be used by individual managers to target specific messages to specific individuals. At present, this hard data is used solely for personal issues, e.g. assessment of suitability for career progression, etc. If the information were used as a basis for improving the communication process, then individuals, teams, managers and leaders would have a much easier time in getting through to people.

To take a specific example, where hard data of this nature can be extremely useful, any one of the classifications from the management models on team characteristics will provide a basis for very usable information. Say an individual described as creative, innovative, short on attention span, low on detail is, in the terms of Belbin who is well-known for his classification of people's actions within teams, a 'Plant'. This, by itself may be very useful in a team-building exercise, and improve the communication of that microcosm within the organisation. But what about the rest of the organisation? Individual classifications and those for everyone in the organisation can be used for Corporate Internal Marketing. If the need is for one-to-one contact (i.e. internal selling) or written contact (i.e. internal marketing), and the data suggests a certain approach is the one that should be adopted, why not use it?

A quick check on the target market's particular profile, either on an individual, or on larger teams or groups within the organisation, should reveal the approach most likely to succeed. For example, creative individuals or teams are best approached with messages containing lots of 'pzazz', giving a general overview rather than a detailed one, with a short summary instead of long detailed reports.

However, if a heavy, detailed, facts-and-figures-orientated memo comes out, or a long, boring report, then the result is obvious. Does this degree of targeting appear to be taking Corporate Internal Marketing too far? No. It is no different to the messages that management trainers have been preaching for years about interpersonal skills.

Just imagine, if a new team member, manager, supervisor or colleague didn't have to invest the time and effort to build up all the data it takes to establish and maintain good relationships, the savings would be tremendous. It therefore follows that all the data collection in training rooms, in assessment centres, would and should be usable on a day-to-day basis, as it is for the particular need at the time.

To take another example of a personality profile, if someone likes prior warning about an issue, and doesn't like surprises, what is wrong with that? Why should everyone but the new team member know about it? To have this level of research data on individuals freely available, should not be a fantasy. It will, I believe, be common practice among the most successful organisations in the next 10 to 15 years.

To take this a stage further, the Royal Mail, who are about to enter the 1990s with one of the largest, most co-ordinated approaches to Corporate Internal Marketing, have started to use Actual information in a very specific way. Every individual in the organisation received a targeted piece of communication which allowed, among other things, discounts and offers on various products. There would have been no point in targeting the wrong products, with the wrong style of message. Knowledge of the target market was therefore vital.

The large investment in any exercise like this is the one determining factor for suggesting that a more sophisticated research- based approach is taken to Corporate Internal Marketing. The other element is the effect on the whole organisation, if the internal marketing message is off target. In an external marketing campaign, the effect of poor marketing certainly adds up, and word of mouth does play an important part, but inside an organisation the speed and impact of good and bad news travels even faster! People even enjoy it if there is a good bit of 'juicy news', especially if someone gets it wrong. Corporate morale, motivation and the strong involvement in the products and services that the organisation offers, are not to be tampered with. Yet, they are the very things that are being tampered with, by people who do not have the necessary information to make quantifiable judgements.

The expenditure on 'communications' is enormous in all organisations. This is true of even the simplest level of people talking to each other. The lack of a data base for most types of communication is frightening. If the same view was taken on the investment in communication, as is taken of expenditure, then there would be a totally different situation today. The trouble is that the 'communication issue', as it has been called in the past, was seen as highly amorphous. So, little could be done in hard, practical terms, apart from the gnashing of teeth and perennial cry 'we're not very good at communicating'.

Now something can be done, research can be undertaken. It can be carried out in a systematic way. It can be tied into the existing data used for other purposes, as in psychometric data, and it can be made generally available.

On a personal level, people should be proud of their individuality. They should be able to expect others to take their individuality into account, as does the external marketeer. The excellent work done on team identification and psychometric tests, and the proposed tests of attitude, awareness and ability should provide powerful tools to assist people in the internal marketing process.

To take this a stage further, at an organisational level, internal data can be used to assist at the macro level of Corporate Internal Marketing, and external type data may become invaluable. One organisation has already discussed the possibility of defining the ACORN profile of the high numbers of temporary staff, and using this in direct mail for recruitment.

The move towards this much tighter targeting is happening to an increasing extent in external marketing. Rather than waste money on advertising in media such as national newspapers and TV to reach tens of thousands of people who will never buy the products and services, specifically pinpointed direct mail campaigns are beginning to take over. The same could be true of recruitment.

Does this seem far fetched? What if the recruitment campaign was linked to the external marketing to make it even more effective? What happens when the recruitment sections in the press are so full because of the problems created by the demographic time bomb, that both the cost of insertion and of repeating the advert make it so difficult to attract people?

Finally, now that the mainstream external advertising agencies are recognising that recruitment advertising is lucrative, that it must conform to corporate branding, and that the adverts must be targeted to hit home, it won't be long before they will be asking for as much information as possible about the internal target markets. If none is forthcoming, they will have the ideal excuse for not providing the right adverts. Money will be wasted. In the business climate of today, wasted money becomes a priority. If a pro-active approach to research is not taken now, a reactive one will soon happen. Organisations that get their recruitment right today will be further down the path tomorrow.

The methods of research

Having established the basis for the data, the next step is to carry out the research. Just as in external marketing there are a number of ways that this can be done. In essence, the research splits into three main areas: Qualitative, Quantitative, and Unstructured research.

Qualitative research is carried out one-to-one, or in small groups where the findings are intended to produce 'in-depth' analysis of the respondents' views. Quantitative research provides a representative sample size sufficient to make the data that is required reliable. I have called the remainder Unstructured simply because the data is collected *ad hoc*. This category includes anecdotal data (often very powerful within organisations), unsolicited views, such as letters in staff newspapers, feedback from briefing groups and casual conversations where opinions are generated, hardened, and so on.

The whole basis of successful external marketing comes from *effective research*. The same must be true of Corporate Internal Marketing. It is worth spending some time on one of the methods of research within organisations to appreciate the power and complexity of using it as part of the internal marketing mix.

One of the most powerful of these methods is that which centres around gaining solid qualitative data. It was developed by my team within Human Resource Development Limited. The technology is copyright, but a description of the benefits will suggest how this type of research tool can be used.

Many thousands of man-days have been spent, in a wide variety of situations, using this research method. It has assisted many organisations in gaining a tremendous insight into the hearts and minds of the individuals working in them.

To best explain this, an extract from a launch booklet about the research is provided. This spearheaded a much bigger programme for Renault Truck Industries, a company forced to go through massive cultural and structural change. The brief at the start of the 1990s was simple. Become efficient, or manufacturing moves out of the UK. The introduction of the change began by first telling the people that the new 'Business Development Programme' centred around them, and therefore their needs. This ran alongside the sales needs and structural needs. All three were paramount in starting the process of turning the company around, and provided the basis for a committed team of people.

The changes that the organisation had to go through were driven by the new managing director, whose brief from the foreign parent company was simple – be profitable or we close the manufacturing side of the operation and transfer it to another country. The timescales were short, against a declining market and a worsening economy. The focus on the three areas of sales development, organisational development and people development meant just about everything was a major area of scrutiny. To introduce the beginnings of the organisational change, an announcement was made that a large percentage of the workforce would be offered voluntary redundancy. The situation became increasingly difficult because the percentage and number of volunteers didn't match.

It is against this type of backdrop that the data provided by a research programme can produce the key 'hot buttons' that will motivate the individuals who do want to stay and give their all. Not all organisations are facing this amount of change over such short timescales, but the example provides a compression of many of the problems organisations do face.

The letter from the managing director puts the need for research into context.

'Firstly, we get a cross-section of you together – volunteers only in a number of workshop groups, away from the company, to discuss the issues affecting you and your thoughts and ideas about the company in general.

Secondly, a questionnaire is put together from the findings of these workshops, and given to everyone else to fill in, confidentiality assured – of course!

From these findings we can immediately tackle the real issues and start off with the training, development and reorganisation as appropriate.'

(For the complete statement see Apendix 1)

This is an example of the Qualitative and Quantitative research that can be undertaken. It also serves to show that because the internal target market is static, the research itself can produce the initial PR to a campaign.

In addition to the base data, the research can be used to test the rest of the process in the internal marketing mix. This testing can be from initial concepts, to final artwork, just as the external marketeer will be constantly checking the views of the external customer on all aspects of the products and services. What is even more important about the research process in the internal marketplace, is this aspect of the static nature of the market. Every move to do some internal research will almost inevitably produce two things – awareness of what is going to happen, leading to advance PR, and ownership of the solutions, brought about by involving people. Both of these are extremely useful to the internal marketeer.

Analysis of the data

The research data, be it quantitative, qualitative or unstructured, will have provided the basis for some sort of analysis. At this stage, both experience and subjective judgement will take over. It is not just the figures that are important, but the interpretation of them, which will drive any decisions to act, invest, or direct efforts in other directions.

One of the main ways of interpreting data, however, is through comparisons, both with past data, to give trends, and with other organisations' performance to give indicators of success levels. The MORI research for Esso, as previously mentioned, is a good example of the latter. The problem with the new discipline of Corporate Internal Marketing is that the lack of investment in research in the past, and the comparative crudity of the measurement and information produced means that there is a lack of both base and reliable comparative data.

There may be plenty of 'Attitude Surveys' lying around in large organisations, but are they under constant review? Do they form the basis for ongoing research? Are they used by the board as part of the performance measures of the organisation? Are comparisons made with other organisations?

The answer to all of these questions tends to be no, in large organisations, and almost invariably no, in small organisations. Yet the external marketing departments in both large and small organisations would not move without the data. The reason is simple, external marketing is all about being close to CUSTOMERS. It is because the organisation does not see its internal people as customers that there is no perceived need for research. The exception has tended to be when large amounts of money were going to be spent on specific campaigns. It was then felt worthwhile to check on the size and extent of the problem, so that it could be tackled in the best way. These included Customer Service, Quality, and programmes of Change (of whatever nature), e.g. JIT, IT. The time has come when internal market research should be a continuous activity within the organisation. Only reliable data will prove the effectiveness of the total approach to human resource development.

Piecing the facts together

Attitude surveys are not enough. A structured approach to four key areas of data is required. The four A's are Attitude, Awareness, Ability, Actual.

Attitude is the first area to tackle to get people in the organisation feeling positive. There are a dozen attitudinal factors.

Awareness is beginning to become more important as education and society has changed. People demand information and involvement. Modern communication, democracy, new teaching approaches, all produce a need for an awareness of why things are done externally. The same is true internally.

Ability was the traditional domain of training departments to tackle. The education and communication of skills requirement is greatly enhanced by marketing them as products.

Actual data, such as psychometric tests, should be freely available to assist everyone in the communication process. External data, such as ACORN and Lifestyle will become increasingly used to assist the process and attract new people.

14 | *Elements of the internal marketing process*

Introduction

The data has now been collected, it has been analysed and the recommendations have been produced and agreed. What next? The process of getting the internal products and service to the internal market place now comes into play.

This internal marketing process must incorporate all of the elements of the 'internal marketing mix'. The order in which they develop will flow very much in the same way as external marketing. Many of the processes are also happening consecutively. These processes are looked at separately later in the book, but they must all be taken into account as part of a complete process.

For instance, at the creative stage, the conceptual input for design, title and copy ideas will have to be based on the needs of the organisation, as well as those of the individuals. It is the internal marketing mix which is crucial to the process of matching resources and relationships.

This process is not restricted to large-scale campaigns. As is indicated by the model, any element of matching the needs of the organisation and the individuals must flow through the internal marketing mix. This means that any communication, from a conversation to influence someone, to a memo, to a large-scale internal marketing campaign, should be able to be run through the internal marketing mix to gain maximum benefit.

Before this happens, some defining of the problem that needs to be communicated must be done. For example, if the issue that needs to be internally marketed is the result of an existing problem, what sort of problem is it? Is it quality, that is, quality assurance; is it a drop in production, e.g. lack of motivation, poor morale, etc.? If, however, it is an organisational issue, then the process will be different. Without going into detail the methods for highlighting problems are well covered in training programmes on 'Problem Solving'. They provide methods for defining problems, facilitating decisions, and planning to prevent future problems. Methods such as Ishikawa's fishbone are helpful (it helps by detailing in diagrammatic form the central issues and the sub-issues that feed off it whenever there is a problem).

Too often in marketing, many of these techniques are little known, and less used than in other areas of management. There is a tendency to look for solutions without having fully defined the problem, the concerns, or having established other likely solutions. A typical example of this might be, 'sales are down in the north'. The solution jumped on immediately is an increase in marketing activity, such as advertising. But the real problem may be, for example, that the northern retailers have heard a malicious rumour that makes them hold off ordering (this situation did occur in an organisation in which I worked). The *real* problem needs real problem solving techniques to arrive at a solution.

If, however, the problem does not have a definable solution, other than recognising that something new is required, this technique is totally different to analysis – it is called creativity, one of the main ingredients in the internal marketing mix.

Creativity

It is for their creativity that most advertising agencies are known and upon which they build their reputations. Increasingly, the other services which they once provided in-house are being farmed out to freelance people or to sub-contractors. This includes everything from artwork to print and media buying. The one service that tends to stay within the agency and be guarded jealously, is the creative function. This is simply because it is the one service upon which all the others hang. The mysteries and aura built up around the creative aspects of advertising are fuelled by the often temperamental and outlandish dress or behaviour of these 'artistic types'.

Whole campaigns and millions of pounds can be based on concepts which the average person might feel incapable of dreaming up. Yet these ideas, in essence, have to be totally understandable by the target market in order to create the desire to purchase or increase the propensity to purchase. They are perceived to be clever because of the underlying awe of creativity. Whoever would have thought of selling off British Gas through a campaign featuring a character called Sid and whom nobody ever saw? The very simplicity of it captured the imagination of millions of people. A star was born.

But why bother with Sid, or any new idea in the first place? Why can't all campaigns be the same? Why not a whole series of simple messages produced in black and white on A4 pieces of paper? Why the colours, the designs, the humour, the sex, the fantasy, the enticements, the songs, the music, the well-known actors, the appealing children, the animals, the cartoons, the new campaigns, the revamped products and services, etc.? It is because people get bored very quickly. They are soon 'switched off' by seeing the same thing again and again.

How then does this equate with Corporate Internal Marketing? The comparison with the continuous and monotonous A4 pieces of white paper should not have been lost on anyone. They are called memos in business.

The amazing thing about this method of reaching a target audience is that in comparison to the level of sophistication attained by external marketing, the memo is about as exciting as the 'Situations Vacant' in the local newspaper. They may be fine if you are desperate for a job and scour every inch, but if you have a job already then the chances of your reading them are very slim indeed! And today, most people who have jobs are very busy. The use of the memo, or similar pieces of communication, creates a second comparison with that of external advertising. Not only is the quality of the advertising message usually very good, but the targeting of the message also ensures that the message hits home. The same cannot be said of much of the internal communication that takes place in organisations today.

Additionally, the consumer is not hit with products and services that the manufacturer feels he might like to sell. They are targeted with products and services that research says they want to buy. This means that the organisation starts off at a major disadvantage, if all it does is attempt to push its needs to the individuals within it as was seen with the Top Ten products and services on p. 131, at least individuals' needs can now be assessed and met, alongside these of the organisation.

Finally, the creative process in external marketing usually lies with the naturally creative people. They have also been trained to apply their talents to the needs of the advertiser. How does the average individual suddenly become a creative person, as well as having all the other internal marketing skills? The answer is that, like every other skill, creativity can be taught.

The lessons to be learned on creativity are amazingly powerful, and there are many excellent books on the market, notably *The Innovation Handbook*, by Vincent Nolan. Others include *The Creative Manager*, already mentioned, and *The Colours of Your Mind*, by Jerry Rhodes and Sue Thane. In fact the increasing number of books and courses suggest that the importance of creativity is now being recognised. The main reason is to help ensure that more people in the organisation come up with the next best-selling product, but the spin-off in terms of the personal creativity need for internal marketing is just as valuable.

The fact that one of those previously conservative institutions, banks, namely National Westminster, actually trains many of its employees in creative thinking using Jerry Rhodes, further suggests that there is growing recognition of its importance.

Having pointed out that creativity can be learned, it is worth mentioning one of the main obstacles to it which will decrease more and more rapidly in The Employee Revolution. As individuals become more sought after, and therefore much stronger in their position *vis-à-vis* the organisation, the biggest inhibitor to creativity will begin to disappear. That is fear. It is the fear that has already been discussed; it prevents the mind from reaching outwards to new methods, coming up with odd suggestions and even contemplating bizarre ideas – the basis for creative thinking.

Add to the removal of this fear the ability to stir the creative juices, and soon stimulating internal marketing messages will come pouring out. As one of the delegates on a creative and innovation workshop once said, 'It is like being on another planet'. The comment itself symbolises the strength of the course.

The techniques of creativity include that well-known activity, brainstorming. There are a number of others, such as one that we call 'no no's', where the word 'no' is barred. An even more potent technique is not just to stop the no's but to get people to piggyback on other people's ideas. This can be done simply by introducing the words 'yes ... and ... '. For example, 'Yes, that is excellent and it could be even better by doing ... '. The opposite to this, which is the norm in most organisations, is 'no ... but ... '. For example, 'No you can't do that but you can try my idea'. The difference is worlds apart; the effect on individuals is a joy to watch.

So, creativity becomes important at every level. It is useful every time that pen is put to paper. The external marketeer has only words and ideas by which to sell the products and services: the internal manager in the role of the internal marketeer is in the same boat.

To give some idea of the creativity which can be applied to the internal market place the centre pages in this book show some of the materials used in internal marketing campaigns and the creative titles, designs and layouts, and so on. The imaginative use of many new ideas in putting across the products and services that an organisation has to offer are only now beginning to blossom. The 1990s will see a move that will put internal marketing on a par with the sophistication, excitement and creativity found in external marketing. To do that of course, some key individual decision makers are going to have to see the benefits of Corporate Internal Marketing; but the moves are strong enough now to suggest that it is only a question of time.

It is a pleasure to see the reaction of people to creative internal marketing: for example to training games, to exciting and different internal videos to motivation schemes, as well as to the large, often very creative and well designed, corporate programmes. These tend to be the ones that have the creative three-word titles, often with the word 'people' in them. This is not surprising, as the biggest need that individuals have is for help with the things that affect them, e.g. 'Where People Matter', the Royal Bank of Scotland; 'People Like Us', Bass; 'Putting People First', British Airways; 'The Right People', Esso; 'People Development Programme', Butlin's. Other successful examples but without the word 'people' in them are: 'Shades', in Top Shop; 'Who Cares Wins', in Unigate Dairies; 'A Leap in Sales', in Gardner Merchant. In summary, creativity will and must become a skill used by everybody.

Mock ups, scamps, visuals

Tom Peters talks of quick tests for new ideas. These must happen before large investments are committed and time is wasted in getting products and services to the external market place only to find that nobody wants those particular products and services. The advertising world has been practising this action well before Peters. With so much at stake in terms of the production costs of advertising, distribution costs, and the reputation of the products and services, quick tests of creative work are essential.

The methodology is very simple; rough designs are produced for research. These can be of the brand identity, a copy line, an advert, a poster, etc. These are the visuals or, in very basic form, scamps. In addition to the visuals, rough examples of the actual packaging, and sometimes the unproduced product, can be prepared. These are the mock-ups. Finally, the TV advert can be visualised in a sequence of cartoons, called a story board. These can then be filmed and a demo track, called an animatic (an animated u-matic), produced to see what the effect will look like. The processes described are not only for internal use; they are used for testing on customers.

The same creative work and ideas for Corporate Internal Marketing can be visualised and tested internally. There needs to be constant research of scamps, visuals and story boards for videos.

Mock-ups can also be produced, for example of the internal support material for a large training programme like workbooks, trainers, guides, and so on. The days of shelves of internal training and product information manuals all looking the same are over. If the organisation is to put across its products and services in a dynamic and targeted way then every form of internal marketing material must be looked at.

The person who walks through the door at nine o'clock may have spent the previous evening watching a multi-million dollar movie with incredible special effects. They may have awakened to break-fast TV with wonderful holiday adverts for the Bahamas. They may have read the colour tabloid on the way to work. They may have been given a free colour magazine as they came out of the tube station. Then they sit down to another badly written, boring letter. Next they try to read through an impenetrable manual. The contrast is startling.

This is not overstating the case. The average person in the UK is subjected to up to 2000 advertising images every day. It is not difficult to see why internal communication is seen as poor in most organisations! It is through a new creative approach to Corporate Internal Marketing that individuals will sit up and take note of the information they are expected to absorb. In addition, they will appreciate the care and investment that is being made in internally marketing the products and services. There are, however, a number of other steps to take before they become products and services.

Innovation

Some people believe that there is a surfeit of good ideas but not enough of them get to the market place. This is the process of innovation. It is interesting that the only thing stopping innovation happening is people. It is the jealousies, the fear, the 'not invented here', the misconceptions, etc. that stop ideas becoming reality.

Once again, as with creativity, problem solving, decision making, planning – and all other business disciplines – the process is trainable. The culture which allows it to happen also needs to be right. This may take longer to engender, but many organisations, both in the East and the West, have proved that continuous innovation, both for the internal as well as external market, can be sustained. It is the job of the marketeer to ensure that new products and services are steered through the internal and external maze of human and other obstacles. This is also true of the internal or external products and services. The innovation process is critical.

Edward De Bono, in his book *The Six Thinking Hats*, highlights the main problem with innovation. He points out that at any one time the individuals who are involved in the process will almost invariably all be thinking totally different things about the ideas before them. His recommendation is to orchestrate the process so that everyone exposes their core attitude, or mode of thinking to others. It ensures that attitudinal barriers are not raised through lack of understanding. Thus, he created six coloured thinking hats. The easiest one to explain is the black hat. If you are wearing this, you are telling others that you are going to oppose the idea, or a part of it. It is exactly the same as saying that you are going to play 'Devil's Advocate'. If everyone knows where you stand, they are less likely to get upset about what you say – which is exactly why people do warn you that they are going to play Devil's Advocate! This highlights one part of a process – exposed for all to see.

What is therefore critical to the innovation phase is that it is put through a process or structure. This helps steer it through the tortuous maze of people's reactions. It is not a fanciful notion on De Bono's part: innovation is crucial to the activity in both the internal and external marketplace. Personal experience of being involved in the development of a training product that produced a process for innovation, is that if it is ignored or circumvented the idea will almost invariably fail. No matter how brilliant the idea, how creative the concept in the internal market place, there are even more enormous hurdles to overcome than in getting products to the external market place.

Branding

The 'three-word titles' of the large Corporate Internal Marketing campaign have already been mentioned. If these are given a specific logo, or even an effective typeface, they can often form the basis of the brand identity of the products and services on offer. Just as Mars, Coca-Cola, Persil, etc. form the brand names of the external products, so too can internal products and services be branded. The branding process occurs when the device used to signify it is constantly used to reinforce the identity of the product. This can be on the covers of the training manuals, on the notepaper used to send out any information, on the posters to put on the staff room walls. And so the brand is built.

Once established, the range of products on offer under the brand identity can grow. This further reinforces the strength of the brand and lets the internal target market know that the organisation is serious about the products and services it is delivering.

Under the brand of the 'People Development Programme' at Butlin's Holiday Worlds, every aspect of the Top Ten products and services has been addressed and put into the programme. The beauty of a campaign of this nature is that there is every reason to tell the external market place about it. If customer service is part of the brand, then it is worth capitalising on this. The Royal Bank of Scotland use the internal brand as a strap line on all their external advertising, i.e. 'Where People Matter'. This, of course, further builds the internal perception about the importance of the campaign. It also creates a level of customer expectation which drives the people in the organisation to try to deliver.

The strength of an organisation, indeed its financial value, is now recognised to be in its brands. Takeovers and mergers happen to create opportunities for the brands to be further exploited. However, very little attention is paid by the acquiring organisations to the strength of the human resources. Even less attention is paid to the strength of feeling internal people have towards the internal brands, and the products and services they comprise. This is a massive oversight. If the people are only one-third of the equation where customers, the organisation and people are important then it is still a very large percentage. It is these internal people who are internal customers. Internal customers don't just buy products and services – they buy brands.

The next move after creating a brand for a programme of change, e.g. people development, customer service, etc., is to create brands for the ranges of internal products and services. These can then be linked by a corporate style. The individual products and services can reflect this style while having their own unique identity. This is entirely consistent with external marketing.

Referring back to the model, it can be seen that there is a very clear-cut segmentation of the overall products and services that are on offer, i.e. vision, structure, plans, practices. This segmentation provides its own brands.

Vision, Mission, Values   An example of this is Esso. Used in their external marketing campaign, the branding signifies the overall intent of the organisation. Very simply, this is done through the words 'Quality Service Value'. The title is then used extensively in the internal marketing campaigns, and helps to build an overall identity to the external campaign.

In the example of Renault Truck Industries, quoted earlier, an organisation faced with massive change or losing its British manufacturing base, the overall brand used is under the banner 'The Business Development Programme'. This has been added to a further strap line, 'Investing In Our Future'.

Structure   Sadly, few organisations pay much attention to branding their structure. Renault have had to highlight this area out of necessity. 'The Organisational Development Plan . . . Investing in Us', forms the basis for structural changes, and ties in with the overall title.

Plans   The same holds true for plans, as these are often very poorly marketed. This is covered in Renault by a key strategic plan that will ensure their survival as a manufacturer, 'The Customer Development Plan . . . Investing In Sales'.

Practices This is an area of little shortage of brands. Many switched on training businesses would clamour to add the names of their brands, and many excellent internal brands that have been developed could be added. I have already written about some of those brands and mentioned one called Shades. Shades is an overall brand for a colour-coded method of tackling a number of attitudinal based issues. These issues include customer service, innovation, telephone skills. Developed by Human Resource Development Ltd, Shades provides an umbrella for a number of products viz:

Shades The overall brand of a colour-coded attitudinal system. It is aimed at developing internal and external customer service skills. The brand has a registered trade-mark to protect it.

Tones The telephone skills product that allows people to deal with sales and other telephone calls.

Solutions Now Based on Shades, providing an alternative approach to De Bono and Rhodes. It is a colour-coded creative and innovation process.

Corporate Colours To overcome the major disadvantage of the one colour method of communication, i.e. white paper, this product colour codes internal memos. It creates a highly visual process for internal marketing.

All these products under the brand title of Shades, have been commercially produced for the external market place. The same process however, should take place with internally produced products.

Internal products will come from those who provide the products and services. They should all be put through the internal marketing mix. This will ensure that they come out as branded. The products could include many areas such as training, development, etc. (see the Top Ten). All of these products and services, if given to external marketeers, would have been put into the marketing mix long ago! The process of looking at internal products and services in the same way needs to happen automatically.

Every action to build the internal brands within an organisation must be seen as adding financial value to it. As soon as that can be proved, then the case for investment becomes financial, not intuitive, and the position of Corporate Internal Marketing takes on the same strength as external marketing.

Packaging

I use the term 'packaging' loosely here to describe the methodology for putting the organisation's products and services across. In Corporate Internal Marketing, the product is invariably in the form of words, i.e. mission statements, strategic plans, training information. These words need to be packaged in such a way so that the customer is tempted to buy the product.

The packaging may be as simple as a memo, or it may be a totally co-ordinated range of material from a video to a trainer's guide. See the checklist below showing a range of options open and the varying degree of sophistication in production methods.

Packaging checklist, including quick reference on production options

Paper based

Memos: typewriter/word processor/desk-top publisher
Letters: as memos/printed b&w/one to four colour
Headed paper circulars – as letters
Posters: silkscreen/litho/line (i.e. simple artwork); half-tone (i.e. including photography)/full colour/special colour (often for corporate logos)
Reports: as posters/gloss covers
Manuals: as reports/ring bound/dividers/laminated pages/stapled pull-out sections

Filo-faxes: as manuals
Magazines: as per the massive variety in external publishing
Newsletters: as letters
Newspapers: as per external publishing/one, two, four colour
Books: hardback/paperback
Charts: as letters
Certificates: as letters/special stock paper (e.g. parchment)
Brochures: stitched/loose
Mailshots: as per external marketing
Presenters: binders/flip packs

Visual material

Overheads: handwritten/as letters
Slides: photographic/artwork/typeset/computer generated
Flip charts: hand written/machine copied from original
Presentation panels: using blown-up artwork, photos, etc.
Lasers (often used at conferences)

Audio

Cassette: location/studio

Audio visual

Video: low band/high band/shot on film/converted to U-Matic,
   VHS/displayed on monitor, giant TV, video wall, screen/location/
   studio/vox pops, i.e. people in the street interviews
Film: as per video when converted to video
Slide tape: screen and audio cassette/also can be converted to video
Computer-based training: computer generated/also video based
   (see video)

The nature and extent of the packaging will be dependent on a
number of criteria. A few examples will illustrate 'the needs that
arise' and the packaging produced to meet them.
   A favourite piece of internal marketing, which went through all
the stages of the internal marketing mix in an exhaustive develop-

ment programme, is the Gardner Merchant merchandising package. The creative and innovative processes were at work during the whole development period because it was the first time anything like it had been introduced into the organisation. In short, it was a game, to be played by managers and staff in each of the contract catering establishments! It was considered not only an exciting and novel way of putting across a very important message to over 20,000 people, but the initial tests also showed that the learning and retention levels were higher than with most conventional training. In addition, although the number of messages to get across was considerable, the time taken to absorb them was much less than would have been taken in any normal method of training.

The packaging of the concept was crucial. If the internal target market felt in any way that they were being talked down to, or that the message was somehow being trivialised then the substantial investment could have been wasted. The people involved in the project would have a difficult time also, because their credibility would obviously be affected.

The game (see middle section colour photo) was given a brand name, intended to be strong, memorable and to indicate what it was supposed to achieve. It was called IMPACT. To add credibility to the brand, during a brainstorming with the client, the first letter 'I' was changed to a £ sign, thus it became £MPACT. To further explain the basis of the product, the strap line was added, 'The Science of Merchandising'. This added to the strength of the brand by pointing out, via the word 'science', that it was based on researched information. Indeed a very large investment over a six-month period in a number of trial sites produced enough computer data to prove that the concepts provided very impressive, sustained results.

The key to the findings was that there were six main areas that managers should look at in their merchandising, i.e. the way they lay out their products. Each of these areas had sub-sets of actions that needed to be taken. The central concept was provided by the customers, who themselves were split into three types. The way that the counters were physically spaced and positioned produced buying patterns that affected the amount that the customers could spend. Confused? So would anyone be. The permutations of 36 ways of laying out product, three types of customer buying pattern, and endless ways of laying out the restaurants would have been extremely difficult to put across. The size of the problem was compounded because Gardner Merchant has over 2000 sites, geographically spread, with as many different styles of operation, each operating to satisfy a different client company.

Given so many different permutations the creative use of a game with cards, board and dice allowed each of these factors to be separated, yet instantly linked in the mind of the player. The element of chance reflected the real world, and the element of luck produced one of the main human motivators – the competitive spirit.

The packaging of the solution was also user friendly. Everyone knows how to play games. The alternative was to have people sitting in long training sessions. The thorough testing of the game produced a product which worked well. This was vital. People will often look for any excuse to put down things which fundamentally challenge their *modus operandi* and their beliefs and behaviours. In addition, when talking about research, the advance warning of things which are going to be introduced provides its own PR. The 'buzz' went around the organisation that the new training was going to be a game that was fun! All of this was part of the process.

The packaging comprised the box, with a colourful design that was thoroughly researched (in fact everything was researched and tested). This came with a separate pad, used to draw alternative restaurant layouts. Inside the box were coloured pens, used to differentiate the most lucrative counters, and the flow patterns of customers. The cards produced the innumerable permutations of key areas of impact of merchandising on customers. A dice represented how much is spent on the items chosen. Finally a scoring pad kept a record for the players. Who says the often incredibly complex world of business need be boring?

Another example of packaging a complex product is the Esso, 'The Right People Programme' which was targeted at the independent dealers. The issues to be tackled split into three critical areas for the business. These were, and will continue to be, recruitment, induction and retention.

The solution was to provide a user friendly guide, which was heralded by a pre-release mail shot. The creative element once again was strong, using a series of cut-out people all joining hands with their arms held high, as if jumping for joy. This symbolised the power of having people that are motivated.

The guide was unlike anything that Esso had ever produced. It featured lots of graphics in full colour, line illustrations, photographs, and large type, all with bullet points rather than wordy paragraphs. Once again, the style was researched and adapted to the internal target markets.

The guide was designed to be readable either in short sharp bursts, or from cover to cover. Later research showed that the experienced manager dipped into it, and the newer manager tended to use it as a complete learning package.

Research from external marketing shows that the attention span of people is reducing all the time. This meant that the guide had to have a succession of bite-sized messages. Each of them had a hook that, for example, made things easier or simpler for the busy manager. The sections were kept short, and examples of any administrative procedures were always shown as handwritten forms as if another manager had filled them in. This obviated the feeling of the procedures being imposed from above.

As an added learning aid – and an advert for those who wanted to know what the guide was all about before committing themselves to reading it – a cassette was issued. This could be played in the car. It contained an interview featuring an unbiased third party experiencing the same problems of recruitment, induction and retention. This was Paul Chisnall, the Personnel Director of Trusthouse Forte Airports. He commented on the fact that the biggest difference in the customer's mind between organisations all competing for the same revenue, is the level and quality of customer service. This needs to be given by well-trained and motivated staff.

Rather than sending everything at once, another guide in the series, was issued some six months later. This allowed time to fully research the impact of the first and to incorporate the findings. Both guides then formed the basis of a workshop, allowing the managers to discuss the most successful methods they had adopted and to hone their skills in some of the new techniques. These workshops were also put into test and marketed to the managers.

Both of these examples serve to illustrate the creativity that can be applied to packaging internal products and services.

Corporate Internal Marketing and the small organisation

Often at seminars people ask, 'What about the smaller organisation which neither has the need for large-scale productions nor the budget?' While the budgets may not be as large, the need for a similar approach to Corporate Internal Marketing is vital. The person in the smaller organisation is no different. The external marketing influences are just as strong, and their needs and wants are much the same. It may also be that the person in the smaller organisation will have had large organisation experience. They may be used to a degree of sophistication which makes them difficult to satisfy. The small organisation cannot afford to ignore internal marketing.

The answer to what seems like a problem lies in the advent of desk-top publishing (DTP for short). By using simple practices like printed headed paper to give a greater degree of perceived accept-ance, and with the relatively low cost of laser printing and high-speed photocopying, the smaller organisation has no excuse for boring internal marketing. The investment will certainly be greater than before, that is when producing that simple and usually boring typewritten piece of A4, stuck in the same ring binder as all the other pieces of paper. But is it the investment which is the issue, or the return on that investment?

DTP is beginning to open new worlds to every internal marketeer. Everyone can have the capability at their fingertips to be able to put information across in a way that will not only be readable but also enjoyable. Coupled with improved skills in Corporate Internal

Marketing there will be no reason why every individual in an organisation should not be treated to a high degree of targeting.

The fact that all the other elements of packaging are not available, not just the sexy manuals, but also the videos, games, cassettes, etc. make it even more important to try to use the technology that is affordable.

If you are still in doubt about the relative effectiveness of some of the pieces of communication your organisation processes, you only have to look at all the work and time wasted on some of those training manuals that are now propping open the doors. How often are they read? How much is put into practice? How often do people ask for more? Additionally, how much do people complain about 'poor communications' even when you have been pumping out memos, manuals, etc. at a very rapid rate? You try to keep up with the pace of change going on, and the increasing demands of customers on quality, service and value, yet the level of communication is still not good.

The introduction of the internal marketing practices into small organisations does work. The difficulty with quoting small-scale examples is that no one has heard of them, and the co-ordinated approach happens slowly. If, however, it is going to take British Airways 12 years to get where it wants to go, then it is obvious that large organisations are faced with difficulties as well. It isn't just large budgets that make Corporate Internal Marketing work; it is the Attitude, Awareness and Ability of the individuals in the organisation!

Test marketing

The external marketeer will have a variety of methods for test marketing at his disposal. These will include one-to-one interviews, small groups in people's houses, large tests of people pulled into halls, through to actually launching the product on the market in a test area. This is normally a TV area or, more recently, on a global scale, testing a whole country prior to an international launch.

The same methods of testing different numbers of people are also available to the internal marketeer; the differences encountered when researching target markets are two-fold. The first comes from a major flattening of external cultural differences. These differences which exist between individuals externally are flattened through the superimposition of the corporate culture internally. The wide variety of styles and approaches that need to be adopted by external marketing is therefore reduced.

Secondly, the internal target markets are used to a relatively unsophisticated level of Corporate Internal Marketing. This allows greater leeway in what is acceptable to the internal market place, e.g. corporate videos do not have to match the quality of TV adverts. Nevertheless, it won't take much of an improvement in internal marketing for the 'Oliver Syndrome' to start happening. The cry will not, however, just be 'More!' It will also be 'Better!'

It is vital to test the creative inputs in the internal marketing mix. This often applies to the later stages as well, such as final artwork and on into the actual usage of the product.

As has already been mentioned, there is another benefit to internal testing of the various stages. The closed loop of communication that exists within an organisation soon allows the grapevine to work. The structured internal marketing methods create instant awareness of the fact that something good (or bad) is going to happen. By putting concepts into test, the badly conceived elements will quickly be spotted. Hopefully, this will prevent mistakes occurring.

The final benefit gained from test marketing is a sense of ownership from those being tested. The internal marketeer can also claim a high level of internal involvement, especially to those who are not tested.

So what is done to test the concepts, designs, packaging and ultimately, of course, the product itself – be they new training methods or the mission statement?

Basically, testing is either done on a one-to-one basis, or in group discussions. I am not going to discuss in detail the techniques that are used. Suffice to say that many of the skills are those used by most training specialists. Depending on the complexity of the information that is required, this can be handled internally, or by the outside organisation responsible for the research.

Launching new internal products

If handled correctly, the initial PR about something new to hit the organisation can be done via the testing. This can be supplemented with further PR via the communication channels that already exist, for example briefing groups. The warning to anyone considering this route is to watch out for the 'Chinese Whispers' that occur. There are often massive distortions and attitudinal additions that are used to provide personal and political benefit. In short, verbal communication, such as cascading through briefing groups is dangerous.

Other existing channels are the use of internal newsletters or newspapers. However, it is worth remembering that these traditional channels do have a reputation of often being just propaganda.

If the products and services to be launched warrant special attention, then it is usually best to plan each based on its own merits. The methods that can be used to get across new products are no different to external marketing.

Teasers

These are short, sharp messages, often incomprehensible, warning that something is about to happen. They are used extremely successfully in external marketing and can be used as effectively in the internal market place. The Esso teaser has already been mentioned. Another example is a poster declaring 'WATCH THIS SPACE!'. There are many reasons for using this technique, but it must not be overused. As with much of the rest of this newly emerging discipline, if seen too often, it will be perceived by some to be full of hype, and a waste of money.

Conferences

These are an excellent way of highlighting a subject's perceived importance within an organisation, because of the impact that conferences can generate. Their strength is that they can start to tackle Attitude. They are not very good, however, at creating deep understanding. Neither do they allow the involvement people need to develop new skills. In other words, they don't address Awareness, and Ability.

As increasing numbers of people recognise the need to do more than just touch the surface of the human resource development issues in the organisation, conferences may not necessarily diminish in number, but they may well diminish in importance.

Events

Not quite a conference, because the audience does not just sit in rows listening to speakers. The event can have lots of participants. There is usually more involvement from the audience, rather like a TV game show. They rely very heavily on good quality presenters or even actor(s) to provide a high level of excitement. They have their place in the internal marketing mix but, again, absorption is sacrificed for impact. If impact is required then fine, but if all the excitement is created from watching and not doing, then very little will be absorbed.

This type of training event, where a lot of ground is covered in a short space of time, is often described as a Chinese meal. At the time you enjoy it and feel quite full, but it doesn't take long to be hungry again and forget that you have just eaten. These are usually held for 50 to 100 people, over one or two days, using a 'sheep dip' approach. For smaller numbers – say up to 30 – using a workshop style approach with less hype and more involvement provides a high degree of absorption as well as impact.

Workshops

This method of imparting knowledge and of changing attitudes is beginning to take hold. Once, they were seen as a very expensive way of putting things across. The view now is that they are one of the most cost-effective and powerful tools at the disposal of the organisation.

The participative nature of workshops is the one sure way of creating the right environment for individuals to teach themselves. They have the time to think things through, and other people's views provide an excellent stimulus. With no more than 12 people, the amount of ground that can be covered in a structured environment can be enormous.

Workshops are not necessarily training *per se*. It may be that the products and services being launched are simply a new approach not requiring any new skill input. It may be that a transference of ownership of responsibility is necessary and the implications need to be thought through. The environment that needs to be created is one of open debate, healthy cynicism, honest feedback and a testing of the products and services to ensure they stand up to the needs of the people who will be using them.

Bottom-up commitment from leaders

The launch of new products and services must be seen to have one key ingredient – commitment. That is why the external marketeer will spend a substantial part of the first year's marketing budget on the launch. The PR, the launch event, the launch advertising will create impact and demonstrate the commitment in the new products and services to the external market place.

The same must be seen internally. Whether it is the launch of a new lunch rota in the stores department or a major initiative on quality, the internal market place will be looking to see the level of commitment that the organisation and the individual managers and leaders place on it. This is why bottom-up commitment is vital. If it is not seen from the beginning, it is easy for the individuals to self-justify that they do not have to take it on board.

Is this preaching to the converted? Are your leaders committed? In many organisations the word commitment is mistaken for enthusiasm. Leaders can be very enthusiastic that something is done, and continue to be enthusiastic. However, it is the amount of time they devote, and not just the amount of mental energy, that is the key to demonstrating commitment. No launch, whatever size, will be successful without the commitment of the appropriate leader.

Top-down commitment from customers

If customers are the most important focus of the organisation, then any new products and services launched must have an effect on them.

There is every reason for showing some top-down commitment, either physically, or in the content of the launch. For example, if dealers or agents will benefit from a new level of customer service then invite them to share in the process. It is only by being closer to customers that the organisation gets it 'right first time' in delivering its products and services.

To take another example, in the external market place the motor show is aimed at both dealers and customers. Opinion gathered at these events is vital in planning the on-going marketing. The same could happen internally, and indeed is starting to happen. At the moment, it may be with closer ties such as dealers and also with suppliers; but in the future what is to stop panels of external customers from being part of the research and launch of major Corporate Internal Marketing campaigns? The customer supplier chain should not be a concept: it should be a reality!

Within my own organisation, we have initiated meetings of key customers, potential customers, and suppliers, to discuss the issues that we face in meeting their needs. This provides a forum for everyone to improve by learning from each other. Like everything else, especially when you are busy, it is not easy to devote the time. But who said business is easy?

The distribution process – people

The biggest difference between Corporate Internal Marketing and external marketing has already been hinted at. It was demonstrated how even something as simple as a piece of test research can have implications such as informing the organisation of what is happening. Whilst things have to be kept under wraps within external marketing, the closed loop and much smaller numbers involved in the internal market place make internal marketing very involved with the people aspects of the organisation.

In external marketing the attention is focused on the needs and demands of customers. There is, however, very little need to take into account the multitude of day-to-day factors that affect the actual life of the customer.

In the internal market place, the factors which affect the day-to-day life of the individual are the very ones that are being marketed. Add to this the complex inter-personal relationships, inter-departmental relationships and inter-organisational relationships that exist. Other factors such as union involvement will also impact on the Attitude, Awareness and Ability of the individual

It does not stop there. It is only by using the people in the organisation to assist in the distribution of the products and services that the internal marketeer will succeed. A good advertising campaign will have a media mix that ensures the message is delivered a certain number of times. The consistency of delivery is never in question as the mechanical or technological process will not alter it. The internal distribution process must use people as an integral component. It boils down to a comment that I hear time and time again: 'If only we had more good managers'.

It is only when the people in the organisation are all capable of practising internal marketing that any sort of guarantee can be made about the quality of delivery of internal products and services.

The logic of this has been stated at every twist and turn in this book. It is demonstrated in the logic that everyone is a customer. The resulting need must therefore be for sales and marketing skills. It is demonstrated by the recurring themes of understanding people and being able to meet their needs. These themes run throughout virtually all training programmes on management and leadership. It may be that it is a rose by any other name – but is it any less valid?

The net result is that the distribution channels for Corporate Internal Marketing will make or break any of the internal products and services. This of course is no different from external marketing; it is just a different ball game. People are not very often the distribution channel, unless of course they are trained sales people.

Conferences/Events/Workshops

These were discussed under the launch of new products and services, but may be just as valid for regular updates, for motivation exercises and for improvements to existing products and services, which do not have to be new to be under discussion. The ability of the presenters and facilitators will determine the impact on the individuals involved. The rest of the organisation will then be affected.

Training

Very often there will be a large training element attached to the distribution of internal products and services. In addition to this, individuals in organisations today are putting training (and development) very high on their list of needs. Organisations are also recognising that they must put their training needs high on their list of priorities if they are to survive. Matching the two needs may not be difficult to start, given a low base. Tight training budgets result in individuals looking elsewhere if their training needs are not met.

In distribution terms, it is becoming increasingly clear to all levels of management that training individuals in all aspects of the three 'A's is not the responsibility of the training department. It is a management responsibility. This means that they are now responsible for the delivery of the internal products and services that are necessary for the survival of the organisation. This, for some, is a major attitudinal shift in itself. Once again it is people who will be delivering the marketing: in this case, the managers.

Team briefing

My views on one-way cascades are probably clear by now, but it is worth repeating that they do have their place. They can be made interactive and can improve the absorption of information on the products and services being delivered.

Individual meetings

Individual meetings require a whole host of skills. These form the basis of many training programmes, which are all ultimately aimed at getting individuals to practise the tasks necessary for the organisation to succeed. People will fail to buy into the organisational products and services without continuous input. The management and leadership skills needed include delegation, motivation, coaching, counselling, presentation, to name but a few. If the quality of the product, for example leadership, is not delivered to individuals, the Corporate Internal Marketing of other products and services will be adversely affected.

All these people aspects have to be taken into account in the internal marketing mix. It is no use delivering a sexy package of training and development if the distribution channel cannot handle it. It is equally valid if the internal target market cannot handle it.

Does this sound reasonable? Of course it does. People cannot operate without the input and output of people skills. These skills have been classified by using many different titles. These include such tried and tested techniques as Situational Leadership and its populist derivative One Minute Management, and the alternative process driven approach of Performance Management.

However, none of these skills or practices admits that internal people are customers! But if this is now accepted, then matching their needs with products and services requires another skill used in a one-to-one or small group situation – selling!

Corporate internal selling

The interesting phenomenon that exists in the UK is that because of our reserved attitude, we cannot cope with accepting the fact that we have to sell to be successful. The image of the double glazing salesman with his foot in the door makes us shudder. We feel uncomfortable with the notion that people have to be persuaded to accept something by influencing them. Selling might be all right for the people on the road, but it's not something that internal people would feel necessary or even desirable.

What people do seem to be able to cope with, but in essence is the same thing disguised under a softer title, is the fact that they have to 'sell themselves', or even softer still, they have to 'sell their ideas'. It is fascinating to see the different interpretations of these three titles – selling; selling yourself; selling your ideas. The net result is exactly the same, but if the internal individual finds it more acceptable, and buys into the concept, albeit as a result of ignorance and prejudice, then there is every reason why the apparently 'softer' titles should be used – it's called psychology, and that is what forms the basis of marketing and selling!

Another interesting thing about coming out front with the acceptance of internal selling, under any of its three titles, is that the corporate language about the internal customer is immeasurably strengthened. Once again, both Crosby and Peters stopped short. Just as Corporate Internal Marketing is the process for matching needs of organisations to groups of targeted individuals, so corporate internal selling is the distribution channel that puts the message across on a one-to-one basis.

Organisations put considerable resource into their external sales activity – they know that they have to. They know that customers need persuading; they know that customers need to be handled with professional expertise; they know that the skills of the good salesperson will produce a whole host of benefits including loyalty, confidence, trust, information and of course revenue. The salesperson in turn is targeted, feels motivated to achieve, knows the power of speech, body language, persistence, and so on.

If the model of Corporate Internal Marketing is correct, then it follows that every action by every individual in verbally putting across the products and services of the organisation, in one-to-one or small groups, must be selling. So why is it that they have been disguised under totally different names like inter-personal skills?

In many situations it may appear that selling skills are not required, e.g. when interviewing, appraising, coaching. But these are the very situations where selling is crucial. There is always something to be sold. The specific skills involved in delicate people situations would almost invariably be enhanced by the skills of selling.

This book is not the platform for discussing Corporate Internal Selling in depth. Suffice it to say that if you regard the innumerable sales books and sales training programmes as evidence of the breadth and depth of the subject in external terms, then there is a long, long way to go internally.

Much could be done to co-ordinate the many leadership, management and people skills using the more assertive banner of Corporate Internal Selling. The experience of many organisations, especially in the financial and retail sectors in training and developing their front line individuals to sell to the customer, demonstrates the benefits to be had if everyone in the organisation is skilled in Corporate Internal Selling. In short, once internal marketing is recognised, we are almost forced to buy into internal selling, and to reaping the tremendous rewards that will follow.

If you are not convinced, below is a list of the powerful techniques that enhance the skill of using words as the vehicle for getting things done. This means every manager, leader, supervisor and many, if not most, other individuals in the organisation can benefit. They are classified under the ABC of selling, the Approach, the Buy, the Close. You don't have to understand or appreciate the benefits of using the techniques and skills in the list. They serve to illustrate to those who have not got a sales background the extent and depth of knowledge that exists in this field in understanding and using psychology to succeed in the external market place. The same can be done internally.

A word of warning however: the methods of delivery of these techniques and skills cannot simply be transferred from external sales to internal sales. To put not too fine a point on it, if internal people had to face some of the styles and methods adopted to motivate external salespeople they would be put off selling for life! Targeting of the internal selling message is likely to be a delicate affair.

The ABC of corporate internal selling: Some of the techniques and skills

A   The Approach

ATTITUDE TO SELLING – positive approach, goal setting, accepting rejection.

INDIVIDUAL CUSTOMER RESEARCH – assessing background, needs, personality, style of approach.

PLANNING THE INTERFACE – use of selling time, setting meeting objectives, arranging daily priorities, the 80/20 rule of effectiveness, pre-arrival activities.

UTILISING PERSONAL STRENGTH AND PAST EXPERIENCE – establishing track record, projecting image, using personality, social strengths, contacts.

REHEARSING – acting the part through preparation.

INTRODUCTION – remembering names, establishing rapport, creating confidence, backing off, adapting to different customer styles.

USING THE POLITICS AND POSITIONS POSITIVELY – establishing relationships, levels of authority, approaching decision makers and influencers.

CREATING BUSINESS AND PERSONAL RELATIONSHIPS – establishing personal details, status, allies, enemies.

CREATIVE STARTS – using visuals, stories, questions, revealing information, testing knowledge.

B The Buy

MEETING THE CUSTOMER ON EQUAL TERMS – meeting negatives, meeting aggression, etc.

IDENTIFYING THE IRRATIONAL NEEDS OF CUSTOMERS – using kudos, reassurance, past experience.

BODY MANAGEMENT – sex, staying in charge by being relaxed, eye contact, gestures, expressions.

VOICE MANAGEMENT – volume, pitch, variety, emphasis.

POSITIVE SIGNALS – expecting the order, assumptive statements, writing notes.

QUESTION TECHNIQUES – general, specific, controlling, bonding, open up, close down, thinking time, getting 'yes', testing feelings, steering.

REFLEXIVE LISTENING – playing back, building common understanding, confirming, enhancing the need, inserting alternatives.

UTILISING THE CUSTOMER'S SENSES – visual, touch, sound, ownership through involvement.

THE HOOKS – the nice thing for them, the benefits.

THE FACTS – what the products and services comprise, the features.

C The Close

HANDLING OBJECTIONS – the positive approach, agreeing, acting.

TRANSFERRING REJECTION – moving the barriers, alternative solutions.

ASKING FOR THE ORDER – overtly and covertly.

NEGOTIATING – A SUBJECT IN ITS OWN RIGHT!

AGREEING THE 'INVESTMENT' – the acceptable language of selling yourself.

Internal marketing and sales support material

Given the low base among managers of awareness of the need to market or sell the products and services of the organisation, support material is vital. This is especially true as their attitude and ability in this activity are at a very low base. This material is also needed to support the internal marketing and the internal selling. The size and scale of many organisations mean that even with a good level of attitude, awareness and ability, there will always be constraints that necessitate strong support. These include the levels of people's ability to deliver, and the time constraints which prevent the same degreee of preparaton that can be given by specialists.

These are exactly the same arguments that are used for the production of external sales and marketing support material. The salesperson needs a presentation kit, just as the shopkeeper needs point-of-purchase material to build the display. This doesn't mean that the salesperson or shopkeeper will use the material; indeed millions of pounds are wasted. What is hoped for is that it will persuade them to stock, sell and display the main product on offer. If they do use the material that is often a bonus!

The internal marketeer must do the same. The sales process must be enhanced. The internal salesperson will have more credibility and more confidence in delivering the message if they have support material to help them. The internal customer will be impressed by professionally produced material, and will be more confident in the person's commitment to selling the products and services.

Having run many workshops to introduce various changes in organisations, I can testify to the relief of the attendees when they realise that they don't have to deliver the often complex messages without the backing of internal marketing support material. What does this include?

Support material – trainer/facilitator guides

Traditionally, trainer guides are wordy tomes. They are often highly unusable and scribbled and scrawled all over by the trainer or presenter. In short, as a product in their own right, they do not meet the customer requirements.

They require considerable effort and time to produce. The core product may in itself be excellent, but the lack of budget and internal marketing input often means they lie on shelves, only to be reinvented by someone else who is unaware of their existence. The wasted investment in training and development in this area is frightening. It is no wonder that the move within training departments is away from being producers to being buyers of material. The next move, to further prevent reinventing the wheel and being able to get instant access to products and services already developed, is towards contract training. This will perform the same function as all other contract services and allow the organisation to concentrate on its core business. The same will, of course, follow with internal marketing and all the support services it needs.

More support material – videos/cassettes/workbooks/posters/leaflets/mailshots/teasers/letters/magazines/books, etc

There are lots of ways of supporting the internal marketing and selling process. These are so familiar in external marketing, albeit using different terms, that their use in internal marketing can be equally valid. The way they are put together and used in the internal market place may be different, but essentially the same psychological base exists. So, TV adverts are effectively the same as corporate videos – both are trying to sell something using a highly visual and auditory medium. TV documentaries are, in essence, the same as video training programmes. Overheads and slides are like posters. Newspaper articles are the same as memos: they may have calls to action, provide information, generate enthusiasm, tell bad news. Radio provides comparisons with both fixed messages like cassettes, and the live interactions happening all the time with individuals. Just like newspapers, they provide comment, news, information, entertainment, etc.

The use of magazines and books is an interesting and new development in Corporate Internal Marketing. In exactly the same way as these are used externally, they can be used internally. Magazines, for example, produced for individuals, with stories, offers, hints, problem pages, etc. giving the opportunity to get across corporate messages without ever once mentioning anyone in 'management', far less the chairman, could be one of the strongest media used for cultural change.

Using these to get across key training messages like product knowledge, negates the need for producing the unreadable and unread reference documents, so prolific in organisations today. The Royal Mail, Trusthouse Forte, and Woolworth have all invested in this internal medium; and they are sure to be the first of many.

The same argument for the use of magazines to supplement the distribution media in the internal marketing mix is also true of books. If *The One Minute Manager* was one of the most popular of all management books, why was this? Because it was short, simple, and based on a soap opera style of story. The same could and should be done for organisations with similar messages to portray. In many ways the training video already does this, so why not a different medium which will appeal to a different target customer? Books, based on stories, or even text-book style, also allow much greater flexibility in reading and speed of absorption. They can be easily produced in one colour, and in many cases drastically enhance many of the messages that an organisation wants to portray, but usually ends up doing so in more indigestible reports and manuals.

In summary then, without the marketing and sales support the internal marketing and sales process is doomed to fail!

Internal promotions

No matter how successful a product is, its sales must be supported at some time with some form of promotion. In external marketing this type of activity, along with PR, is termed 'below the line' advertising. The sales promotion industry has changed from being the poor relation to one of the key elements in any marketing budget. The type of support given through promotion can be seen on virtually every product in the land, and increasingly it is moving into the services that are provided, from dentists to solicitors. There is nothing wrong with this type of support; the only problem is that it suffered, and still does, from the plastic daffodil image of the 1960s, where the 'free offer' bore little relationship to the product being promoted.

Today's external customer is still looking for something 'extra', but the tendency now is to provide added value rather than price cutting. The same is true of the needs of the internal market place. The customer can be tempted to make additional purchases, or to buy a trial purchase through promotional offers. In the same way as externally, the quality of these promotions must be good, and relate to the product they are supporting.

But beware, people may be taken in once, sometimes twice, but never a third time. So what is it that the internal customer will be attracted to in promotional terms?

The answer can be summed up in one word – recognition. Anything which enhances the products and services of the organisation by providing recognition will create an instant hook to increase the propensity to buy, such as the following:

Certificates Whether these are internal or external certificates, as long as they have to be earned and are perceived to improve the status of the individual, then they are an excellent method for promoting.

It must be noted that the reason why they motivate people is not just pride, but an increased potential for reward and for better prospects either inside or outside the organisation. There is no sense in denying the individual the visible signs of success that increase their personal marketability. The organisation can only hope to retain their services through everything else it does.

It is for this reason that accreditation is now high on the list of priorities of individuals.

Accreditation The added value that comes from learning new skills and receiving external recognition provides an excellent promotional platform for organisations. The current UK scheme that is attracting much attention from employers and employees alike is NCVQ: the National Council for Vocational Qualifications. Under this scheme an employer can have a training programme certified as being pertinent to others in the same sector, or sectors with the same needs. The certificate shows a level of competence which is marketable when looking for a new job, or used as a bargaining tool for a pay rise.

The same is happening at lower levels in the organisation, i.e. managers and leaders! The MBA is a promotional offer of many organisations targeted at managers, allowing the managers free time and financial assistance, e.g. course fees, and even sending them abroad to study.

Badges The armed forces have proved the strength of this pro-motional incentive – a free badge or stripe with every promotion. They are worn with pride when they are well deserved. The same can be equally true internally. There are many organisations which provide badges for all sorts of achievements. In Trusthouse Forte, for example, there are training badges, service badges and badges for winning internal competitions such as sales. In the words of Tony Monnickendam, in his days as Director in Charge of the Motorways Division, 'Badges are excellent as long as the wearer doesn't end up looking like Idi Amin!'

Incentives/Prizes This is a dangerous area in terms of the spend and effectiveness of promotional offers. As long as the individual receives constant and effective verbal praise and 'small' signs of recognition, the often vast sums spent on providing incentives can be put to much better use. This is at least until the time when the actual products and services are sufficient in themselves to motivate.

One organisation is spending millions on the type of incentive that is akin to the ones used for external sales forces. The size of the rewards, and the fact that not all the target market can actually win them can result in two things happening. The award itself is insufficient to suggest it's worth it, and the failure to win the award is probably more demotivating to the losers than the positive effect on the winners.

In the words of the person responsible for this, 'we have created a beast which we keep having to feed, that we don't want in the first place'.

In addition to providing good products to motivate there is another way of providing the recognition people need. This comes from the instant praise and recognition type management technique that has its roots in performance management and *One Minute Management*. This powerful tool, used in many organisations, suggests that not only can a great deal of promotional money be saved, but also the response of individuals can be so much greater.

We have observed in many organisations that the most successful levels of individual and team motivation do not come from the long-term expectation of promotional incentives and rewards, they come from the immediate praise of the manager and instant recognition. This may include small promotional incentives such as badges, pens, gifts vouchers, etc.; but the key is not in the amount, it is in the immediacy of the praise.

This is a purely personal view, but I believe that an alteration of management style, together with some small token of recognition would either produce the desired result if no promotional incentive is being offered, or save considerable sums where it is being offered.

Budgets Tom Peters strikes again! If it is now recognised that to succeed in the external market place investment in new products and services is vital, then why should the internal market place be any different? The products and services that the organisation offers today will not only appear to be 'old hat' relatively quickly, but will also be highly likely to be out of date in terms of what they are supposed to deliver. Given the ever-increasing speed of change of external products and services, the internal market place must move just as rapidly. Together with the many other forces of change, such as mergers, acquisitions, privatisation, etc., the chance of stability in the internal market place is slim. Whether it is mission statement or training programmes, the forces of change will affect them. To create new products and service the internal marketeer will have to put the whole process of innovation into the internal marketing mix. This will include constant research, testing, repackaging, relaunching, redistributing, and repromoting. These have all been discussed already. They need to be happening constantly with existing as well as with new products and services.

The big difference between internal marketing and the world of external marketing is that quality and quantity of the input and output are vastly different. This shouldn't be the case. Indeed, the demands of the internal marketplace will soon be such that the quality of internal marketing will have to strive to be as good as it is externally.

The 'Catch 22' of Corporate Internal Marketing is that, no matter how good you are, the external marketeer has been at your target market before you. They will invariably have bigger budgets, which means that the internal perceptions are likely to be coloured by the level of sophistication they are used to externally. No matter how hard you try, they will very quickly expect more. The 'Oliver Syndrome' will affect every organisation as it strives for excellence and quality in Corporate Internal Marketing. Indeed, the better you get, the more they will expect. Why not? If something is good you can hardly expect people not to want more!

That is the bad news. It will form part of the frustration to be felt by the internal marketeer. The poor budgets in this area and the constant reduction of them when times get tough, will continue to be the norm until Corporate Internal Marketing's worth is recognised.

The good news is that the rewards in trying to catch up with the external marketing will produce the host of benefits discussed throughout this book. These benefits will be felt by the individuals, the organisations, and society as a whole as production, profit, efficiency, motivation, etc. increase.

There can be no doubt that The Employee Revolution is taking place in a big way. It is happening not only in the UK but throughout the world. The only doubt now is how soon and in what way will organisations match the needs of the individuals to the products and services of the organisation, in order to meet the needs of its customers.

Corporate Internal Marketing is already a major topic of debate in the United States and in continental Europe. In external marketing our advertising industry leads the world. Can we produce the levels of attitude, awareness and ability in the UK to build a service industry which meets the needs of today's and tomorrow's organisation in the global market place for Corporate Internal Marketing?

The jigsaw is complete

CREATIVITY

A process that can be learned by everybody – once the fears and inhibitions are removed. The skill will be vital to stimulate people with new messages and new internal products and services.

INNOVATION

Another vital process that turns good ideas into products and services.

PACKAGING

From memos to videos the quality of the medium tells the user the commitment behind the message.

TEST MARKETING

Test the issues before communicating. The benefit is that this can be used to create good PR prior to launch.

LAUNCHES

The decision needs to be made between impact and absorption. More and more organisations are recognising that absorption is the real requirement. This means targeting smaller groups in workshops.

DISTRIBUTION

The manager is the key. The channels use are therefore not the static ones of internal marketing.

CORPORATE INTERNAL SELLING

One of the key skills of externally pushing products and services should be transferred internally, i.e. selling.

INTERNAL MARKETING AND SALES SUPPORT MATERIAL

The sales people need support; the marketing messages need support. They cannot do it alone.

PROMOTION/INCENTIVES

Promotions, like Certificates, add value. Incentives are only needed when the product or service needs support.

BUDGETS

Without these nothing will happen. This area is only only new, it is generally unbudgeted unless it comes under training. The budgets will often in future be the first to be cut!

15 | *SWOT analysis*

No self-respecting marketeer would miss the opportunity to use one of the well-established 'one minute marketing methods', the SWOT analysis. Well, maybe they would, but it is included anyway as it provides an excellent summary. It can be used by those trying to influence the board or others of the 'Strengths, Weaknesses, Opportunities, Threats' of Corporate Internal Marketing.

Strengths of Corporate Internal Marketing . . .

- There is an almost universal acceptance of the principles and practices of marketing.
- The language created by external marketing provides the same base for the language of Corporate Internal Marketing
- 'These concepts (i.e. Product, Price, Promotion, Distribution) are familiar to executives; and what is perhaps more important, they make it legitimate to tackle such issues as barriers and culture mismatch in a systematic structured way.' Extracted from *The Sunday Times*, 10 September 1989, 'Good Plans Need Internal Marketing', by Professor Nigel Piercy.
- The threat of having to learn something new, in order to survive the rigours of management and leadership, is considerably reduced.
- Every individual will be able to see the large benefits that Corporate Internal Marketing will bring. These will be manifested in terms of new and improved products and services from

the organisation. They will enhance its image, speed its introduction and encourage personal commitment to the process.

- The model allows any organisation to start at any point of entry.
- Badly targeted and poorly produced and supported products and services should become a thing of the past.
- The acceptance of individuals as people who do not automatically respond to directives just because they are paid to work means that much greater thought, time, effort and money will be put into all areas of 'communication'.
- With strong data bases the risk of getting it wrong is reduced.
- Just as external marketing produces the process to create and sustain high levels of motivation and commitment to products and services, the same is true of the Corporate Internal Marketing process.
- The strongest assets of organisations today are their brands. The same can be true of internal brands.
- The attraction, retention and input of individuals will be enhanced through the desire to keep buying into the internal brands rather than risk changing brands and going to other organisations.
- The marketing of better targeted products and services will be enhanced by the promotion of them, which at the same time will reduce the need for unnecessary incentive schemes.
- The price of not adopting internal marketing can be expressed as the cost of mismatching the resources and the relationships and the consequent failure to deliver the products and services to the external customer. This is ultimately the biggest single strength of Corporate Internal Marketing.

... and the weaknesses

- The main difficulty with introducing and practising Corporate Internal Marketing lies with middle management. They are under threat from the flat, and flattening structures. They are the main constriction in an 'egg timer' effect on the channels of communication. They see the role of 'managing' as a role of 'controlling', the easiest thing to control being information and communication. Any move to open up these channels will be seen as a bypass.

- There is a strong management perception that high investment in people is not cost effective and is risky. This will prevent the true introduction of Corporate Internal Marketing.

- Traditionally the first budgets to be cut in times of trouble are Training and then Marketing. Training products, as the fundamental basis of Corporate Internal Marketing, make it an easy target for the accountants, and hard-pressed managers. They will slash the budgets when times get tough.

- The investment needed to be effective looks large – especially in countries like the UK where the internal investment in people (ie mainly in training) has been low.

- The business discipline of Corporate Internal Marketing is new, with few practitioners.

- Although based on the principles of marketing, the vast difference with Corporate Internal Marketing is that the distribution channels for the products, services and the information are fundamentally through people. In other words, not through newspaper columns or TV adverts. The belief that 'The PR or advertising agency will handle it' is likely to lead to some very expensive mistakes. The results of agency led campaigns can be massive impact but very little absorption.

- The role of many training people, some of whom have become trainers often for the wrong reasons (in this business equivalent of a backwater), will not have given them the depth of knowledge, experience, confidence or standing to deal with this issue.

- The very nature of Corporate Internal Marketing makes it very high profile, and therefore very risky.

- The strategic importance of the issue will mean a much greater understanding and time commitment from already busy people – even though they might see the longer term rewards.

- Payback, like marketing, is often easy to see instinctively but difficult to prove financially.

- The effectiveness of the investment in external marketing is often in question: 'I know 50% is effective – but which 50%'? The same will be true of investment in Corporate Internal Marketing.

- Marketing, as a discipline, involves the future, and therefore 'change'. Inherently, people distrust both.

Opportunities

- With many organisations now having learned the lessons spelt out in Tom Peters' books on 'Excellence', they are concentrating on the perceived key issue of customer service. The acceptance of internal customers might exist because of Crosby and others on quality. However, without the knowledge of how to integrate and implement both of these, as well as absorbing other major changes such as JIT, information technology, innovation, etc., the going will be tough.
- The opportunity is there to gain a major competitive advantage through practising Corporate Internal Marketing.

Threats – to the organisation that doesn't practise Corporate Internal Marketing . . .

Without the fundamentals of Corporate Internal Marketing the following problems create the threats to the organisation:

- The 1,000 × 1% improvements in quality can only come from committed people.
- Customers will be attracted to go to the competition if they recognise and offer a better quality internal product/service.
- The opportunity cost of sacrificing good practices, plans and strategies is enormous.
- The psychological cost of not reaching the target audience with the right internal products and services is also enormous.
- The bottom line cost of not having a motivated workforce is well known.
- The failure to communicate provides the incentive to leave.

- The failure to 'buy into' the products and services means they 'quit but stay'.
- The loss of the expertise of the people to innovate, improve, suggest is considerable.
- There is a distancing of the decision makers from the final customer.
- The failure to motivate and communicate means the major leaps forward in innovation from the people will be stifled.

. . . and to Corporate Internal Marketing

- The biggest threat to Corporate Internal Marketing itself will come from the internal power struggle. The likely dissection of a holistic approach will put back its introduction and diffuse its power.

16 | *Coda*

The most fascinating aspect of Corporate Internal Marketing is only just beginning to emerge. It relates to its future position in the organisation. It has its roots in the power struggles and past responsibilities of individuals and departments.

If, for example, in the past, the external marketing department was looking for new products and services to deliver to customers, it did not really consider whether the internal organisation was capable of delivery, except in the broadest terms of production timetables. If there was non-delivery, poor quality, low levels of customer service, or a salesforce not motivated to sell the product, then these were separate issues, to be handled by other departments as a result of the concerns expressed by marketing.

Today, the intense level of competition and the unprecedented levels of quality being demanded means that these internal issues must be addressed by the external marketing department before the event, not after.

Very few marketing directors would have thought, in the past, to ask the personnel director for his input on the strategic and tactical impact that external marketing plans would have on the organisation and the people. Personnel did its thing and marketing did likewise.

Now that the strategic and tactical implications of organisational change, including external marketing plans, can be seen in a holistic way, the interface between internal and external marketing will and must grow, and be formalised.

This is the crux of this book. It is not only about the sexy introduction of creative internal campaigns. It is not only about better internal communications. It is not only about the financial benefits that accrue from motivated workforces.

It is about all of these and more. It is about a discipline that does not necessarily create the internal products and services, but it does ensure that they are the right ones, delivered at the right time to the right target market. This discipline must match the needs of the organisation and the internal market. Crucially, as the needs of the organisation include the external strategies and tactics of external marketing, the two disciplines must work together.

In the same way many of the products and services will ultimately be produced by other means and other functions, such as the board, human resource function, finance, administration, etc. The relationship of the Corporate Internal Marketing function to these departments, must be the same as the one of external marketing to those departments. In external terms, for example, production can only produce what the customer wants to buy. It is the responsibility of the marketing function to determine this. The same is true internally.

The difference in Corporate Internal Marketing is in *matching* – not meeting – the internal customers' needs for products and services with the needs of the organisation.

Your views as a decision maker and influencer will shape the future destiny of this emerging discipline. Your actions and attitudes will help create the right environment which recognises that The Employee Revolution has taken place. The processes of establishing the internal customer is crucial to creating the new internal 'citizen' just as the French Revolution was. You will be able to ensure that the way to succeed in the external market place will be to create and nurture the internal market place.

To do that you and everyone else in your organisation must take on the mantle of facilitator between the needs of the organisation and the individuals. If the organisation size demands it, then the structure also needs to incorporate a department responsible for Corporate Internal Marketing. As has happened in the Midland

Bank and the Royal Mail, its function would be to match the strategic and tactical needs of the organisation to those of the people, be the influences internal or external.

In summary, the only way to establish and maintain the products and services that match the needs of the individual to those of the organisation is by Corporate Internal Marketing.

Are you ready to introduce and join The Employee Revolution, or will it happen to you like it did to the French 200 years ago?

Appendix I: Extract from the Renault Trucks Business Development Programme

D. Merz

Managing Director

15th January 1990

Dear

The last few years have been tough for all of us here at Renault Truck Industries in the UK.

The redundancy announcement, and and other changes as well as the lack of long-term planning have caused us as a company, to feel rather insecure and unsettled. This is understandable.

However, what I'd like to do in this letter is share with you my optimism for our future.

I'm going to call this the "Decade of Confidence" and I hope that by the end of this letter, you'll understand why.

Your Senior Management Team have now been briefed on my vision for this company's future, and now it is the time for everyone in the organisation to share in it too.

"I want to develop an organisation, with the focus on customers and an obsession with quality. It will have a flatter, less bureaucratic company structure, where people talk to one another openly and freely and call each other by their first name. There will be fewer of us working here but those that do, will be better trained, more skilled, have a greater opportunity to develop thoroughly, and in general have improved pay and conditions. A good team spirit will be fostered with improved communication and involvement for everyone. I believe there must be an end to the discriminatory practices and policies and in general terms, we need to create an organisation where motivation and morale thrives".

THE
PEOPLE
DEVELOPMENT
PROGRAMME
Investing in You

THE
ORGANISATIONAL
DEVELOPMENT
PROGRAMME
Investing in Us

THE
DEALER
DEVELOPMENT
PROGRAMME
Investing in Our Customers

THE
BUSINESS DEVELOPMENT
PROGRAMME. *Investing in Our Future*

The only way to achieve all this is with **Your Involvement, Your Ideas, Your Skills and Your Commitment!**

The first stop in all of this is to introduce you to **The Business Development Programme,**"Investing In Our Future".

This is the name we are giving to an ongoing programme, designed to help us achieve our goals.

This programme takes into account the 3 fundamentals that go to make up any company.

Customers

People

Organisation

 CUSTOMERS

We've already started to address the customer issue with **The Dealer Development Programme, "Investing In Customers"** and when this reaches its climax, we will be sharing the findings with you all.

 PEOPLE

Nothing is achieved within an organisation without it investing in its own people. With this in mind **The People Development Programme, "Investing In You"** is born. This will address the training, development and communications of all levels of people within the organisation.

We have plans for management training, supervisory training, team training, and individual training and that's just the start!

THE
PEOPLE
DEVELOPMENT
PROGRAMME
Investing in You

THE
ORGANISATIONAL
DEVELOPMENT
PROGRAMME
Investing in Us

THE
DEALER
DEVELOPMENT
PROGRAMME
Investing in Our Customers

THE
BUSINESS DEVELOPMENT
PROGRAMME.
Investing in Our Future

ORGANISATION

To meet these goals, as I've said we need flatter structures, with more open communication channels. These will effect our plans and our working practices. All of this will be addressed in **The Organisational Development Programme, "Investing In Us"** which will operate in conjunction with the other programmes.

The first stage in all this is to get to grips with your views, attitudes and ideas to make all of this work.

To do this, we have asked a group of consultants, from a company called Human Resource Development (H.R.D.) to research all this and put forward your findings to help us all focus on the way forward.

They will be looking for volunteers to take part in one day workshops, to put forward your views and perceptions about the company.

About 15% of the company will take part in these and everyone else will receive a questionnaire to fill in.

Please volunteer to take part in all this - it's your future, and I very much want you to discuss your thoughts and ideas, openly and freely.

This will be a very exciting time for all of us!!

From the findings, HRD will assist us in focussing on the areas you feel are important and provide the training, development and opportunities that will match your needs with those of the company.

THE
PEOPLE
DEVELOPMENT
PROGRAMME
Investing in You

THE
ORGANISATIONAL
DEVELOPMENT
PROGRAMME
Investing in Us

THE
DEALER
DEVELOPMENT
PROGRAMME
Investing in Our Customers

THE
BUSINESS DEVELOPMENT
PROGRAMME. *Investing in Our Future*

Please tear off the final section of this letter and give to your manager if you would like to take part in the workshops by Tuesday 16th January 1990 as our first workshop will take place on Thursday 18th January 1990.

Here's to a great future together.

Yours sincerely,

Dieter Merz

- -

I would very much like to take part in the workshops to take place in January and February.

Name .... Dept.........................

THE
PEOPLE
DEVELOPMENT
PROGRAMME
Investing in You

THE
ORGANISATIONAL
DEVELOPMENT
PROGRAMME
Investing in Us

THE
DEALER
DEVELOPMENT
PROGRAMME
Investing in Our Customers

Appendix II: Introduction to the theories behind Corporate Internal Marketing *by David Maitland*

One of the major attractions of the internal marketing concept is the vastness of the theoretical and conceptual dimensions associated with it. It crosses almost every discipline in business in the same way that marketing does. In this short chapter, which is aimed at the undergraduate or student looking for an upbeat introduction to some of the concepts, it is only possible to skim the surface of some of the conceptual issues of the subject, so there is a danger that there will not be enough for the academic and too much for the interested theorist.

It is not intended to be a purely academic thesis, although a great deal of research has gone into its production. However, it does aim to link the concept of internal marketing portrayed in this book to a number of other areas of theory, highlighting some of the issues that result. It will provide lots of references for further study, although these are limited in the text to make reading easier. It will also put the concepts expressed earlier into some kind of context and focus on four main areas and their relationship to internal marketing.

1 Marketing Theory
2 Organisation Structure
3 Organisation Communication
4 Human Resource Issues

The angle from which one examines internal marketing depends to a large extent on one's level of analysis and what one hopes to get out of the process. This chapter aims to provide an overview of four of these areas.

The concepts associated with marketing are by no means new. It began to grow as an acedemic subject after the Second World War, although it was not really until the early 1960s that the concepts of marketing as we know it today began to appear (Levitt 1960). In fact, it is not until the late 1970s and early 1980s that marketing academics began to tackle some of the issues surrounding marketing within the organisation (Anderson 1982; Dawson 1969, 1980; Deshpaude 1982).

Towards the late 1980s, the area of internal marketing has begun to gain importance in its own right within the literature (Flipo 1986; Gummesson 1985, 1987; Piercy and Morgan 1990b). However, it still remains largely a practitioner's 'sport' primarily practised by the human resource consultants as part of Organisation Development or Customer Care programmes.

The concept of internal marketing is still being defined and the areas of focus still being explored. It does use concepts from Organisation Development, and also from pure marketing, but the idea of internal marketing also differs in many respects. Certainly current thinking appears to be moving towards focusing on the issues of how to do it, rather than what it is (Bonoma 1985, Piercy and Morgan 1987), and this book is another example; although as shall be seen, with a rather different approach.

Marketing theory and internal marketing

Why internal marketing?

The concept of internal marketing really began to appear in marketing literature in the US and the UK in the late 1980s (Flipo 1986; Gronroos 1985; Piercy and Morgan 1990a). Interest in the concept of internal marketing according to Piercy and Morgan really developed from the realisation that marketing strategy, to succeed, required support from the organisation as a whole and the people within it. They identify that the firm's marketing strategy is not isolated from the rest of the firm, in so far as the firm's marketing strategy needs to be mirrored by an internal marketing strategy. In effect, the internal marketing strategy markets to the internal customers (Peters and Waterman 1982) to ensure that the external marketing strategy is effective.

This preposition is also the basis of this book and forms a cornerstone to the author's ideas and strategies. It is certainly the fundamental answer to the question: 'Why bother about internal marketing?' However, although the reasons for doing internal marketing come from this base, the methods and approaches differ widely according to one's area of concentration, and one's ultimate aims and objectives.

THE USE OF MARKETING TECHNIQUES

The use of marketing theory in internal marketing implies that concepts which are appropriate to external marketing can be used internally.

It is important, however, at the outset to state Piercy and Morgan's main criticism of current marketing theory (Piercy and Morgan 1990b) that there is a lack of appropriate tools and implementation skills available within the body of research to make even external marketing appropriate to practitioners in the industry. This particular problem is what makes this book and the author's approach to the issues so useful since it is a practical response to the problems of internal marketing, a 'how to to do it' book.

The use of external marketing concepts on internal marketing allows direct comparisons. There are four main elements to the internal marketing mix:

1   PRICE   This is the opportunity cost of undertaking that strategy. It is easily said, but the problem is slightly more complex. The sorts of opportunity costs involved are potentially at both a group (e.g. union or work group), or individual level. They include the cost of changing work practices, pay structures, customs and norms.

2 PRODUCT This is primarily the marketing strategy itself, e.g. a Customer Care or 'Excellence' programme. Some of the implementations of product revolve around the need to change technology, organisation structure, and resource allocations to fit the product into the organisation.

3 PROMOTION This is really about communication and messages. It is an area which will be tackled later in some detail. It is perhaps the most easily identifiable and tangible aspect of the internal marketing mix, but as this author has identified, can present some unusual problems because it happens within the organisation.

4 PLACE This is linked, to a large extent, to promotion as in many cases the internal marketing programme is actually about changing views and approaches. We can identify 'place' issues around channel elements of product promotion such as meetings, seminars and training sessions.

The Market is another key area of analysis. The market for the internal marketer is the whole organisation, and in the same way as external markets can be segmented, so can internal ones. The author has shown some of the ways that internal markets can be segmented. Internal market segmentation is in its early stages of development and so sophisticated methods are not yet available. However, some of the key variables must be:

- Power – the ability to influence decisions.
- Organisation linking pins for information. These are individuals whose role in passing information is vital, e.g. a director's secretary.
- High users of a product, e.g. front-line staff in customer care programmes.

PROBLEMS USING MARKETING THEORY

One can identify numerous similarities between external and internal marketing and apply many external marketing concepts internally. However, it is important to highlight some of the key problems in directly applying external concepts internally.

The organisation is unlike any other market. It has its own structure, function and purpose in a way that external markets do not have. It has authority patterns, power relations, and communication flows which are not repeated within markets externally. There is legislation which will alter the organisation as a market in a way that it will not do externally, e.g. employment law. Lastly, there is often an historical context within an organisation which needs to be accounted for in any analysis.

The human resource issues will be dealt with in some detail later; however, at this stage it is worth highlighting some of the key issues around the subject of human resources. The employment contract is probably central to any analysis of human resource issues. Marketing theory is ill-equipped to deal with a market where all the segments have a contractual relationship and, more importantly a psychological relationship with the employer (Argyle 1983). In addition, there are individual relations issues which will influence internal marketing strategy, not just in the sense that unions are like a large consumer group in a market, but also in the relationship between employer and employee or marketeer and market.

Power and authority relations within an organisation will influence the use of external marketing theory within the organisation. Etzioni's work on organisations in the 1960s (Etzioni 1975) shows the variety of power and authority patterns within the organisation. These patterns are complex and constantly changing, which makes internal markets different from external ones. This area is certainly accepted by current writers in the field of internal marketing (Piercy and Morgan 1990b), but the analysis of this factor is limited to its being a barrier to communication or implementation. It could be argued that power relations within the organisation are the key to successful implementation of internal marketing strategies and so a rather deeper analysis of this area is really required.

The structure of an organisation can be seen as important to internal marketing strategies. Some work has been done in this area, notably Chandler (Chandler 1962) who explored the relationship between an organisation's strategy and its structure, and Cravens (1986) who focused more on marketing strategies and how they are influenced by organisation structure. In this context however, we are really interested in some of the effects of organisation structure on internal marketing strategies. This will be dealt with later, but at this stage suffice to say that the way a firm is structured will affect marketing strategy internally in a way it does not externally, if only to the extent that functional or geographical organisation structures affect communication processes. This is emphasised by Cravens' work (1986) on external marketing strategy.

ADVANTAGES OF USING MARKETING THEORY IN INTERNAL MARKETING

There are a number of advantages to using external marketing concepts internally. In the first place, it is highly acceptable to those involved. The concepts involved are straightforward and there is a limited cost in transferring concepts internally. For example, market research techniques are directly usable within the firm, and are often used in the form of quality circles, or I.Q. workshops (H.R.D. 1987). In many cases the techniques when directly applied are easily understood by managers involved. There is no learning shift required for marketing or for another function to use the concepts.

The use of external marketing concepts also allows for a direct link to marketing strategy, which ensures that the two strategies fit quite clearly together and form a common strategy. The author in this book has used many underlying marketing concepts to ensure that internal marketing concepts can link closely to external marketing strategy. Marketing concepts also legitimise the process of internal marketing and make it acceptable to the organisation as a whole (Piercy and Morgan 1990b). This is important, because it is clear that marketing strategy is accepted by the organisation as being vital for its success (Cravens 1986), and so using marketing terminology and concepts when discussing internal marketing provides a measure of legitimacy in its use.

External marketing concepts also help to provide an overall focus to an internal strategy and ensure that important areas of that strategy are not ignored. It is easy at one level, as this author suggests, to concentrate on the channel, the medium (i.e. in which the message is delivered) and message considerations, e.g. the company newspapers, or briefing groups. But at this level it offers only a limited view of the problems and issues involved in internal marketing. The wide focus over macro and micro level issues which exist in using marketing concepts allows the analysis and implementation to be clearly identified. However, it is also the concepts' major limitation in that it fails to focus on other issues such as human resources because the concepts do not allow it to do so. It is this issue that this book attempts to tackle.

Pure marketing theory, when applied to internal marketing, has its benefits in terms of ready-made language, legitimacy and links to business strategy, but, it fails to take account of issues related to human resources, organisation structure, and power relations. The author, in this book, has focused on a number of these issues, although his concentration is practical marketing linked to human resources rather than any overall theoretical view. The key advantage of using marketing theory in internal marketing is that it can use the implementation techniques which are beginning to be developed. The author has also provided a framework which adds to those implementation tools and fits well with other similar developments taking place in the area of internal marketing.

Organisation structure and internal marketing

One of the key variables in any internal marketing strategy and one clearly identified in this book is the organisation's structure (Cravens 1986). The issues which result from an organisation's structure can be looked at from a number of levels. On the one hand, there is the organisation chart level, and on the other hand there is the relationship between internal marketing and organisation theory.

At the organisation chart level, a divisional structure such as that found in the Rank Organisation will make internal marketing more complex for a number of reasons. Firstly, there are often no clear lines of authority between divisions who operate to a large extent as isolated business units. Secondly, the objectives and goals of units within a divisional structure are likely to be different because they are in different markets and different business areas. Thirdly, technology is likely to be different between business units. Fourthly, relations and authority patterns will be different within the separate units. The list is endless.

Weber (1947) is a good example of the early work in organisation theory. His ideal type of bureaucracy was based on formal authority structures with clear specialisation of functions and defined spans of control. Positions with 'bureaucracy' tend to be hierarchical with formal lines of communication and strictly followed written rules enforced by formal management control systems. It is possible to identify a number of organisations today which exhibit features of Weber's bureaucratic ideal type, e.g. civil service, the army, banks.

The implications of this model of internal marketing are several. In the first place, the ideal type of bureaucracy would preclude any attempt to appeal directly to the workforce in the way which, say, Michael Edwardes did at British Leyland. Internal marketing would need to involve formal hierarchical communication flows. Secondly, internal marketing under a Weberian model would involve the 'translation of rules and regulations in written downwardly directed communication' (Euske and Roberts 1987, p. 43). The formal organisation structure theories tend very much to concentrate on the channels of communication and so one would expect interest in terms of internal marketing to focus on segmentation brochures, memos, briefing groups and training sessions. Subtleties like the market and internal market planning would be seen as irrelevant, as the variables of timing and content are not seen as important (Euske and Roberts 1987).

One of the useful areas of formal organisation structures to internal marketing is the concentration on control systems. An area of weakness to internal marketing is its non-involvement in control. One of the differences between an internal and an external market is that one can control it to a greater extent and use power relations to enforce the desired results. This is very much linked to the idea of 'what gets measured gets done'. Although one is trying to match the needs of employment to the business strategy, there is clearly a place for Taylor's (Taylor 1911) view of 'downward persuasive strategies in implementing (the) mental revolution' (Euske and Roberts 1987, p.43). It is important while not overestimating the importance of control in internal marketing, also not to ignore it.

The work group and the informal relations within an organisation will have a major influence on internal marketing strategies in a number of respects. Firstly, internal marketing implies a theory of orientation to human activity in the firm (McGregor 1960) although it is now clear that internal marketing and its communication implications are more complex than theory Y would have believed. Secondly, Schein (1965) wrote that groups highlight the problems associated with the conflict of interests between individuals and organisations. This area is explored more closely in the human relations section of this chapter. Schein's response is towards internal marketing. Lastly, in the area of work groups and human relations is the idea of the organisation 'linking pin' (Likert 1967) where there are key individuals within the organisation who act as links between work groups and are therefore potentially key targets in any internal marketing campaign as their influence is likely to be very high. Examples of such organisation 'linking pins' would be the technician between the workshop and shop floor or the training officer between different levels within the organisation which he tutors.

The human relations approach to organisations would be more appropriate in internal marketing because it emphasises trust, supportive relationships, and informal networks, an understanding of which is essential to internal marketing.

Systems theory is another area of organisations which has implications for internal marketing practice. Open systems theory (Katz and Kahn 1966) requires that organisations interact with their environment in order to function. The relationship between the organisation and its environment is mediated through boundaries which are semi-permeable. In people functions, the boundary is crossed by boundary spanning roles: for example, the salesman who enters customer organisations to sell products. Systems theory addresses the processes which occur within the organisation and identifies those which have been shaped into regular patterned activities that have structure.

The concept is an important one because of the holistic concept identified at the start of this book. The extension of the holistic concept is that if one changes one element of the system, there will be implications for all other aspects. From a human resource point of view, if you change the recruitment strategy and get better people into the organisation, there will be some effect on how much you have to pay, the training and career implication etc. So, from an internal marketing point of view there are a number of implications or results from adopting the approach. Firstly, the management style of the firm needs to reflect the internal marketing approach. This is really a distribution element in external marketing terms. For example, one wouldn't promise 200g cans of beans and provide 180g cans and expect to get away with it. Secondly, the whole organisation needs to practise it, and this is perhaps where culture comes in. The main reason for all parts of the organisation being involved is that without this, other artificial boundaries will be set up within the organisation. The result may actually be worse than if there were no attempt to market internally, as efficiency between parts of the organisation would get worse rather than better.

The essence of the holistic model and the systems approach is that it implies that internal marketing must come from the top. If the use of internal marketing is going to have implications for the whole organisation, then it must be planned for and carefully controlled to ensure that the messages and results which occur are planned and fit into the overall strategy of the firm. Furthermore, it is for the firm to ensure that all departments or parts of the firm are working towards the same direction, and boundaries do not occur within the organisation from misdirection and power relationships.

A second reason for the top-down approach is that the approach of the internal must match the external marketing strategy (Piercy and Morgan 1990b). One of the areas which are normally moulded by the organisation is its boundary spanning roles into the environment, i.e. those roles in the organisation which are in contact with suppliers and customers. This is often done via the external marketing strategy and its communication. For many service organisations however, such communication is made impossible. Imagine a servicing business or catering where over 75% of the employees will be in contact with customers or in boundary spanning roles! The need for internal marketing to meet organisation objectives is highlighted in this form of operation as the only means of ensuring that the external marketing strategy is achieved.

However, as Tom Peters identifies with his internal customer supplier chain, one of the main implications of an organisation becoming 'customer facing' is that *all* parts of the organisation must become 'customer facing' because, as systems theory suggests, boundaries with the organisation will be created which are potentially more damaging than losing the competitive edge by not being customer orientated!

As this book has suggested, and is implied by Peters and Crosby, it is important to take an overall view of the issues involved in internal marketing because changing one is bound to influence many other issues, as they are all inter-related in some respect.

One of the problems of starting from a customer care angle and launching a customer care programme as the start to an internal marketing campaign is that it actually starts at the wrong end and misses out a large number of levels, issues and problems in between including, in many cases, the views of middle management. An appreciation of systems theory may well account for the success or failure of any organisation's campaign or strategy and certainly represents one of the strengths of the approach, as outlined in this book.

One last area which is discussed in this book, and is highly relevant to a theoretical overview, is the concept of organisation change and the implications for internal marketing. Greiner (1972) identifies that organisations proceed through a life cycle in which different management styles and approaches, and different communication processes occur to bring about the required results. In internal marketing terms, it would be important to know the stage at which the organisation was in order to identify implications for the internal marketing strategy. For example, the move from entrepreneurial to managerial control due to the increased size, variety and complexity of an organisation, is bound to have implications for internal marketing strategy.

Organisation communication theory and internal marketing

One of the main components of internal marketing is its communication, in fact in essence internal marketing is all about communication, and specifically organisation communication. The best authors in this subject are certainly Fisher (1978) and a book edited by Jablin, Putnam, Roberts, and Porter (1987). The four perspectives outlined below are taken directly from these authors and a far more detailed analysis of the communication issues can be found within them.

1 Mechanistic perspective

This sees communication as essentially a transmission process in which a message is sent along a channel. The focus of the communication process is the channel and what happens in that channel or on that channel. The message is important in that it travels in the channel and the encoding or decoding elements of a communication system are relevant only in that they link to the channel.

This theory is interested in a number of aspects to the communication process. Firstly, fidelity, which relates to how accurate the message is at two points on the same channel. This naturally relates to the internal marketing process in the sense of 'being sent down' or 'passed up' through several layers. Secondly, there are breakdowns and barriers which stop or impede the transmission process. Cultural differences are an ideal example of these barriers in internal marketing terms. Thirdly, there are gatekeepers who act as a relay of information. The secretary is an example of this. The gatekeeper concept ties in with the linking pin concept covered earlier. The gatekeeper can in reality enhance or suffocate the message and so in internal marketing terms they are potentially a key focus for the internal marketer.

The main uses for internal marketing of the mechanistic perspective lies in its focus on message and channel considerations. It therefore focuses on the key promotion and distribution considerations of an internal marketer, and looks at the effects of methods used to transmit information concerning the product and how clearly it is received.

However, although the theory examines how well the message is received, there is a clear problem that the mechanistic perspective is unable to help in the area of how well the message has been understood. The essence of the internal marketing programme (at its most cynical) is in explaining the company's approach and matching as far as it is possible the needs of the individual employee to the organisation's needs. This is primarily a qualitative exercise and cannot really be encompassed within the mechanistics perspective.

2 Psychological perspective

The psychological perspective focuses on the influence which the individual has on the communication process. It consists of the attitudes, beliefs, values, and perceptions of individuals and their effect on 'What information is attended to, conveyed and interpreted [and] how this information is processed' (Jablin, Putnam, Roberts & Porter 1987).

If one can imagine the value of stimuli which affect us each day, the psychological perspective aims to examine why we take notice of some things and not others, and then how it is processed for use. In some respects this perspective is useful for internal marketing because it focuses more on the receiver of the message than on the content or channel considerations associated with the message. This is useful because it is the alteration or adoption of the needs and attitudes of the individual in the organisation that is the aim of the internal marketing process. It becomes a useful concept when one examines the individual relationships within the process of internal marketing especially if one examines the use of briefing groups and other direct face-to-face marketing techniques where the relationships between individuals, communicator and communicatee become vital to success.

3 Interpretive-symbolic perspective

This perspective views communication as a key variable in forming and maintaining the organisation. It is based on the work of Boulmer (1969) and Mead (1934) on symbolic interaction which sees communication as mediated through a series of shared meanings and symbols. Thus under this perspective, in order to be able to communicate effectively with a group, the internal marketer must be able to use symbols and meanings which can be interpreted and understood by the group. An ideal example of this is the many cigarette advertisements which can only be really understood by cigarette smokers, or those who can relate to or have an understanding of the cigarette smoker.

This perspective suggests that employees act as a result of interpreting a message or action. The response to a particular internal marketing message will be dependent on the meanings which that message has for an individual or group. The meanings which a group has for a particular message will be dependent on a wide number of factors, such as culture. These symbols and values are interpreted by the group to define its meanings.

One of the main implications of this perspective for the internal marketer is that the same message or approach is unlikely to be acceptable to the whole organisation. This author has clearly identified that the approach of the internal marketer must vary according to the audience being addressed. Under this perspective, different groups tend to interpret situations differently because of where they come from and the way in which they attach different meanings to the same things. For example, compare the meaning of profit to the trade unionist with that held by the board of directors.

4 Systems perspective

The essence of the systems perspective relates to the discussion earlier on systems theory in organisations. This perspective sees the communication process as a system. It tends to focus on how 'the categories form sequential patterns of message behaviour' (Jablin, Putnam, Roberts & Porter 1987, p.30). There are many similarities between this perspective and the discussion earlier on systems theory. The implications are similar and so it would add nothing to the analysis to discuss this area further.

The main value of these perspectives to the study of internal marketing is that they allow a focus on a variety of aspects of the communication process involved in internal marketing. They are able to form theoretical bases for further study, and more detailed analysis of specific areas of the internal marketing communication process from a variety of angles.

Internal marketing and the human resource function

An understanding of the relationship between internal marketing and the human resouce function is fundamental to success at internal marketing. As this author identifies, the differences be-tween an organisation and an external market are so large that without that understanding of the organisation's human resouces, any internal marketing exercise will fail. In simple terms this will be because internal marketing matches individual and group needs to those of the organisation. The internal marketer must, therefore, tackle issues of industrial and employee relations: pay, recruitment, training, development, etc. It is not possible, as this author also suggests, to separate areas which are so interlinked with the indi-viduals' and groups' needs from any discussion of changing the needs themselves. So, as this author has done, it is vital to examine the implications of internal marketing and the human resource function.

Internal marketing implies a particular relationship between employer and employee. This can probably best be explained by examining some of the perspectives which can be taken towards the relationship between employer and employee, and relate them to internal marketing and its use within the organisation. An ideal text for exploring these issues and perspectives is *Understanding Indust-rial Relations*, Chapter 3 (Farnham and Pinlott 1979).

The internal marketing approach assumes that there is some measure of common interest between employer and employee. It also assumes that their needs are relatively similar and that to a large extent any differences between the two points of view are caused by a lack of understanding. Moreover, a further implication of the internal marketing approach is that it is the employee whose needs must change, or who must understand the position of the employer because it is the employer who is reacting to changes in the business environment which require strategy changes.

The last paragraph clearly fits the unitary perspective of individual relations where the organisation is seen as having one common purpose. There is no conflict of interest between employers and employees because they both have the same aims in terms of production and profit. Managers who hold this view talk about the company as a team rather than as two sides. They would also argue that the firm requires strong leadership in order to ensure that tasks required for the firm to survive do occur. Internal marketing in this instance would be seen as a very limited exercise of 'selling' the wishes of senior management to the workforce. At best, the internal marketing concept would be about communication, ensuring that employees understood what the common interest was and what their part in it would be.

The result of senior managers holding this viewpoint is that internal marketing would take the form of company newspapers and briefing groups where the company view would be stated and explained. The need to do research into employee needs would not arise because of the assumption that all employees accept that the needs of the company must come first, and that the employees' needs are the same as the company's.

This view of the relations within industry is common in the United States where management prerogative is absolute in many of the states. Many organisations do not recognise the existence of any conflict of interests between employer and employee which might lead to the creation of a trade union. For example, in the US only 18.2% of employees were in a union in 1985 compared to 50% in the UK. In this situation it is easy to understand why the concept of internal marketing has taken off in the United States, and why it has had only limited success in the United Kingdom.

However, the focus of internal marketing in the United States is different from that expressed in this book. Little attention is given in the transatlantic literature on internal marketing which focuses on market research within the firm or the more qualitative issues of what should be discussed within internal marketing strategy. The focus in the United States is more towards the clarity of the message to ensure that it gets through, rather than the requirement to match the needs of employees and the company.

The view discussed in this book appears to fit into a different perspective of industrial relations, that of pluralism. The pluralist perspective bases its analysis on the fact that there are groups within the organisation who have different views and interests. The successful operation of the firm requires that all those groups work together in harmony. This view is the basis of consensus management. To give an example, a firm which employs skilled craftsmen and labourers would need to appeal to these two groups in different ways. Their interests and values are likely to be different in a number of respects. Firstly, the craftsmen have a position to maintain. Secondly, their skills are possibly more transferable between firms. Thirdly, they will have experienced life differently. In symbolic interactionist terms, they will respond to symbols with different meanings than those to which labourers respond, e.g. in the technical language which they use.

If one takes the perspective that an organisation is full of competing groups with different power relations and different needs, as this book has implied, then the area of internal marketing takes on a new meaning. It is no longer purely a top-down selling or information process, but becomes a dynamic two-way communication process which attempts to build understanding and trust between groups so that the organisation as a whole can move towards its strategic goals. The internal marketing process, as discussed in the book, requires a level of market research, and market targeting; but most of all, it requires a focus which forms the basis for all the important organised activities, a basis for the organisation language, and a basis for the entire culture of the organisation. Although not unifying the different groups within an organisation, the internal marketing process will at least provide a measure of understanding and trust between the groups to allow the organisation to progress and gain competitive advantage.

The final perspective which needs to be examined is the industrial conflict perspective. This view suggests that in the West, conflict between employers and employees has become institutionalised and socially regulated and so has become accepted in its correct form. Conflict between employers and employees is natural in a part-capitalist society in its new form, primarily because of the more socially mobile society and a more diffuse distribution of power. Accepting this view, individual conflict is axiomatic; it is only the forms it takes which change to any degree (see R. Hyman 1975)

The internal marketing concept as discussed in this book could be argued to be a new form of institutionalising of the conflict between employers and employees. It certainly provides a new set of tools and relationships which would allow employers to communicate and bargain with their employees. As this author has suggested, the concept is potentially a strong tool to compete with the traditional industrial relations concepts. The Corporate Internal Marketing concept, it could be argued, is partly a reaction to changes in society to a more individualistic approach, requiring a move away from the formal, large union organisations which currently exist, to the highly flexible organisation-centred approach of Corporate Internal Marketing.

The other key issue in terms of human resource and Corporate Internal Marketing is the employment contract. The one big difference between internal customers and external customers is the contract under which the two groups operate. The existence of the employment contract fundamentally changes the relationship between the internal and the external customer and the organisation. There is a contract in most cases between the organisation and an external customer, but there is not necessarily the psychological contract which exists between employer and employee (Argyle 1983). In many cases, work provides a person with identity or purpose. At the very least, it provides a person with a means of living. The employment contract is far more than an agreement to work at a set of tasks for a set period of time per week, for an agreed set of benefits. The contract also involves duties of employer and employee towards each other. For example, the employee's duty to obey his/her supervisor while at work.

The psychological contract between an employer and employee requires that the approach towards internal marketing needs to differ from external marketing. The situation is in some respects simplified because the contract places similar duties on employees and provides a structure that is absent from the external market. However, on the other hand, the contract makes internal marketing more difficult than external marketing because the internal needs of employees within the organisation are more fundamentally linked to that organisation.

One of the major difficulties of any internal marketing approach which relies solely on marketing concepts for its base is that the language and concepts available cannot be related into the human resource approach. The concepts are designed for external use, and require major overhaul to suit the internal market. The internal customers are fundamentally different to external customers and so the application of similar concepts will not necessarily have similar effects, and application of principles rather than techniques have a much greater chance of success. However, as this author has suggested, it is the combination of marketing and human resource principles which go to form Corporate Internal Marketing as a concept and a useful tool for organisations in change.

Summary

It is possible to identify a number of theoretical strengths in the approach taken by this author.

In the first place, the book is a very practical approach to the problems of internal marketing. It provides tools, procedures and practices to help internally market to employees. There is a great deal of theory on subjects such as organisations, culture, communication, buyer behaviour, etc., but little practical base to these theoretical approaches.

The absence of a theoretical body of internal marketing knowledge is perhaps a function of its 'newness' as a concept. It is important for the future that this knowledge is built up. As the author suggests, it is not purely about applying marketing concepts within the organisation, nor is it about adapting concepts used in human resource management. It is a combination of the two with a clearly separate conceptual basis.

A further strength of Corporate Internal Marketing is its systems approach to the subject, which ensures that the entire concept and its implications for the organisation are examined as a whole rather than in parts. One could examine the internal marketing concepts at a variety of different levels, from the individual to the organisation. The system's approach allows a measure of that analysis without the associated theoretical difficulties of meanings for individuals. The systems approach with Corporate Internal Marketing provides an overall approach to internal marketing; it allows the different relationships within the organisation to be examined as they relate to each other, and analysed as separate units when necessary.

Finally, the Corporate Internal Marketing approach is clearly within the pluralist perspective. The issue of improving organisation efficiency and effectiveness depends, to a large extent, on communication. Corporate Internal Marketing argues that mutual understanding and trust between employer and employee is the major issue addressed through internal marketing and one of the key variables to success of the external marketing strategy.

The Corporate Internal Marketing approach to internal marketing helps to provide a common language between the organisation's people and external marketing to form the basis of the relationship between matching employee needs to those needs created by the external marketing strategy.

References

ANDERSON, P. 'Marketing, Strategic Planning, and the Theory of the Firm' *Journal of Marketing*, Vol. 46, 1982, 15–26.

ARGYLE, M. *The Psychology of Interpersonal Behaviour.* London, Penguin Books, 1983

ARGYRIS, C. *Personality and Organization.* New York, Harper & Row, 1957.

ARMSTRONG, D & DAWSON, C. *People in Organisations.* Cambridge, Elm Publications, 1985.

ARNDT, J. 'The Political Economy Paradigm: Foundation for Theory-marketing', *Journal of Marketing*, Vol. 47, 1983, 44–54.

BONOMA, T.V. *The Marketing Edge – Making Strategies Work.* New York, Free Press, 1985.

BOULMER. *Symbolic Interaction – Perspective and Method.* Englewood Cliffs, Prentice Hall, 1969.

CARNEGIE, D. *How to Win Friends and Influence People.* London, Cedar Books, Revised edition, 1981.

CARZON, J. *Moments of Truth.* Cambridge, Massachusetts, Ballinger Publishing Co., 1987.

CASCINO, A.E. 'Organizational Implications of the Marketing Concept', in E.J. Kelly and W. Lazar, eds. *Managerial Marketing: Perspectives and Viewpoints.* Homewood, Illinois, Irwin, 1967.

CHANDLER, A.D. *Strategy and Structure.* Cambridge, Massachusetts, MIT Press, 1962.

CRAVENS, D.W. Strategic Forces Affecting Marketing Strategies', *Business Horizons*, Sept-Oct 1986, 77–86.

CROSBY, P.B. *Quality is Free.* New York, New American Library, 1979.

DAFT, R.L. & WEICK, K.E. 'Toward a Model of Organizations as Interpretation Systems', *Academy of Management Review*, 9, 1984, 284–295.

DAVIS, K. 'A method of Studying Communication Patterns in Organizations', *Personnel Psychology* 6, 1953, 301–312.

DAWSON, L.M. 'Marketing for Human Needs in a Humane Future',
Business Horizons, June 1980, 72–82.

DAWSON, L.M. 'THE HUMAN CONCEPT. NEW PHILOSOPHY FOR BUSINESS',
Business Horizons, December 1969.

DESHPANDE, M. 'The organisational context of market research use',
Journal of Marketing, Vol 46, No. 3. 1982.

EUSKE & ROBERTS In: Jablin, F.M. et al (eds) *Handbook of Organisation Communication*, London, Sage, 1987.

EVANS, R & RUSSELL, P. *The Creative Manager.* London, Unwin Hyman, 1989.

FARNHAM, D & PINLOTT, J. *Understanding Industrial Relations.* London, Cassell, 1979.

FELDMAN, M.S. & MARCH, J.G. 'Information in Organizations as Signal and Symbol', *Administrative Science Quarterly*, 26, 1981, 171–186.

FISHER, B.A. *Perspectives on Human Communication*, New York, Macmillan, 1978.

FLIPO, J.P. 'Service firms: Interdependence of External and Internal Marketing Strategies', *European Journal of Marketing*, Vol. 20, No. 8, 1986, 5–14.

FOSTER, R.N. *Innovation – the Attacker's Advantage.* London, Pan Books, 1987.

GOLDRATT, E & COX, J. *The Goal.* Croton-on-Hudson, New York, North River Press, 1984.

GREINER, L.E. 'Patterns of Organization Change', *Harvard Business Review*, 45(4) 1972, 119–130.

GRONROOS, C. 'Internal Marketing – Theory and Practice', in Thomas M. Bloch, Gregory D. Upah and Valerie A. Zeithaml, eds. *Services Marketing in a Changing Environment*, Chicago, AMA, 1985.

GUMMESSON, E. 'Using Internal Marketing to Develop a New Culture – The Case of Ericsson Quality', *Journal of Business and Industrial Marketing*, Vol. 2, No. 3, 1987, 23–28.

HAGE, J., AIKEN, M. & MARRETT, C.B. 'Organization Structure and Communication', *American Sociological Review*, 36, 1971, 860–871.

HOPKINS, T. *The Official Guide to Success.* London, Granada Publishing, 1985.

HOPKINS, T. *How to Master the Art of Selling.* London, Collins, 1982.

HRD (1987) Unpublished research.

HYMAN, R. *Industrial Relations: A Marxist Introduction.* London, Macmillan, 1975.

JABLIN, F.M. 'Task/Work Relationships: a Life-span Perspective', in M.L. Knapp & G.R. Miller, eds., *Handbook of Interpersonal Communication* (pp.615–654). Newbury Park, California, Sage, 1985.

JABLIN, F.M., PUTNAM, L.L., ROBERTS, K.H. & PORTER, L.W. (eds) *Handbook of Organisation Communication*. London, Sage, 1987.

JOHNSON, S & WILSON, L. *The One Minute Sale Person*. London, Fontana/Collins, 1985.

KANTER, R.M. *The Change Masters*. London, Unwin, 1983.

KATZ, D & KAHN, R.L. *The Social Psychology of Organisations*. New York, John Wiley, 1966.

KOTLER, P. *Marketing Management: Analysis, Planning and Control*. London, Prentice Hall, 1984.

LAWRENCE, R.R. & LORSCH, J.W. *Organization and Environment: Managing Differentiation and Integration*. Cambridge, Massachusetts, Harvard University Press, 1967.

LEVITT, T. 'Marketing Myopia', *Harvard Business Review*, July–August 1960, 45–56.

LIKERT, R. *The Human Organization*. New York. McGraw-Hill, 1967.

MALTZ, M. *Psycho-Cybernetics*. Hollywood, California, Wilshire Book Company, 1960.

MARCH, J.G. & SIMON, H.A. *Organizations*. New York, John Wiley, 1958.

MCGREGOR, D. *The Human Side of Enterprise*. New York, McGraw-Hill, 1960.

MEAD, G.H. *Mind, Self Society*. Chicago, Chicago University Press, 1934.

MINTZBERG, H. *The Nature of Managerial Work*. New York, Harper & Row, 1973.

MONGE, P.R. 'Systems Theory and Research in the Study of Organizational Communication: the Correspondence Problem', *Human Communication Research*, 8, 1982, 245–261.

MUDIE, P. 'Internal Marketing: Cause for Concern'. *Quarterly Review of Marketing*, Spring/Summer 1987, 21–24.

PETERS, T.J. & AUSTIN, N. *A Passion for Excellence*. London, Collins, 1985.

PETERS, T.J. & WATERMAN, R.M. *In Search of Excellence*. New York, Harper & Row, 1982.

PIERCY, N. 'The Marketing Budgeting Process: Marketing management implications', *Journal of Marketing*, Vol. 51, no. 4, 1987, 45–59.

PIERCY, N. 'The Role and Function of the Chief Marketing Executive and the Marketing Department', *Journal of Marketing Management*, Vol. 1, No. 3, 1986, 265–290.

PIERCY, N. 'The Role of the Marketing Department in the UK Retailing Organisations', *Internal Journal of Retailing*, 1990 (In press).

PIERCY, N & MORGAN, N. 'Internal Marketing: Making Marketing Happen', *Marketing Intelligence and Planning*, 1990a (In press).

PIERCY, N. & MORGAN, N. 'Internal Marketing: Strategies for Implementation and Organisational Change', *Long Range Planning*, 1990b (In press).

PIERCY, N. & PEATTIE, K. 'Matching Marketing Strategies to Corporate Culture: the parcel and the wall', *Journal of General Management*, Vol. 13, No. 4, 1988, 33–44.

PUTNAM, L.L. & PACANOWSKY, M.E., eds, *Communication and Organizations: An Interpretative Approach*. Newbury Park, California, Sage, 1983.

REDDING, W.C. 'Organizational Communication Theory and Ideology: an Overview', in D. Nimmo, ed. *Communication Yearbook 3* (pp.309–341). New Brunswick, New Jersey, Transaction, 1979.

RHODES, J & THAME, S. *The Colours of your Mind*. London, Fontana/Collins, 1988.

ROBERTS, K.H., O'REILLY, C.A., BRETTON, G.E., & PORTER, L.W. 'Organizational Theory and Organizational Communication: A Communication Failure', *Human Relations*, 27, 974, 501–524.

ROGERS, E. & AGARWALA-ROGERS, R. *Communication in Organizations*. New York, Free Press, 1976.

ROGERS, E. & SHORMAKER, F. *Communication and Innovation*. New York, Free Press, 1971.

SCHEIN, E. *Organizational Psychology*. Englewood Cliffs, New Jersey, Prentice Hall, 1965.

TANNENBAUM, A. *Social Psychology of the Work Organization*. Belmont, California, Wadsworth, 1966.

TAYLOR, F.W. *Scientific Management*. New York, Harper, 1911.

TOWNSEND, R. *Up the Organization*. London, Coronet Books, 1970.

TRUJILLO, N. 'Performing Mintzberg's Roles: the Nature of Managerial Communication', in L.L. Putnam & M.E. Pacanowsky, eds, *Communication and Organizations; an interpretative approach*, (pp.73–97). Newbury Park, California, Sage, 1983.

WEBER, M. *The Theory of Social and Economic Organization*. New York, Free Press, 1947.

WEICK, K.E. *The Social Psychology of Organising*, 2nd edn. Reading, Massachusetts, Addison-Wesley, 1979.

Index